To
Cathy
co worker in public
Health
Dr Sam Tate

VET SQUARED:

MEMOIR OF A VETerinarian
& AIR FORCE VETeran

Dr. Samuel W. Tate

DORRANCE
PUBLISHING CO
EST. 1920
PITTSBURGH, PENNSYLVANIA 15238

Dorrance Publishing Co
585 Alpha Drive
Suite 103
Pittsburgh, PA 15238
Visit our website at *www.dorrancebookstore.com*

ISBN: 978-1-6376-4259-7
eISBN: 978-1-6376-4575-8

VET SQUARED:

MEMOIR OF A VETERINARIAN & AIR FORCE VETERAN

DEDICATION

Samuel L. Tate, Captain, USN, Ret.

Andrew J. Tate, Lieutenant Colonel, USMC, Ret.

INTRODUCTION

I was born in late December 1941 at the Norfolk Naval Hospital, Portsmouth, VA, now known as the Naval Medical Center Portsmouth. My Aunt Hope Falconer, who did not have a driver's license, drove my mother, Edna Frederica Tate, from our home at Wards Corner in Norfolk. I have been told that I was almost born on the ferry from Norfolk to Portsmouth. My father, Claude Stratton Tate, Jr., Petty Officer First Class, USN, was serving on the USS Pocomoke (AV-9) stationed at Argentia, Newfoundland, tending seaplanes scouting for German U-boats. Two years before that he was on the USS Mugford (DD389) in the Pacific commanded by LCDR Arleigh Burke, who became the US Chief of Naval Operations and the namesake of DDG-51, the lead ship of the class of guided missile destroyers. My father met me for the first time when the USS Pocomoke came to Norfolk in January 1942 for maintenance.

My brother, Claude S. Tate, III, was born in September 1943, also at the Norfolk Naval Hospital. Our father was stationed at Naval Station 117, Trinidad in the British West Indies and was a chief petty officer. He was able to get leave to visit us. My mother, Stratton, and I lived the war years on Louisiana Drive, Norfolk, just three houses from my grandmother Dorothy, Aunts Dolly and Hope, and Uncle Percy. My grandmother was the manager of the civilian cafeteria in the Fifth Naval District Headquarters building at the Norfolk Naval Base. After WWII, we moved eleven times, and I went to nine different elementary schools and two high schools. We lived in Rhode Island, Virginia, Texas, California, and Massachusetts.

My sister, Dorothy L. Tate, was born in November 1954 at the Newport Naval Hospital while we were living in Somerset, Mass. Both Stratton and I had our tonsils removed at that hospital. Our father was on the pre-commission crew of the USS Wilkerson (DL-5) being built in Boston, Mass.

My father retired from the Navy in 1957, and we moved to a new house in what was then Princess Anne County and is now Virginia Beach, VA. The three of us siblings went to Princess Anne High School.

Stratton served in the Army at Fort Belvoir, VA, during the Vietnam War. Dorothy Lou was commissioned in the Navy after graduation from Old Dominion University and retired at the rank of commander (05).

All photos, unless otherwise annotated, were taken by Dr. Tate or are from his collection.

PART 1

BECOMING A VETERINARIAN

VETERINARY CAREER

My career in veterinary medicine began in the summer of 1960 with Dr. Benjamin Y. Ward at Boulevard Veterinary Hospital on Virginia Beach Blvd in Norfolk, VA, after I graduated from Princess Anne High School. Dr. Ward was a navy pharmacist mate in WWII. He graduated from the University Of Georgia College Of Veterinary Medicine using the GI Bill. He first operated a mixed practice in Kinston, NC.

Boulevard Vet Hospital started out as a gas station at Davis Corner just over the VA Beach city line. In 1960 it was one of the only two veterinary hospitals from there to the oceanfront. There were also two doctors who recently graduated from University of Georgia, John I Gray and William Lee. Both would be elected president of the Virginia Veterinary Medical Association (VVMA). My position was kennel boy, which had three ranks: Pooper Scooper, Super Pooper Scooper, and Super Duper Pooper Scooper. I learned new tasks through on-the-job training to what nowadays is considered a veterinary assistant. That includes holding animals for examination, blood draws, and positioning the X-rays, graduating to assisting in surgery, and preparing surgical packs.

I was working one evening with Dr. Gray when this older, well-dressed lady presented her Boston terrier for examination. The scrotum of his testicles was inflamed, swollen, and painful.

Dr. Gray, "Ma'am, your dog has a severe case of scrotal dermatitis."

She responded, "You mean on his balls?"

The red flush of embarrassment started at Dr. Gray's eyebrows and went over the top of his bald head. John is still a good sport when I tell that story at VVMA meetings sixty years later.

SHOOT A HORSE

Dr. Ward asked me to go with him one evening to attend a down horse. In addition of getting the euthanasia solution he retrieved his .45 pistol from the safe. The horse belonged to Judge Kellam, and Dr. Ward had been trying to get a permit to carry a hand gun. He wanted to show the judge that it was necessary to do so. We arrived at the stables at Princess Anne Court House about dusk. Judge Kellam had already decided it was time to let go of the very old, sick horse. The lighting was very poor in the stall so a lantern was brought in. Dr. Ward knelt down and placed the muzzle of the pistol in the appropriate spot on the head of the horse and pulled the trigger. Nothing happened. It's no telling how old the ammunition was, maybe WWII. He ejected the bullet and tried again. This time he achieved the desired results. Dr. Ward then said to me that we needed to find the ejected bullet because if the owners burned the straw, someone could get hurt by an exploding bullet. So we crawled around on our hands and knees in the lantern light feeling through the straw until we found the bullet. Judge Kellam approved Dr. Ward's hand gun permit.

TIMBER

There was a dead pine tree at the back corner of the outdoor runs. Recognizing my scouting skills, Dr. Ward asked if I could cut it down to make it fall away from the runs. I notched the trunk at the bottom on the side of the direction I wanted it to fall. Then I cut above it on the opposite side. What I failed to realize was that the tree already had a slight lean towards the runs. Thomas, the kennel man, was in the runs attending to dogs when the tree came crashing down. Thomas hit the deck. Fortunately the tree compressed the fencing only about two feet, and neither Thomas nor the dogs were injured.

GEORGE

Dr. Ward had a myna bird named George. George's cage was located in a corner of the waiting room of the veterinary hospital. George had the ability to mimic Dr. Ward's voice in several situations. The sound of the front door to the hospital opening would trigger a pronouncement from George, "Ring the bell and have a seat." The client, looking around the waiting room and not seeing anyone, would follow George's instruction. Dr. Ward also had a dachshund named Hansel. A human whistle would trigger George to whistle and command, "Here Hansel, here Hansel." When Hansel was present, he would run around the room looking for Dr. Ward. Dr. Ward's maid would talk to George while she was ironing, and George mimicked her voice as well.

George would stay at the hospital when Dr. Ward was out of town. It was my job to feed George. Some of his treats were peeled and sliced apples and white grapes. One day, I had a plum for lunch and I gave George a slice. Within about ten minutes, George was frantically flying around in his cage and spurting diarrhea as he went. He then fell to the bottom of the cage on his back with his feet pointing upwards and kept repeating, "Squawk, squawk, squawk." I took him and his cage to the wash tub to be cleaned. I also had to clean the wall and floor in his corner of the waiting room. George recovered, and I never varied his diet again.

Unfortunately, another kennel boy held George too tightly and he suffocated.

AMMONIA

I assisted Dr. Ward in surgery for a spay on a dog on a Friday morning. We placed the dog on a mat on the floor of the storage room just off the surgery room where I could watch her as I cleaned the instruments. Dr. Ward planned on leaving at lunchtime to spend the weekend at his cottage in Nags Head, NC. He left me and another kennel assistant to do the afternoon feeding, cleaning of the outdoor runs, and closing the hospital. Roache was a Norfolk City fireman and worked at the hospital when he was off duty. He said his name was pronounced "Rocky."

I finished cleaning the surgery instruments and prepared to mop the floor. I opened the cabinet under the counter where the sanitizer was stored in one-gallon glass bottles. When I took out the bottle in the front, all the bottles behind it shifted forward; the bottle in the far back was partially sitting on the frame of the cabinet. When all the bottles shifted, that bottle slid off the frame and hit the concrete floor and broke. The room was immediately filled with ammonia fumes. Roache called the fire department and reported the spill. He left before his fellow firemen arrived because he did not want them teasing about the incident for the rest of his career. I evacuated all the dogs from the inside kennels to the outside runs. The firemen arrived, assessed the situation, and set up exhaust fans. They also vacuumed up the liquid ammonia. One fireman came out carrying the surgery dog. She was trembling because she was coming out of anesthesia. Fortunately, she was all right. Dr. Ward had a fish tank in his office. Apparently the water absorbed some of the ammonia fumes and all the fish died. Dr. Ward returned on Monday with sunburn and related that his boat had sunk. I told him about the ammonia incident and his dead fish. He said we handled the situation without any major loss and his fish tank was minor compared to his boat.

I worked for Dr. Ward all three years I went to Old Dominion University and the summer at the end of my first year at Michigan State. Dr. Ward and I never discussed that I might work for him after graduation, but I think it was a mutual expectation. I know he was disappointed when I joined the Air Force. He retired and sold the practice to Dr. Constance Pozniak, who later became the first female president of the VVMA. In 2007 I saw an advertisement on the marquee for a kennel boy. I said to the office manager I was interested in applying for my old job. Dr. Pozniak got a great laugh out of that and hired me to do relief work for her a couple times.

OLD DOMINION UNIVERSITY

ODU did not have a pre-vet program so I was in pre-med along with Jim Pauley, a Princess Anne High School classmate, and Harvey Phillips. The three of us had student jobs with Dr. David Soneshine in his tick lab. Dr. Soneshine had a National Institutes of Health (NIH) grant in conjunction with Walter Reed Medical Center to study the environmental factors that affect the prevalence of brown dog tick, *dermacentor variables*, and the vector of Rocky Mountain spotted fever.

Our job was to raise ticks in the lab for his experiments conducted with temperature, carbon dioxide and humidity variations. He had female ticks collected in the field engorged with blood in vials. These females would lay their eggs in the vials which then hatched to larval stage. We would count the tiny speck of rust-like larvae on white filter paper with a camel hair paintbrush into groups of one hundred and pour them into another vial. We had mice suspended in little cages over individual water tanks. We would sprinkle the one hundred larvae on a mouse to feed. We then collected and counted the larvae and stored them in vials until they metamorphosed into nymphs. Then the feeding process was repeated and the nymphs became adults, which were then used for the chamber experiments. So, we not only had to care and feed the ticks we also had to care for the mice. All of this was conducted in one of the few air- conditioned facilities on campus, so when we finished our work we would stay in the lab to study in a cool place. One day Jim Pauley poured a vial of tiny specks in a book I was holding on my lap. I thought it was tick larvae. He laughed at my reaction, then told me it was only rust. I got even by placing a dead rat in his gym bag on his motor scooter. I didn't know the rat had lice.

Jim Pauley became a dentist and practiced in Portsmouth, VA. Harvey Philips became a veterinarian and practiced in Ashland, VA. He was the brother-in-law of Dr. William P. Knox, who I worked for in Yorktown, VA when I retired from the AF and completed my refresher courses at Virginia Maryland College of Veterinary Medicine (VMCVM) in 1988.

I started exploring veterinary colleges after my freshman year at ODU. Virginia had a regional contract with the University of Georgia where most VA residents went. However, that also eliminated the colleges that had their own regional contracts. Georgia had a requirement for agriculture courses that were not offered in the summer there or at VA Tech. The University of Illinois required two semesters of a foreign language. Michigan State University accepted students with less than four years of college if they met all the science prerequisites and could take the agriculture course in the first year of vet school. I applied to MSU in my third year at ODU and was placed on their alternate list. I enrolled in summer school for French I, along with Jim Pauley, planning to take French II in the fall to meet Illinois' requirement.

I was coming home from class when my mother greeted me, "Michigan State called, and you have been accepted and need to be there in two weeks."

"But I don't have any money for tuition." (I paid for three years at ODU with the money I earned working for Dr. Ward)

Mom said, "Call them back and say you are coming. We will figure out the finances."

I thought it would be nice to have an Associates of Arts Degree to show for my three years at ODU, but it was too late to be awarded in 1963. So, they sent it to me in 1964. Thus, my transcript looks like it took me four years to earn a two-year degree.

I packed my clothes and a borrowed microscope in my father's WWII sea trunk and rode the bus to East Lansing, Michigan.

MICHIGAN STATE UNIVERSITY

I lived in Emmons Hall on the far side of campus from the veterinary college during my first year. I rode my bike to class. Bob Crenshaw, who was a herpetology major (amphibians and reptiles), was my roommate. He kept a rattlesnake in a pillowcase in our room. One day he was showing it in another room and it got loose and went under a desk. Another hall mate came in to see what was going on, heard the snake's rattle, and left in a hurry. Bob graduated in December and went to South America. He returned in the spring with some snakes he was trying to sell to exhibits, including a twenty-foot anaconda.

HOUSE OF EMU

Emmons Hall was two stories high with two wings, thus it had four floors each with a name beginning with the letter "E." My floor was House of Emu on the first level facing the Kellogg Hotel and Conference Center across the street. Our resident advisor (RA) was Andy McEntée from Grosse Pointe, Michigan. He was majoring in criminal justice and tried to act the part. He was also the captain of our flag football team in intramural sports. As RA, Andy had a single room in the center of our floor across from the incinerator room. My floor mates and I hatched a prank to paper Andy's room. Several of us received hometown newspapers, which we began saving. We knew that would not be enough so we started "collecting" the bundles of the student newspaper delivered to the dorms. We colluded with an RA from another floor to let us in Andy's room one weekend while he was home in Grosse Point. We opened the newspapers and balled them up starting at the door. We had the room packed wall to wall and floor to ceiling. We exited the room by the windows.

We anxiously awaited Andy's return on Sunday night. He unlocked his door, but it would not open into the room. He set his bag down, put his shoulder to the door, and forced his way in. At first he was furious and ranted up and down the hall banging on doors that we were hiding behind. He went back to his room and pulled out some of the newspapers and read the banners, "*Virginia Pilot* – Sam Tate, *Grand Rapids Press* – Tom Prescott" and so on. We started emerging from our rooms and all had a big laugh. We then began helping Andy clear his room. The papers became waist high in the hall. We started stuffing them into the trash incinerator across from Andy's room. We heard sirens as the fire department arrived. Someone in the Kellogg Conference Center saw flames coming from the chimney and thought Emmons Hall was on fire. The firemen explained how dangerous it was to stuff paper into the incinerator with all that paper in the hallway. They called the campus public works who brought a dumpster for us to put all the paper into.

Andy returned from another trip home to find a puddle of water under his door. Opening it, he found a snowman in his room.

Andy had light switches in his room that controlled the lights in the hallway. He would dim the lights in the evening as a reminder to be quiet because people were studying. The lights would be dim day and night the entire exam period. We changed the fluorescent tubes so that no matter which switch was turned on the light intensity remained the same. It took Andy a few tries before he figured out what we had done.

DEAD HORSE

During my first year at Michigan State, the entire veterinary college was housed in Giltner Hall. The first floor on the front of the building was at ground level, while at the rear the basement was at ground level. The large animal clinic was at the end of one wing on the first floor. There was ramp driveway from the clinic doors down to a very large paved lot below. Access to the necropsy lab was the through that lot and to the left. One day, two seniors were moving a dead horse on large, low hand cart. The head of the horse was slightly over the edge. When one of them released his hold on the handle to close the barn door, the cart got away from them. It rolled down the hill, and the head of the horse slammed into the side of a car parked at the bottom. The police report for the damage to the car read, "Hit by a dead horse."

WHERE IS THE HORSE?

The gross anatomy lab was a two-story room in the basement of Giltner Hall. There was a rail in the ceiling that ran into the cooler for storing large animal specimens, which hung from chains so that the specimens were in an upright position. Students were allowed in at night to study, and one student was responsible for the key and to make sure everything was put away. The evening before the final exam we decided to play a joke on Dr. Tickemyer. We hoisted the animals all the way to the ceiling where they would not be seen as one entered the room unless they were looking at the ceiling.

HUMANITIES vs. SOCIAL STUDIES

American History was required in high school as social studies. I was exposed to American History by my family's travels throughout the United States during my father's navy career. So when I went to ODU, I decided to explore European History. When I arrived at MSU, I was told that I was deficient in social study credits. So I enrolled in American History 101. The first quarter ended before Christmas vacation. We had to remove everything from our dorm rooms so that they could be thoroughly cleaned. I went home to VA Beach. I posted my grades on my bedroom door. I had earned an A in American History and highlighted on my report card. I received mostly Cs and some Bs in my vet courses. My dad wrote the following note on my report card: "I thought we sent you there to be a veterinarian, not a history major."

CASE REPORT

Also during my freshman year, I wrote a case report based on my experience as a veterinary assistant with Dr. Ward. The article was published in the student periodical *M.S.U. Veterinarian* in the spring of 1964 edition. I had a special connection to this Bassett. His owners were members of my church and their teenage children and I were in the youth group together. In reflecting on this case, I now see it as a harbinger of future cases such as CORN COB and one many years later when a Labrador retriever ate the entire beef roast, including the netting.

CASE REPORT:
OBSTRUCTION OF THE GASTRONINTESTINAL TRACT BY GOLF BALLS
Samuel W. Tate*

On August 9, 1962, a two-year-old male Bassett Hound was brought to an out of state veterinary hospital for the purpose of being bathed. The owner mentioned that the dog had been vomiting the day before and had not eaten for a day or so.

HISTORY AND SYMPTOMS

This dog was first a patient of the hospital when it was seven months old. At that time he showed symptoms of vomiting and diarrhea. A fecal examination revealed no evidence of parasitism. The animal was treated with penicillin and antiemetic tablets with favorable results. For the next fifteen months the dog continued to have spells of vomiting, diarrhea, and impacted anal sacs. He would often show listlessness and posterior soreness which would be relieved by expressing the anal sacs and administering Sterane. [1] His last such period of these symptoms was in June, 1962.

On August 9, the dog's temperature was normal. His anal sacs were expressed and contained much fluid. Because his temperature was normal, he was bathed and released on the same day.

*The author is a freshman student in the College of Veterinary Medicine, MSU.

---

[1] *Chas. Pfizer and Co., Inc.*

DIAGNOSIS

On August 11, the Bassett was returned to the hospital. The owner complained that the vomiting was more violent and the dog still had not eaten. A radiographic examination was ordered and an 8" x 10" radiograph was taken of the lateral view. The radiograph showed three round objects about 3.5 cm. in diameter in the stomach.

TREATMENT

The patient was prepared for surgery. He was anesthetized by an injection of Pentothal[2] in the cephalic vein. The abdomen was clipped and scrubbed with Nolvasan.[3] A midline incision was made and the peritoneal cavity exposed. Upon entering the stomach, two golf balls were found in the fundic region and another was found blocking the pylorus. The golf balls were removed and the stomach wall was sutured. The peritoneum, muscle layers, and the skin were then sutured. The patient was given dextrose intravenously. Penicillin was also given at this time. The patient's recovery was good and he was eating solid food on the second day following surgery, so he was discharged.

On August 17, the animal was again returned to the hospital. The vomiting has become more severe than before and contained bile. The dog was very weak and in a state of shock. He had lost a considerable amount of weight. Another radiograph was taken. A 14" x 16" cassette was used to obtain a view of the entire abdominal cavity. The second radiograph showed an object about 3 cm. in diameter in the lower abdominal region.

The patient was tranquilized with Sparine.[4] The surgical field was prepared as before and a local anesthetic was given. An incision was made in the inguinal region to the right of the midline. The peritoneal cavity was opened and the obstruction was found about three inches anterior to the ileocecal junction. A fourth golf ball was removed and the incision was closed. Post-operative care consisted of dextrose given intravenously and penicillin.

---

[2] Buck and Sons
[3] Fort Dodge Laboratories
[4] Pitman-Moore Co.

A mineral oil enema was also given. The patient was removed to the recovery room where he died that night.

SUMMARY
All four golf balls were minus their exterior layers and consisted of just the rubber cores. The one found in the ileum had ruptured, expelling its soft core into the intestine. The source of the golf balls without covers was not determined from the history.

Although the balls could have been palpated, the possibility of foreign objects was overlooked because the symptoms were the same as the animal had shown throughout his life. It was not determined if the four golf balls were present at the beginning or ingested after the bathing was performed. By the time the second operation was performed, it had been ten days since the patient had eaten any substantial amount of food and was therefore a poor surgical risk.

The possibility of obstructions in the gastrointestinal tract is often overlooked by practitioners and "shot-gun" remedies being used, the animal is temporarily relieved with antibiotics. This case points out the importance of an early and correct diagnosis after a complete examination. Certainly every dog that is brought in cannot be radio-graphed just because it has an intestinal upset. However, all possibilities would be examined and the animal should be watched very closely for new complications.

MARRIED MY HIGH SCHOOL SWEETHEART

I married my high school sweetheart, Shirley Spangler, after my first year at MSU. Dr. Ward loaned us his cottage at Nags Head, NC, for our honeymoon. That summer we lived in a one-bedroom cottage on Norview Avenue, Norfolk, VA, while I worked for Dr. Ward, and Shirley continued at the *Virginia Pilot* newspaper. We then moved to married housing at MSU. Shirley got a position as secretary in the Department of Romance Languages typing papers for graduate students in languages she couldn't read. Samuel L. Tate was born in May, 1966.

We moved across the street to a two-bedroom apartment. On the second floor was a balcony the entire length of the building. I was awarded the Charles Pfizer Scholarship (based on need) at the Michigan Veterinary Medical Association meeting that summer. I paid the hospital bill for the delivery with the scholarship.

CORN COB

My partner and I were assigned a Walker hound as one of our first cases in small animal clinics. He presented with symptoms of vomiting, poor appetite, and weight loss. Abdominal palpation was normal, but its mucus membranes and white of the eyes were yellow (icteric or jaundiced). We had just completed the course in infectious diseases and our thought of a deferential diagnosis immediately went to hepatitis, so we moved the hound to isolation. We started it on IV fluids and antibiotics.

The next day the dog was not much better and turning more icteric. We palpated the abdomen again and found a mass. We took the hound to radiology.

Dr. Mostowski asked, "Does this hound live on a farm?"

We said, "Yes."

Dr. Mostowski nodded. "He ate a corn cob."

The X-ray showed a foreign object in the small intestine so we scheduled the hound for surgery. Sure enough, there was a corn cob in the duodenum right where the bile duct empties. The corn cob was blocking the bile duct causing bile to back up into the liver, which was causing the jaundice.

SPLAT

During another small animal clinic rotation we were assigned a Dachshund belonging to the director of the Student Health Clinic, Dr. Feurig. The dog was very obese and being treated for a luxated disc. We were doing hydrotherapy in a bathtub to exercise his legs. We took him out of the tub and placed him on a stainless steel exam table. My classmate who was holding him let him go in order to reach a towel to dry him off. In the split second that took, the dog propelled like a seal off the table and SPLAT on the floor. We put him back on the table, and he was dead within minutes. The necropsy showed he died of a ruptured liver that was extremely friable due to fat infiltration (fatty liver).

STUDENT JOBS

I worked several part-time jobs in the vet college during my second though fourth years. My first jobs were with the husband and wife team of Drs. Rodger and Esther Brown. I helped him prepare anatomical specimens for a lab he taught. Esther ran the histology lab where technicians prepare tissue samples to be examined under the microscope. I cleaned the lab on evenings and weekends. Esther was also in charge of pre-vet student orientation during spring break. My job was to usher them to various stations around the campus and answer their questions about student life in general and the vet college specifically.

Our class moved to the teaching hospital during our third year and used a locker room on the second floor. I took over management of the student laundry account. All student overalls and scrubs had the student's name and a red tag to separate them from the faculty. The MSU laundry would deliver all the red-tagged clothing, and I would distribute them to the students. I collected the laundry fee from each student, paid the laundry, and retained five cents per article for managing the account.

I became an assistant in the graduate pathology lab on the top floor of Giltner Hall my third year. This lab supported all the research projects of the PhD candidates in vet pathology. At first my duties were to wash and autoclave all the glassware. All test tubes and petri dishes that contained pathogens had to be autoclaved before they could be discarded. I also performed mathematical computations on a calculator for their statistical data. The position expanded to taking care of the animals in the various research projects.

There was a herd of about twenty goats in runs in the basement of Giltner Hall. I would move one goat to an empty run so I could clean the run, and then move it back. I then repeated the process until all the runs were cleaned. I would then take all the waste in a wheelbarrow out to a dumpster then feed and water all the goats. I was also caring for about a hundred guinea pigs at a barn on the research farm. They were in large metal bins with bedding. Each bin had to be emptied and cleaned twice a week in addition to feeding and watering the guinea pigs daily.

My most interesting and intensive job was taking care of specific pathogen free (SPF) piglets at nights and on weekends. There was a controlled environment building on the research farm that housed these animals. The potential for infection by several pathogens complicates the study of the effects of one specific pathogen on organs and tissue; thus, the use of SPF pigs. The sow would be prepared for C-section, which would be performed in a vinyl "bubble." The piglets would then be passed from the surgical "bubble" into stainless steel kennels in a vinyl pressurized isolator. There were four piglets per isolator in two sets of two kennels. Each isolator had a set of arm's length rubber gloves built in both sides. Access to the interior was through a round air lock in the front of the isolator, about twenty inches in diameter and six inches deep. The outside and inside covers were vinyl discs held in place by rubber bands about the width of a bicycle inner tube.

The care and feeding process began by removing the outside air lock cover, placing sterilized cans of formula on the shelf in the air lock, and replacing the outer cover. Then I would place my arms in the gloves in the side of the isolator, remove the insider cover, and bring the canned milk in. The next step was to empty the waste from the pans under each kennel into the empty milk cans from the previous feeding with a large bulb syringe. The piglets were fed by bottles that hung in the door of their kennels every four hours. The bottles would be refilled and the empty cans left in the isolator. The cans with the waste would be placed in the airlock and the inner cover secured. The outside cover was then removed, the waste cans taken out, and the outer cover replaced. The process took about twenty minutes per isolator. Sometimes Shirley would go with me, and it was easier for two to manipulate the airlock.

RADIOLOGY EXAM

During our junior year, radiology was taught in the large classroom on the second floor of the teaching hospital. Dr. Mostowski projected slides of radiographs on a screen in the front of the room. Many of us had difficulty visualizing the abnormalities, especially those of us who sat towards the back of the room. The final exam for the course was conducted the same way. Fifty percent of the class failed which never happened before. I was one of those that failed. Failing a course meant falling back a year. Sandy Chesnut had completed the Army ROTC program and was commissioned as a second lieutenant in armored instead of Medical Services Corps because he wanted to be where the action was at summer camp. If he were held back a year he would have to go on active duty. The faculty decided to give us a second exam because it was too disruptive to have half of the class not advancing to the senior clinics. Dr. Mostowski provided us with all the original radiographs so we could study them on the view boxes in our spare time. The makeup exam was scheduled for two weeks using the view boxes.

It just so happened that the exam was at the same time as the American Veterinary Medical Association (AVMA) in Louisville, KY and most of the faculty was gone. Some of the senior interns monitored the exam. Lo and behold, half of those taking the makeup exam failed again. I passed. When the faculty returned, they decided to give another makeup exam at which every one passed, including Sandy.

DEAD COW

I was on farm ambulatory service the first term of my senior year, the summer of 1966. Dr. Sam Getty was our instructor. He was always complaining that the motor pool didn't provide spare tires in our vehicles. He had experienced flat tires several times and complained about time lost waiting for a repair truck.

One hot summer day we were going out to a farm with a sick cow. We were pulling a mobile cattle chute; its tires were so bald we could see the cords. When we got to the farm the cow was dead. The farmer wanted it necropsied. We loaded the cow into the chute with the aid of a wench. We then got on Interstate 96 about ten miles from campus when a tire blew on the chute. Dr. Getty called the motor pool on the radio. They said to leave the chute there; they would send a repair truck, fix the tire, and tow it back. Dr. Getty never mentioned the dead cow.

Not only did they put two new tires on the chute, they put a brand new spare tire in the van.

ARROGANT PROFESSOR

We got a call to treat a herd of Chalet cattle belonging to a MSU professor in another college. We went to his farm just inside the twenty-five-mile practice limit. He told Dr. Getty the cattle were on another property of his just a few miles away. Although it was beyond our practice limit, Dr. Getty agreed to go because otherwise we would have lost out on that instruction time. The professor had several rolls of snow fencing he said we would need. We loaded them on the chute. About twenty head of cattle were in large pasture with a wooded area at the far end. We set up the snow fence using the pasture fence as one side of a funnel leading to the chute. We then went out on foot and began to quietly herd the cattle towards the opening of the funnel. When the lead cow got there she bolted, and the rest of the cattle followed her down into the woods. Dr. Getty was already perturbed with the professor about stretching the twenty-five-mile rule, and this was the last straw. We hooked up the chute and left the professor and his snow fence and cattle.

Dr. Getty submitted a bill for the farm call. The professor refused to pay it. The university garnished his pay.

HANDWRITING ON THE WALL

January 1965 I was in my sophomore year in Veterinary College. I was reading the news section of the Journal of the American Veterinary Medical Association (JAVMA). It had an article every year with a table that showed the enrollment in all the veterinary colleges by class and sex. In the bottom right corner of the table was the total number of male students in the class of 1967. Two pages over was an article about the US Army Veterinary Corps and how many veterinarians the army was going to draft in 1967. The two numbers exactly matched.

My goal had always been to go into small animal practice, maybe where I worked as a student in VA Beach. However, the handwriting was on the wall that military service would come first.

Coming from a military family dating to the Revolutionary War, I had no qualms about serving my country but had no desire to do it in the Army.

There was an Air Force Reserve Officers Training Corps (ROTC) unit on campus, so I went to see what they had to offer. They told me about the early commissioning program. I would be commissioned as a second lieutenant (01) in the Medical Service Corps and be exempt from all training and not subject to the draft. Upon graduation I would be commissioned a first lieutenant (02) in the Veterinary Corps with promotion to captain (03) after six months on active duty. In the military there is this thing called "longevity." Military pay is based on both rank and longevity. So, my longevity would start with my commission date as a second lieutenant. My promotion to captain in October 1967 coincided with two years longevity, which gave me a whopping pay increase.

I discussed the situation with my wife, Shirley, and we decided it was the best course rather than wait to be drafted. As it turned out six of my classmates were drafted by July 1967 and visited me at Lackland AFB while they were in training at Fort Sam Houston for the Army Veterinary Corps.

CATTLE DRIVE

Before I could sign up for the Air Force I had to complete a four-page statement of personal history (DD398). I sent it to my mother to provide the information for the nine places where I lived and the fourteen schools I attended since 1950. I also had to have a physical. The ROTC unit scheduled me for a site in Detroit. I didn't realize until I arrived at seven in the morning it was the induction center and most of the people there were draftees. Before I could state why I was there, an army sergeant directed me to a cubical in a large room with a hundred or more inductees. On the table in front of me was an aptitude test. I raised my hand and a sergeant came over. I told him I didn't need to do the test and said I was there for a commissioning physical. He asked, "Why didn't you say so?"

I replied, "I wasn't given a chance." He told me to follow him. He sat me down in a room with those school desks with the writing surface attached to the back. The military medical history form was on the desk, and a sergeant in a white lab coat was in the front of the room with a pointer and a huge wall chart of the medical history form.

He started to speak, "Okay, you's guys, do not get ahead of me. In the first block, write your last name first! (Pause) In the second block, write your first name last. (Pause) In the third block, write your middle initial. If you have no middle initial, writes NMI." (Pause)

I raised my hand. He barked, "What do you not understand?"

I replied, "I already have the form filled out."

He said gruffly, "I told you not to get ahead of me."

I replied, "They gave me the form at the ROTC Unit and I filled it out."

He asked, "What are you here for?"

I replied, "A commissioning physical."

I was sent to another room and told to strip to my underpants and shoes. I got in a line to have blood drawn and afterwards I was given a urine specimen cup. When some of the men released the pressure on their arms to urinate in the cup, they ended up with blood on the floor. Next station was the physical exam. I finished the cattle drive before noon but was not entitled to the free lunch because I was not an inductee.

JOB HUNTING

At MSU half of the rising senior veterinary students take their clinical rotation in the summer in order to maintain operations in the teaching hospital. In return they graduate in early March instead of mid-June. I opted for the summer rotation. I advised the AF Military Personnel Center (MPC) at Randolph AFB, San Antonio, TX, that I was to graduate in March and would be available to immediately enter active duty. They replied that they could not tell me yet when I would be scheduled for the Medical Officer Basic Course (MOB). It could be anytime between August and December 1967. So in January I started to interview for a temporary position. I interviewed in four practices in Michigan and Indiana. I couldn't find anyone to take me on for such an undetermined time.

I called MPC again. I explained my situation – that I had a wife and child and that I could not find temporary employment. They still could not give me a definite entry date.

So, I said I had contacted the Army Veterinary Corps, and they said they could take me as soon as I graduate. MPC said not to take any hasty action.

They would get back to me within a week. Sure enough, MPC called and said orders were in the mail for me to report to Lackland AFB, San Antonio, in May for a direct duty assignment, and I was scheduled for four weeks of MOB in August followed by the eleven-week Veterinary Officer Basic Course at Sheppard AFB, Wichita Falls, TX.

FAILURE IS NOT AN OPTION

I was a couple months from graduation in 1967 when the ROTC unit notified me that I needed another physical. They were going to send me back to the cattle drive in Detroit. I objected and said I had grown up in a military family and knew I could get a physical at any military clinic. So, they made an appointment and sent me to Wurtsmith AFB, Oscoda, Mich.

There were four of us getting commissioning physicals. The medical officer called all four of us into his office and closed the door. The major then said, "I was coerced into the Air Force and I have only one kidney. I don't care what I might find wrong with any of you - you are not failing this physical."

We all passed with flying colors.

IS THAT A HORSE?

It was in my senior year of veterinary college at MSU. I was on large animal clinic rotation and I was assigned a donkey. Chester was from the Dearborn Zoo and had granulating sores on all four legs at the fetlocks. This condition is also known as proud flesh and is an overgrowth of granulating tissue. The skin is unable to grow to cover it. The sores were initiated by an insect cuterebra, which lays its eggs in the skin.

I reviewed the literature and found there had been some success using the cartilage of cow's ears to make a collagen bandage. I went to the local slaughterhouse, collected the ears, cleaned and disinfected them, and removed the cartilage. Oh, did I mention Chester didn't like anyone touching his legs? There was no improvement after two weeks.

Next I tried autogenous red blood cells. I drew blood from Chester in a whole blood collection kit with an anticoagulant. I allowed the red blood cells to settle to the bottom and siphoned off the plasma. I then transferred the red bloods cells to a plastic spray bottle. I would squirt the red blood cells on the wounds. After several days, a scab began to form and the skin edges began to epithelize the wound. After several weeks of twice daily treatment the skin had almost covered the wounds.

Then came the long Thanksgiving holiday. I went to my Aunt Virginia's home in Cincinnati, OH. When I returned, Chester had died. They held his body in the cooler so that we could do a post mortem exam. The diagnosis was a rupture abdominal aorta aneurism due to parasitic worms. Totally unrelated to his leg sores.

I got permission to preserve his skull. So for twenty years while I was in the Air Force, Chester's skull resided on my desk. Horse owners seeking free advice about their horse would come to my office and ask, "Are you the vet?"

My replay was "Yes."

Then they would see Chester and ask, "What is that?"

My reply was, "That's the last horse I treated." End of conversation as they made haste out the door.

BLIZZARD

A blizzard hit Michigan January 26 and 27, 1967. The official snowfall in Lansing was twenty-four inches, the most since sixteen inches on March 2 and 3, 1875, and of any storms since 1967. It was the first time MSU closed in its 112-year history. The worst of the storm was the wind causing drifts eight feet deep. We had two feet of snow on our balcony and when we shoved it off, it created a tunnel effect on the apartments on the first floor. It was all hands on deck to dig a path from the parking lot between the two facing rows of apartments to the laundromat and the circle road. It was several days before the big snow-blowing plow cleared the circle road from our complex to Hagadorn Road. To clear the streets and parking lots on campus, the snow was collected in dump trucks and deposited in the lots next to the power plant on Hagadorn Road. That pile of snow was still there when we left MSU in late March 1967.

FIRST TO GRADUATE

The March 1967 class of veterinary students was milling around in the lobby of the auditorium at MSU. We would be leading the procession of all graduates because we were receiving the highest degrees, Doctor of Veterinary Medicine (DVM). The procession marshal came to us asked, "Who wants to lead?"

I replied, "I've been here long enough. I'll go first." I graduated first in my class. You noticed I do not claim to have graduated top of my class.

POST GRADUATION TRAVEL

We left MSU for VA Beach to stay with family while we waited for the time to depart for San Antonio, TX. Then our trip west included an overnight stay with my Great Aunt Julia Jordan in Raleigh, NC, and sightseeing in Atlanta, GA. On our way through southern Alabama on Interstate 65, we saw a sign that read "Florida State Line - 10 miles." I had been in forty-four of the lower forty-eight states, and Florida was one I had missed. We turned off the Interstate onto Alabama Route 21 and crossed the state line two miles south of Atmore, in a rain storm. Shirley pulled into an unpaved lot of a gas station and said, "Open the door and put your foot out so you can say you stepped foot in Florida."

I did as instructed and stepped into a mud puddle.

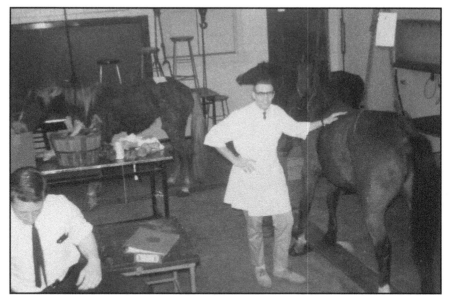

Samuel Tate in large animal gross anatomy, College of Veterinary Medicine, Michigan State University, 1963.

Dr Samuel and Shirley Tate, graduation, March 1967.

PART 2

BECOMING A VETERAN

UNIFORM SNAFU

Lackland AFB, TX
FIRST UNIFORM

I arrived at Lackland without any uniforms since I was assigned directly without going through medical officer basic course where many of officer medics got their three hundred dollar uniform allowance and purchased their uniforms. Master Sergeant (E7) Balsik, Non Commission Officer in Charge (NCOIC) of Veterinary Services, took me under his wing. I received my uniform allowance from the finance office, and he took me to the uniform shop. He picked out a set of blues, two sets of khakis 1505s, two sets of green fatigues, a pair of black shoes, and a garrison hat (also called a wheel hat). He put a special liquid on the visor of the hat to make it shine, and then placed the hat on the file cabinet near the desk of our office secretary, Billie Walker. As my hat was drying, Lieutenant Colonel Hayman was passing Billie's desk and saw my hat. He picked it up by the visor and asked, "What is this hat doing here?"

Billie replied, "That's Lieutenant Tate's hat. Sergeant Balsik was shining the visor until you put your finger prints on it."

SOCKS

I had to pass Billie's desk to get to my office and Lieutenant Colonel Hayman's office beyond that. I came in one morning and Billie asked me, "Doctor, did you get dressed in the dark?"

I replied, "Yes, why?"

Billie replied, "You have two different colored socks on."

DISABILITY

On the 4th of July, I strained my neck when I dove off the high dive at the pool. I went to the hospital and they gave me a neck brace to wear. Wilford Hall USAF Hospital had a lot of senior officers come there to get their separation physicals before retirement. Many of them would get at least a forty percent disability rating and would be able to have that part of their retired pay, tax free.

Several days after my injury, we had a visit by Colonel Griffin, Command Veterinarian, Air Training Command, from Randolph AFB on the north side of San Antonio. As Colonel Griffin passed my space on the way to Lieutenant Colonel Hayman's office, he saw me in my neck brace and asked, "What happened to you, Lieutenant?"

I replied, "I'm working on my retirement disability!"

WICHITA FALLS, TX
RIBBONS

I reported to MOB on Monday in uniform 1505s. There were three of us veterinarians in uniform - everybody else was in civvies. Our course leader was a captain and former enlisted veterinary tech. At the lunch break, he lined up the three of us in the hall and told us the rest of the class would not start wearing uniforms until formal uniform inspection in two weeks. In the mean time we could wear our uniforms if we wanted to but would have to stand inspection by him every morning. No brainer.

The big day of blues inspection arrived. Everyone had a National Defense Service ribbon. But we three lieutenants had additional ribbons from our direct duty assignments. Some of the MDs and dentists were coming on active duty as majors and wanted to know how we lieutenants got those extra ribbons. I replied, "They sell them in the base exchange."

Colonel Wiedman the school commander was the inspecting officer. The first officer he came to was one of the lieutenant veterinarians with the extra ribbons. Colonel Wiedman asked, "How did you earn those ribbons, Lieutenant?"

Caught off guard, he replied "ROTC, sir." Col Wiedman smiled and moved to the next officer.

MCCHORD AFB MAJOR's HAT

In November 1967, I flew from Norfolk, VA, where I situated my family, to McChord AFB, Washington, on my way to Vietnam. I arrived late afternoon the day before my military contract flight and stayed in the Bachelor Office Quarters (BOQ). I arose in the morning and had enough time to get breakfast at the officers' club. It was raining so I wore my rain coat, which I hung in the coat room of the club. After breakfast I put on my rain coat and retrieved my flight cap from the rack above. I went back to the BOQ to get my luggage. I then boarded the shuttle bus to the air terminal. While I was on the bus I was aware the enlisted airmen were snickering. When I got off the bus I put my hand in my right pocket of my rain coat and there was my flight cap with captain's bars. On my head was a flight cap with a major's oak leaf.

VIETNAM POCKETS

The green AF jungle fatigues has lots of pockets. The jacket has two breast pockets and two side pockets. The trousers have two front pockets, two cargo pockets, and two rear pockets. All these pockets have two buttons each, except for the two front pockets of the trousers. That's sixteen buttons, not counting the buttons to close the jacket.

My hooch (quarters) was close to the dispensary (a twenty-five-bed facility). So in the mornings I would drive to the dispensary to pick up distribution (official correspondence). I then would pick up my airmen at their hooch on the way to our office in the sentry dog kennel at the far end of the base. Chief Master Sergeant (E9) John C. Daniels (also referred to as the sergeant major) had his desk next to the rack of distribution boxes; that way he could observe those picking up distribution. He had a very keen eye for how many pocket flaps were not buttoned. I would hear, "Captain Tate, your left rear pocket is unbuttoned. You must set a good example for your airmen."

R & R - HONG KONG
MAJOR GENERAL

Most of our in-country travel was by C-130 Hercules or helicopter, so we would wear our green jungle fatigues. If I was making a connection for an out of country flight, we were required to change into 1505s.

Dan Adona, one of our dentists, and I flew to Da Nang to get an R&R (rest and relaxation) flight to Hong Kong. When I changed into my 1505s at the veterinary office, I realized I had forgotten my metal captain's bars for my shirt collars. The NCOI, a technical sergeant, opened his desk drawer and asked, "What do you want to be?" On display was every officer rank insignia. I could have been a two star (major general) but stuck with the captain bars because that's what was on my travel orders.

SUIT

Dan and I stayed in the President Hotel. The most highly recommended tailor shop of all Hong Kong was on the first floor. The day we arrived we were measured for blue uniforms and suits. Dan ordered shark skin and I a three-piece gray suit. For our last night in Hong Kong we made reservations at a floor show which included dinner at a swanky hotel walking distance from the President. We picked up our tailor-made clothes and were discussing what we would wear to the show. The tailor overheard us and suggested we wear our new suits, which we did. All night we were aware of people staring at us. It wasn't until we got back to our room that we knew why. We still had the tailor's chalk marks on our suits.

R & R HAWAII BUCKLE

I delayed going R&R to Hawaii to meet Shirley until the nine-month point. That way it was easier to cope with another three months separation instead of six. Our hospital administrator, Captain Barry Morrison, and I took a C-

130 from Tuy Hoa to Cam Ranh AFB to catch the R&R flight to Hawaii. There we changed from our jungle fatigues to 1505s. That is when I realized I was missing the blue web belt and silver buckle. I went to the uniform shop. I found the blue web belt but they had no silver buckles. Barry got the idea of using twist ties to hold the belt in place and cover the joint with the foil from a gum wrapper. The first item I purchased in Hawaii was a uniform silver belt buckle.

BEACH ATTIRE

My mother made matching beach attire for Shirley and me to wear in Hawaii. She mailed my set to me in Vietnam without telling Shirley. As we were dressing for the beach, Shirley noticed we matched. She asked, "Where did you get that?"

I replied, "At the Tuy Hoa Base Exchange."

She commanded, "Let me see the label." It read, "Hand Made by Frederica," my mother's middle name that she used for all her crafts.

SARONG

Shirley and I were staying at the famous Coco Palms Resort on the Waialua River in Kauai. Many movies had been filmed there, including *Blue Hawaii* starring Elvis Presley, and where the *Hawaii Wedding Song* was written. Barry Morrison and his wife were staying at the resort where Esther Williams starred in the 1950 movie *Pagan Love Song*. We met them at their resort. After a day at the beach, we were going to dinner. The dining room attire was no shorts. All I had were Bermuda shorts. So we took a bed sheet and wrapped it around my waist like a sarong. We were admitted to the dining room without comment, but I sure got a lot of looks.

GUAM
A GENERAL'S HAT

Part of my "tropical" khaki uniform 1505s was the AF blue flight cap with silver piping and rank insignia on the left side. The silver piping was becoming worn, so I needed a new flight cap. The AF uniform shop was at Anderson AFB at the north end of the island about twenty miles from the main naval base. I found the uniform hat display arranged by sizes. All the hats looked alike to me. After several tries I found one that fit. I took it to the cashier who asked, "Sir is this hat for you?"

My smart-alecky reply was, "Well, it's not for my wife!"

She pleasantly replied, "Sir, this is a general officer's hat."

I was dumbfounded, "All the flight caps there are exactly alike. What are us company grade officers to do for a flight cap?"

She replied, "We get a lot of generals through here back and forth to Vietnam. I can special order you one." I got my new flight cap a month later.

WASHINGTON, DC
EPAULETS

The AF added to its uniform a long-sleeved, light blue shirt with epaulets. There was a cloth rank insignia that slid over the epaulets. It was to replace the shirt worn under the blouse (coat) that had the rank insignia on its epaulets. That way when one took their blouse off in an office setting, their rank could still be seen (That's my opinion, it may not be the real reason, and I was only a major). So, I went to the uniform shop at Bolling AFB across the Anacostia River from the Navy Yard. I found a set of major's epaulets and took them to the cashier who asked, "Are these for you, Mayor?" (Sound familiar?)

I replied, "Well they are not for my wife?"

At which she explained, "These are for a female's uniform."

GERMANY

SUSPENDERS

Every year the U.S. Army Europe (USAEUR) Command Veterinarian hosted a conference in Berchtesgaden for all US and NATO allied veterinarians. In 1982 The Chief of US Army Veterinary Corps, Brigadier General Frank Ramsey, a one star, was a guest of honor. I had served with him on several joint working groups when he was a colonel and I was at NAVFSSO in Washington, DC. I had even taken my boss to the Pentagon for Brigadier General Ramsey's promotion ceremony and appointment as Chief. The last night of the conference was a banquet at which all the ladies wore formals and the officers their service mess dress uniform. The AF mess dress consisted of black trousers held up by white suspenders, a black cummerbund, white pleated shirt, black bow tie, and black waist coat, (black in winter, white in summer) shoulder boards with rank insignia, and miniature medals. Well, I forgot the white suspenders. However, I had a pair of Bavarian Edelweiss suspenders I wore with my lederhosen. (As I mentioned elsewhere, since the US Army assumed all veterinary missions for DoD, there was a concerted effort to have us AF veterinarians transfer to the Army. Those of us who chose not to transfer became environmental health officers in the Biomedical Sciences Corps).

By chance I was in the men's room the same time as Brigadier General Ramsey. I told him I had transferred from the US Air Force. That brought a smile to his face. Then I stuck my thumbs in my Edelweiss suspenders, pushed them out where he could see them, and said, "To the Bavarian Air Force!" He laughed. Then I said, "I came very close to filing out the Army application, but I just couldn't find a pen that wrote green ink." He laughed again and we left the men's room together.

HE'S A LIEUTENANT ALREADY

I had been at Lackland just two weeks when I had a toothache. The dental clinic made me an appointment for 0600 the next day. I arrived to find the waiting area full of recruits all in green fatigues. The staff sergeant at the desk checked me in and said, "Have a seat, Lieutenant." I found an empty seat between two recruits. I stuck out like a sore thumb in my 1505s (khaki) in that sea of green. I noticed most of these recruits had swollen jaws. I deduced they were having their wisdom teeth extracted. After a few minutes, the recruit on my left asked, "Sir, how long have you been here?"

Thinking he meant how long I had been waiting. I replied, "I just checked in."

He clarified his question, "I meant how long have you been at Lackland?"

"Oh," I replied, "two weeks."

He then turned to the recruit on my right and exclaimed, "He's been here as long as we have, and he's already a lieutenant."

DRILL INSTRUCTOR

Lackland was also the site of Officer Candidate School (OCS). It was located on the other side of Interstate 410, at Medina. The base services officer, a lieutenant colonel, invited Lieutenant Colonel Hayman and me to lunch at the OCS dining hall. He wanted too showed off the facility (As far as I remember there were no problems there, so this was not an inspection, just a tour). We went through the serving line and sat at a table reserved for officers. As we were finishing our meals a cadet approached our table. He stated, "Sir, our squadron is ready to return to our barracks and we can't find our drill instructor to march us back."

There was a pause as the two lieutenant colonels looked at me, the only lieutenant at the table. Before either one of them could speak, the dining hall NCOIC spoke, "Cadet, you will find your drill instructor with the other NCOs at the tables behind that white picket fence." I let out a sigh of relief and everyone laughed.

FIRST MILITARY HOP

I needed to take the VA State Veterinary Board Exam in July 1967. The hospital provided me with travel orders, and I was able to catch a military flight from Randolph AFB, San Antonio, TX, to Langley AFB, Hampton, VA. My dad drove from VA Beach to pick me up. The next day, I drove to Richmond to take the exam, which lasted all day and included both written and oral portions. I was the only candidate in uniform. I drove back to VA Beach and spent the weekend. Dad took me back to Langley to catch a hop back to Texas. There were about fifteen of us waiting to board a C-118 Liftmaster, the military version of the four- engine DC-6. The pilot came over and told us there was a problem with the plane. The crew chief could be seen wiping hydraulic fluid from the nose landing gear.

I commented to the major next to me, "I don't think he is going to fix that leak with a rag." The pilot returned and instructed us to load up on the second C-118 in line. We got seated just as fog rolled in off the Back River at the east end of the airfield. The crew had already started the engines, so we sat there idling for about twenty minutes until the fog cleared. We then taxied to the west end of the airfield for takeoff. As the plane accelerated down the runway, it pulled slightly to the right. The pilot throttled back and brought the plane to the east end stating there seemed to be a slight loss of power in one of the right engines. He was going around again for another attempt, which we did with the same results.

He parked the plane at the east end where there was a third C-118 parked. We got our bags and transferred to that one and took off without incident. I was sitting in the back next to a major from Waco, TX. We passed through a thunderstorm over North Carolina, and it got pretty bumpy. The female army medic heading for Fort Sam Houston in the seat behind us got air sick. We landed at Millington, TN, to refuel. The crew chief told us to take our bags with us when we got off the plane. In the time it took us to deplane, there was a puddle of oil on the tarmac under one of the right engines. We went into the snack bar at base operations just as another thunderstorm passed through. It rained so hard one could have paddled a canoe on the runway. The major and I were standing near the pilot watching the rain when the crew chief returned. "Captain Brown, they don't have the part I need, but give me an hour and I can make one."

The major said, "Come on, Doc, we're finding another way home." We walked about two blocks to the Air National Guard flight ops. They didn't have any flights but offered a ride to the Memphis Airport. The major jumped out and went to the Braniff desk. I got the bags and followed. We paid for our tickets and rushed to the gate. We were the last two aboard as the door was closed. The flight attendant seated us in first class. Two weeks later I received VA Veterinary License #912 in the mail.

THE GENERAL'S CAT

One of my duties as base veterinarian at Lackland AFB was to conduct a zoonosis clinic one day a week. It was mostly to provide vaccination of pets belonging to military personnel.

Brigadier General Couch was the commander of Wilford Hall Hospital at Lackland. MSgt Balsick and I attended a meeting where the general was present (I don't remember the circumstances). At the close of the meeting Brigadier General Couch asked me if I would take a look at his cat. He explained it was a stray cat that had been hanging around his quarters. His wife started feeding him and took him in several weeks ago. They had named the cat "Clawed" because he had scratched several people. I was about to say the clinic was only one day a week and he should make an appointment. MSgt Balsick must have read my mind, because he kicked me under the table. I paused for a second and said, "I would be glad to examine your cat at your convenience." He asked if the next morning at ten would be ok. I said certainly.

Mrs. Couch arrived with Clawed at ten the next morning. I was concerned about Clawed scratching people and communicating any diseases. She said he had not bitten anybody, and I dismissed the possibility of rabies because they had observed him more than ten days without him showing any symptoms. On physical exam, I found Clawed was infested with ear mites and had a lot of debris in his ears. I applied some ear mite medication. Clawed shook his head and debris went everywhere, including on my uniform.

Mrs. Couch said, "You should wear a doctor's coat."

I replied, "The hospital supply would not issue me any." I vaccinated Clawed for rabies, several feline diseases, and dispensed medication for his ears.

Within thirty minutes of Mrs. Couch's departure, I got a phone call from hospital supply asking what size lab coats I needed and if I wanted my name and rank embroidered on them.

HOSPITAL FOOD SERVICE

A very large part of my office's responsibilities was food service sanitation. In addition to training food service workers in proper sanitation procedures, it involved doing facility inspections. Although my technicians conducted most of the inspections, I was expected to conduct a certain amount of them, especially follow-up inspection of facilities that were having problems. The hospital food service provides all of the prepared meals to patients as well as operating a dining facility for staff, patients, and visitors. The officer in charge, a major, was a dietitian. The first time I inspected the facility I found some very severe discrepancies in food handling and sanitation. I rated the facility unsatisfactory, which would require my report to the commander, Brigadier General Couch. The major was highly indignant that a lieutenant was telling her how to run her operation. I gave her a copy of the report and left. Within an hour the general's secretary called and said the general wanted to see me in his office right away.

I drove to the hospital and was shown into the general's office. The major was there. Brigadier General Couch asked her, "Are the findings accurate?" She replied that they were but did not warrant an unsatisfactory rating. Brig Gen Couch disagreed with her. He told her she had twenty-four hours to make the correction and that Dr. Tate would perform a re-inspection. If any discrepancies were found, she would be assigned elsewhere. The major did not know that I had treated the general's cat. Not that that had anything to do with it.

BATS IN THE ATTIC

In July 1967, I had been at Lackland AFB, San Antonio, Texas, (the Air Force's recruit training base) for about two months. People were finding dead bats around the base. We collected these bats and sent them to the AF diagnostic lab on base. The report came back that the bats had rabies. I teamed up with Technical Sergeant Messger from the bioenvironmental engineer shop. We located the source to be in the space above the false ceiling in a two-hundred-man recruit training barracks. The square core of the building was constructed of cinder block and housed all the utilities. Projecting from second floor of each side was a recruit housing bay. Under each of the four wings was an open area with a concrete pad for a shaded training area. On the roof where these wings joined the core building was a space covered with copper flashing. The joints at the sides were also closed with copper flashing. In the summertime the heat would cause the edges of the building to expand and compress the copper seals. When the building contracted in the winder the seals fell out, leaving a hole for the bats to enter.

We reported our findings to Brigadier General Couch and the base civil engineers (BCE). The BCE consulted an extermination company in town who said they would tent the building for fumigation. It would take seventeen days and cost sixteen thousand dollars. It was left to myself and TSgt Messger to find a more expedient and less expensive solution.

The first effort was to try to capture the bats in mosquito netting over the exit when they took to flying in the evening for feeding on insects. Of course this was doomed to failure due to the bat's echolocation (sonar)."

Next, we tried forcing them out into the net by using a handheld mosquito fogger. This machine looks like a leaf blower and is powered by a motor that mixes kerosene and a pesticide to form a fog that could be directed towards the bats. We were producing a good amount of fog when the fogger backfired and cause a minor flash explosion in the attic. There was no fire, but it did set off the fire alarm. The TSgt Messger and I exited the building just as the base fire department arrived. The firemen were ready to rush into the building until I told them there were rabid bats in there. We assured the fire chief there was no fire, but as a precaution he went in and confirmed everything was ok.

The next day, TSgt Messger and I went up in the roof of the building and devised a plan for the next attempt. We got a hand pump, a pressurized sprayer, and an industrial sized dry/wet vac. We peeled back the cooper flashing, sprayed the sleeping bats with kerosene, and sucked them up with the vacuum cleaner. Thump, thump, thump…the civil engineers came back later and cleaned out all the guano and sealed all the holes. They also retrofitted all the other training barracks to prevent bat entry. The barracks was ready in only four days vs. seventeen and saved the government sixteen thousand dollars.

SHEPARD AFB, TEXAS
MEDICAL OFFICER BASIC

I left Lackland in August for Sheppard AFB. Shirley and Sam flew back to VA Beach to visit family while I went to school. My boss at Lackland, Lieutenant Colonel Hayman, asked me to give his respects when I made a courtesy call on Colonel William and Mrs. Grau, the veterinary course commander. I arrived on Saturday and made an appointment to meet Col Grau at his residence on Sunday. He told me I needed to call Lieutenant Colonel Hayman on Monday that he had something very important to tell me.

When I called Lieutenant Colonel Hayman on Monday, he informed me I had orders to Vietnam when I completed my training.

Lesson learned - don't make threats to MPC.

Shirley and Sam joined me two weeks later. We rented a one-bedroom apartment off base.

SIR

Our course leader was a captain. Introducing himself the first day, he explained he was a former enlisted veterinary technician. He had completed college and was now in the Medical Service Corps, which was composed of hospital administrators. He then went on to say that many in the class outranked him (Because of their extended residency, many MDs and dentists entered as majors). The captain continued, "However, I am older than all of you and where I come from elders were addressed as 'Sir.'"

HAIR CUTS

Practically all the medics at MOB came directly from college. Some arrived with long hair, sandals, shorts, etc. At the end of the first class, the course leader told all the men to get a haircut (I don't remember about the women.) The base barbershop was next to the exchange at the opposite end of the base from the school. Haircuts were five dollars. The barbers would ask, "Military cut?"

The naive medic would say, "A little here and there."

The next day before dismissing us for lunch, the captain ordered us to file out the door at which he was standing. The men passed by one by one as they were commanded, "Get a haircut, get a haircut, and get a haircut." So, back to the barbershop they would go, spending their lunch hour there and paying another five dollars and again saying a little and here and there. The process was repeated the next day. This time when the barber asked, "You want a military cut?" the reply was, "Yes."

GATE GUARD

I was the senior lieutenant, by date of rank, in my Veterinary Officer Basic Course. Therefore, I was the class leader. My duties were taking attendance and being in charge any time we were in formation. Part of our curriculum involved field trips to food processing plants around Wichita Falls to learn how they operated and what to look for during inspections. On one such field trip, our bus was headed out the back gate of the base. I was sitting in a front seat next to Major Williams. As the bus approached the gate, we noticed the guard was sitting on the ground. Major Williams jumped off the bus and I followed. There was broken glass everywhere and the guard was bleeding from a wound in his right wrist. It appeared he had gone berserk and broke out all the windows in the guard house, cutting his wrist. Major Williams called the security police from the phone in the guard house. I used my handkerchief to put pressure on his wound. I noticed his weapon was still in his holster, motioned to Major Williams, and he removed the weapon. We both received letters of commendation from the base commander.

MAJOR TO COLONEL

The instructors at the Veterinary Offices Course were all majors: Ed Menning, Robert Shannon, James Shuler, Donald Shuman, and Walter Williams. During my career I would have interaction with three of them when they were colonels:

- Ed Menning – Veterinary Corps Assignments, 1071st Medical Services, Squadron Commander (in charge of all operating locations with Navy and Marine Corps) and Assistant Surgeon General for Veterinary Services (also known as Chief of Veterinary Corps)
- Donald Shuman – Commander 1071st
- Robert Shannon – Vet Corps Assignments

IN TRANSIT

After completing my training at Sheppard AFB, we returned to San Antonio. We sold the house in Lakeview and had our household goods shipped to VA Beach. I got Shirley and Sam settled in a one-bedroom apartment about a mile from my parents.

I then flew to McChord AFB, Washington, to catch a military contract flight to Vietnam.

IN COUNTRY

I arrived at Cam Ranh US Air Base Vietnam 20 November 1967. The first thing that hit me was the smell. The second thing was all the empty aluminum caskets in stacks. I could tell they were empty because there were no flags on them. I said to myself, this is for real. The next thing I saw was the Army living like in Matthew Brady's photos of the Civil War.

I caught a C-130 to Tuy Hoa. There all the buildings were metal. I was very thankful I had joined the Air Force and not the Army.

Tuy Hoa Air Base was HQ for the 31st Tactical Fighter Wing (TFW) consisting of three fighter squadrons of F-100's. The squadrons were the 306th,

308th and 309th. They were joined in June 1968 by the two Air National Guard squadrons, the 136th from New York and the 188th from New Mexico. The base also hosted the 38th Air Rescue Squadron (ARS) which flew the HH-43 Huskie light helicopter and the 39th ARS which flew the C-130 Hercules equipped to refuel both helicopters and fixed wing aircraft. The 39th aircraft were also equipped with the Fulton surface-to-air recovery system as seen in John Wayne 1968 movie *The Green Berets*.

The USAF Dispensary was a modular metal structure and was classified as a twenty-five- bed medical treatment facility.

IMPACTED PIG

Several troopers from the 173rd Airborne Brigade showed up at the sentry dog clinic late in November with their mascot, a forty-pound Vietnamese pot bellied pig. They had been in the Battle of Dak To in the central highlands during most of November. They said they had run out of food to feed the pig and that it had eaten mud. It had not pooped for several days. I attempted to check its temperature with a rectal thermometer and found its rectum to be impacted with dirt. I proceeded to give it mineral oil enemas and oral doses of mineral oil. The enemas produced a lot of clay like material. I observed the pig the rest of the day and it started having bowel movements without any difficulty. The oral mineral oil had worked as intended. The troopers returned for their mascot.

I learned from my sources at the 173rd base camp that the troops ate the pig.

PRESIDENT JOHNSON

In mid December 1967 I went to Cam Ranh AB to look at the filled milk plant and to confer with the two AF veterinarians there who were the sentry dog consultants, Capt Bobby Eason and Maj David Wood. The veterinary office was on the top floor of a two-story wooden building that looked like WWII army barracks. It was a long building with a balcony the entire length of the top floor and a drive through port in the middle, which led to the modular evacuation hospital behind it. There were six low, fenced squares of sand in front of the building. As we watched from the balcony, enlisted medics in hospital whites were raking the sand smooth.

Soon after they finished, a flatbed trailer truck came and workers removed all the fifty-gallon drums used for trash cans. Following that was another tractor trailer truck with Vietnamese workers who jumped off the truck with small Christmas trees and a shovel. They planted one tree in each square. Then the medics raked away their footprints.

Shortly after that a caravan of sedans arrived. A bunch of civilians got out and took up positions (Secret Service), and then a blue sedan pulled up the driveway of the port. President Johnson and Vietnam President Ki got out of the car and went through to the port of the main hospital.

There the president presented Purple Hearts to some patients (we could not see that part). The motorcade drove to the other side of the hospital where they picked up the president and his party. Soon after the motorcade left where we were, the truck with the Vietnamese workers came and they plucked the trees out of the sand. Then the other truck came and they replaced the fifty-gallon drums. The medics didn't bother to rake the sand. The event lasted about thirty minutes. The whole airfield was closed down while the president was on the ground. When Air Force One took off it was escorted by two Phantom F-4 fighter jets.

Because the airfield had been closed most of the day, the passenger terminal was packed with troops trying to go up country, including me. I finally got on a C-130 combat loaded. All the web seats were folded up; everyone sat on their bags and held on to straps stretched across the cargo bay.

HOT FOOD

We had forty-seven sentry dogs in our kennels. All the feeding and kennel cleaning was performed by a daytime crew of dog handlers. That way the dogs would get used to multiple handlers and all handlers could work with any dog with few exceptions.

On Christmas Eve the kennel master, Master Sergeant Wilkins, and I wanted to deliver hot meals to our dog handlers at their posts. We loaded a picnic table in the back of the two and a half ton truck (also known as a six by). One of the day handlers drove the truck. I sat next to him in the open cab; Master Sergeant Wilkins and an extra handler rode in the back. We all had automatic weapons. At the dining hall, we picked up the Christmas meal, turkey and all the fixings in Melmac containers for keeping food hot. We drove to each handler's post. The relief handler would take over the dog while the handler would get on the truck and eat the hot Christmas meal at the picnic table.

Everything went fine until we reached the north side of the airfield. About fifty to seventy-five yards of open ground (sand) stretched from the edge of the runway to the perimeter fence. On the other side of the fence was a refugee village of cinder block homes that our engineers were teaching the refugees to build. My female interpreter, Miss Lynn, lived there with her parents. As we are sitting there in the truck, a flare shot up from the village and we are lit up like it was daylight. All I could think of was the line from the 1960 song, *Please, Mister Custer*, "What Am I Doing Here?"

THE TENTS

We had a break lounge in the hospital where the officers would gather some nights especially when new people arrive or others were leaving: Hail and Farewell. Our dental surgeon was Lieutenant Colonel Boxwell who was about five foot five. His deputy was Major Mike Tradarro who was about six foot six. They reminded me of Mutt and Jeff in the comics. Whenever a new officer would arrive, Lieutenant Colonel Boxwell would say, "Mike, tell us what it was like when you arrived in Nam."

Mike said, "When I arrived in 'Nam we lived in tents. The tents had holes in them.

When it rained the tents leaked. The wind would blow sand into the tents and get into everything."

Boxwell asked, "How long did you live in the tents?"

Mike replied, "One night."

Two years later I saw Colonel Boxwell at USAF Hospital, Lakenheath, England.

I saw Mike Tradarro again at Seymour Johnson AFB, NC, in 1986. He was a retired colonel. I saw his obituary in the *Military Officer Association of American* (MOAA) magazine in 2008.

HAIR CUTS

All the operators at the base barbershop were Vietnamese and not very good. Major Tradarro set up a dental chair in his room in the hooch and cut hair to make extra money. He was very good at it. One night, Colonel Evans, the wing commander, was in the chair facing the doorway. Barry Morrison and I were sitting on Mike's bunk waiting our turn. We heard a *thump, thump, thump* in the passageway. The services officer, dressed in combat boots, a short kimono, web belt, and helmet and holding a bayonet all of a sudden jumped into the doorway in a combat crouch. When he saw Colonel Evans, he blurted out, "Is everything secure here, sir?"

PIPE

I started smoking a pipe in vet school. There are two events that stick with me.

In Vietnam I was using my own camera and film to take slides for a course I was preparing for Vietnamese food service workers on base. Since it was official business, I would get the film processed at the base photo lab (they processed all aerial reconnaissance photos). On this occasion I was smoking my pipe. Before entering the photo lab, I tapped my pipe on my boot to get the ash out. I then put the pipe in my pants pocket. I was filling out the form for my film when I felt a warm sensation on my leg. I very nonchalantly asked the sergeant for some water. Thinking I wanted some water to drink, he went to the refrigerator and got some ice water. I said, "Hurry up. My pants are on fire." I burned a hole in my pocket, but fortunately not my leg.

The second incident happened in England in 1970. My office had an NCO, Technical Sergeant Richard Smith, assigned to the Navy Communication Station Thurso near Aberdeen, Scotland. The base had a huge antenna field with the capability to communicate with submarines. He performed all the food inspections at the station and inspected a local meat plant on the approved source list.

Technical Sergeant Smith also inspected a dairy plant in Dunoon on the bank of Holy Lock that was providing fresh milk to the submarine tender and Atlantic Fleet ballistic missile submarines. After I made my staff visit to the two bases with Technical Sergeant Smith, I had to make my report to the Surgeon of Naval Command UK in London. During my visit I also met the dental surgeon, a captain (06). Somehow the subject of pipe smoking came up and the captain commented, "I see you are a man that enjoys eating. If you don't give up that pipe all your teeth are going to fall out." I quit pipe smoking that very day.

Technical Sergeant Smith would serve as my NCOIC on Guam two years later.

BLEACH

The base exchange cafeteria used the three-sink method of washing pots and pans: wash, rinse, sanitize. If the third sink was not heated, then cold chemical sanitizer was used, most commonly bleach. The amount of bleach could be determined with the test strips.

The cafeteria managers were Koreans and the workers were Vietnamese. The first couple times I inspected the cafeteria there was insufficient sanitizer in the third sink. The manager would chastise the Vietnamese. My solution was to paint a red line on the inside of the sink, determine the volume of water in the sink, and calculate how much bleach to add to make the correct concentration. I then took a can and cut it so it would hold the exact amount of bleach needed. I then demonstrated the proper method to the workers.

On the next couple inspections, I found the concentration too high, which would leave a chlorine residue on the surface that could be transferred to food, resulting in food poisoning. I found out why. When I entered the back door of the kitchen someone would say *Boci, Boci* (Vietnamese for doctor). The worker at the pot and pan sink would dump an extra can of bleach into the water. Then it became a race to get to the sink before that happened.

Later in England, I introduced the three-sink method to my scouts. My English assistant scoutmaster, Paul Barber, called it the SWT method: Sure Waste of Time (Pun intended).

WEEVILS

Weevil eggs can inadvertently get in flour during the milling process. After a period of time and under the right temperature they hatch, become larvae, and finally adults. Some species can chew through packages to infest nearby packages while some stay inside the package. Contrary to the popular saying "They are just more protein," there are some people who are affected by the tiny hairs on weevil's surface and develop intestinal problems.

Early in my tour at Tuy Hoa we had a problem with weevils in the sacks of flour for the dining halls. It was expected with the long supply lines from the states and the temperature, but it was not acceptable. Some of the cooks kept the flour stored in the coolers and use a handheld sifter to remove the weevils.

I was told that all our flour was being sifted at the Army supply point that provided all the food for our base. So I drove down there. The quartermaster sergeant was very friendly and gave me a tour. I asked about sifting the flour. He showed me a very large industrial sifter and said they did every bag before issuing it. I stood on a stool and looked in the hopper. It was full of cobwebs. We had a lot less problem with weevils after that.

DEFROSTING MEAT

Wing Commander Col William J. Evans was so concerned about the number of unsatisfactory sanitation reports on the food service facilities that he decided to accompany me on one of my inspections. He chose the enlisted dining hall. Frozen meat was supposed to be thawed in refrigeration in the walk-in cooler. This process took a couple of days and required planning by the cooks. Room temperature thawing was a major discrepancy. As we inspected the kitchen, we came to a bain-marie table with meat thawing in it. The stainless steel table has sides and a hole in one end for drainage. It's most common use was a serving line filled with ice to keep cold food cold. Juice was running out of the meat and down the drain into a large cooking pot.

Colonel Evans asked, "What do you do with the juice, Sergeant?"

The sergeant said, "We use it to braise the roast while they are cooking, sir."

"With the cigarette butts floating in it?" asked the colonel.

I met General Evans (4 star) again in Germany when he was Commander USAF Europe.

A1C SOURWINE

Airman First Class Sourwine was a security police dog handler on the day shift who took care of the dogs. He was a very hard worker, feeding them and keeping the kennels clean. He also brought the dogs to me and held them while I examined and treated them.

The food for our canine sentries came in twenty-five-pound, hermetically sealed steel pails. It was cube-snapped. I had some on my desk when Sourwine came into the clinic. He took one of the cubes and ate it. His reaction was, "That's not very good caramel candy, Doc."

Periodically we would have cookouts for my staff and the dog handlers. We had a big BBQ pit at the kennels. Most of the times we had hamburgers, and occasionally we had steaks. It is not a good idea for officers to do scrounging. It is best left to NCOs. I tried to get a case of steaks from the army supply point at Phu Hep and ended up with lamb roast. When I cut the roasts, the slices looked like prime rib. I marinated them and cooked them on the grill. Sourwine said they were the best steaks we ever had.

Sourwine and I met again eighteen years later at Seymour Johnson AFB, NC. He was a captain and the maintenance officer for an F-4 fighter squadron.

BABOON

We were on main base passing the BX snack bar when Sergeant Andy Sirabyn, my vet tech, and I saw two Army troopers with a baboon on a leash. The baboon had a deformed rear leg. I commented to Sirabyn, "I'll bet before the day is over that baboon will be in our office."

Sure enough, about two hours later, I could see the two troopers and baboon walking down the road to the kennels.

The trooper asked, "Are you the vet?"

"Yes, what can I do for you?"

"Our mascot broke his leg and it healed crooked. Can you make it straight?"

I explained, "I would have to break it and pin it. There would be a very high risk that it would not heal a second time. I observed him while you were on main base and on your way down here. He seems to walk very well."

He said, "But he can't jump as high as he used to."

"How high can he jump?"

"Six feet."

I said, "That seems high enough to me."

39th ARS MOSCOT AND FLIGHT SUIT

I received a call on a Saturday morning that the 39th ARS Mascot had been hit by a Jeep. My examination revealed the dog had a fractured femur of a rear leg. Captain Arnie Miliochio, one of our flight surgeons with some surgery experience, offered to help me with the surgery. He suggested we perform the procedure in the surgical suite at the dispensary. We used a stainless steel intermedullary pin to align the two sections of the femur. The surgery was a success, and the dog recovered very well. On Monday, Major David Rodgin, the dispensary commander, called Arnie and me into his office. He directed that we sanitize the entire surgical suite and everything in it.

The grateful members of 39th ARS gave me a flight suit with my name and rank on it. I wore it on several flights in country. One such flight was to Pleiku to attend to the AF working dogs because the base was temporarily without a veterinarian. We were waiting on the tarmac to board a C-130 with an Air National Guard air crew, commanded by a colonel. The colonel saw me in a flight suit and engaged me in a conversation.

He asked me, upon seeing an F-100 take off, "Do you fly those?"

I answered, "No, sir."

He asked, upon seeing a HH-3 Huskie helicopter fly by, "Do you fly those?"

"No, sir."

He asked, upon seeing a DHC-4 (CV-2) Caribou landing, "Do you fly those?"

"No sir."

Finally he asked, "Well, what do you fly?"

"Would you believe a dog sled?"

He looked confused. "What do you mean?"

"Sir, I am the base veterinarian and I take care of military working dogs."

He asked, "Why are you wearing a flight suit?"

"Because I am flying with you today."

RUSTY 881F

I got a call late at night in April 1968 from the dispensary that one of our sentry dogs had been shot. On the northwest side of the runway was a rice paddy within our perimeter. Rusty alerted the handler to something in the paddy. The handler called it in and a tiger team was dispatched. He and Rusty entered the paddy without backup. When the tiger team arrived, they challenged whoever was in the paddy. The handler heard the challenge, but they could not hear his reply due to the direction of the wind off the sea. So they opened fire. Fortunately for the handler, a M16 round shattered his flashlight on one hip, sending plastic shards into his hand instead of hitting the flare pouch on his other hip.

Rusty was not so fortunate. A M16 round entered his neck on the right side and exited just below the right shoulder. The airmen had controlled the bleeding with a combat pressure dressing.

Before moving Rusty to my clinic, I stared IV fluids and pain medication. We took X-rays which showed a fracture of the upper end of the humerus (large bone in upper leg) with a sizable detached bone fragment. Captain Mike

Sorkin, one of our flight surgeons, volunteered to assist me. Rusty was already on a stretcher, so we loaded him in the back of my pickup truck and drove to the clinic. By this time it was daylight.

I anesthetized Rusty. Sergeant Sirabyn removed the dressing, clipped the hair away from the wounds, and scrubbed the skin in preparation of surgery. Meanwhile, I collected blood from another sentry dog and started a whole blood transfusion. With Dr. Sorkin's assistance we irrigated the wound and legating bleeders as we debrided the devitalized tissue. Next, we drove in a stainless steel inter-medullar pin to align the two sections of the bone. We left the large fragment in place so that it would act as a graft and help in the bone healing.

We then closed the muscle layers, placing rubber drains, and closed the skin. I fashioned a Thomas splint and applied it for more stability. It was now late afternoon. We took Rusty back to the hospital for post-operative X-rays. The fixation was not perfectly aligned, but close enough for bone healing. We transported Rusty back to the clinic. It was starting to get dark.

Sergeant Sirabyn monitored Rusty's recovery from anesthesia. I went to sleep on the floor. I woke up a couple of hours later. Rusty was alert, so we moved him to a kennel. Early in the morning he was no longer laying on his side but on his sternum. A couple hours later he was dead.

A post-mortem exam revealed aspiration pneumonia and blood clots in the pulmonary arteries.

Sergeant Sirabyn would work for me again at South Ruislip, England.

STOLEN JEEP?

Master Sergeant Watkins often let me use his Jeep when my technicians had our truck to perform inspections. On one occasion I was driving his Jeep to the hospital, and I was stopped at a security police roadblock. The airman asked to see my military driver's license, which I produced. Then he asked, "Where did you get this Jeep, Captain?"

I replied, "Would you believe I stole it?" (I tended to be a smart aleck sometimes) I was unaware the purpose of the road block was to locate the stolen Jeeps.

He said, "Please wait here, sir." He took my military license to a master sergeant who then approached me. Now I knew this was getting serious.

The master sergeant asked, "Captain, does this Jeep belong to you?"

"No, it belongs to Master Sergeant Watkins, the sentry dog kennel master. He allows me to use it sometimes."

He said, "Captain, you don't have a M151 Jeep on your driver's license. You need to go to the motor pool and have it added."

On the way back from the dispensary, I stopped at the motor pool. I told the sergeant I needed M151 Jeep on my license. He also added an ambulance and a two and a half ton truck. I couldn't get a forklift unless I took a class.

GRENADE

I took the office pickup truck to my hooch at night. My morning routine was to drive to the hospital to pick up distribution, then drive by the enlisted hooch and pick up my technicians. On this particular morning I hit a pothole. The impact caused the glove compartment to pop open and a grenade rolled out. I dove out the driver's side, and the truck rolled off the pavement into the sand. After several minutes without an explosion, I looked on the floor of the truck and saw that it was a smoke grenade.

I got the truck back on the pavement and drove to the hospital. Our vehicle officer was a first lieutenant male nurse. He was pararescue jumper (PJ) wannabe. He wore a .45 automatic in a shoulder holster. I plopped the smoke grenade on his desk. "What is this doing in my truck?"

He said, "It is in case you break down off base. You can signal and someone will come to your aid."

"Let's get something straight, Lieutenant. I don't drive this truck off base, and if I was broke down off base, I would not pop smoke to let the Viet Cong know where I was."

There were no more smoke grenades in my truck!

US MARINE SCOUT DOG[5]

I got a call on a Thursday night from the hospital that a US Marine and his scout dog had been medical evacuated from Khe Sanh.[6] On the way to the hospital, I wondered why they were evacuated here instead of Da Nang, which was much closer to the main Marine base in Vietnam. The two of them were in a bunker that was hit by a rocket, which started a fire on top of the bunker and melted the tar that was used to waterproof the bunker. The melted tar dripped down on them. Scout's head, neck, and chest were covered with dried blood, but there was no active bleeding. He had patches of tar on several places of his hair coat. Other than tar and dried blood on his uniform, the Marine appeared normal and insisted on going with me to take Scout to my clinic in the kennels. We tried to keep the handlers from other services with their dogs (we treated a lot of Army tracker dogs.). That way the dogs could be more easily controlled during examination and treatment.

Upon closer examination, the only wound I found on Scout was a cut in the tip of his ear (the dog's ear is composed to two layers of skin with cartilage in between. The arterial blood diffuses through the cartilage and is collected by the veins on the other side. There is not a capillary bed like elsewhere in the body. Cuts to the ear bleed profusely. So do foot pads). When Scout's ear was cut, he shook his head repeatedly and blood went all over his head and neck, making him look worse than he really was. Fortunately the tar had not penetrated his hair coat, and there were no burns on his skin. I clipped the tar out of his hair and bathed him. I put a dressing on his ear and taped the ear over his head to keep him from flopping it and making it bleed again. We fed him and put him in a run. Our handlers took the Marine to their hooch, got him cleaned up, and gave him a hot meal. He spent the night with them. On Friday, the Marine came to check on Scout, so I allowed them some playtime in the training area.

That night a group of our handlers took the Marine to the NCO club. After several drinks, the Marine bolted out the door, ran to the beach across from the NCO club, and assaulted a sentry post.

He was restrained and taken to the hospital. On Monday he was medevaced to the AF hospital at Cam Ranh. A couple days later I received a call

[5] I don't recall the dogs name so I'll call him "Scout".
[6] The Battle of Khe Sanh was 21 Jan-9July68

from a Marine general. He wanted to know if they could have Scout back. I said Scout was fit for duty. The general said he would send a plane for him the next day.

FARMER'S COW

I got a request to treat a cow in a village south of the base. It had been shot by a US soldier. It had a wound in the neck halfway between the jaw and the shoulder. It was not bleeding. It was breathing okay and standing. I flushed the wound and gave it an injection of penicillin. It was getting late, and I wanted to get back to the base before dark. We told the farmer I would be back in the morning. When I returned, the cow was dead. I performed a necropsy and determined that the trachea had been penetrated by the bullet and was blocked by froth. I thought that maybe if I had placed a tube through the wound and into the trachea, I might have been able to save her. "Coulda, shoulda, woulda."

I also found various internal parasites plus the cow was pregnant. I knew the amount of the claim against the Army just went up. About a week later I received a call from the Army JAG requesting my report to substantiate the claim.

RAT ON BOARD

I got a call one night from base operations that passengers on a C-130 flight from Taiwan had seen a rat on board. I told them to direct the plane to an isolated spot on the ramp and not to open the doors until I got there. I picked up Captain Will Sappington, the bio-environmental engineer (BEE), and we went out to the plane. We had all the crew and passengers exit by the front passenger door, keeping the loading ramp closed. The main cargo was vehicles. Will and I searched but found no rat. Will set out sticky traps and tracking powder and closed up the plane.

Early the next morning base ops called me again and said the pilot wanted his plane back. Will and I went out and checked the traps and tracking powder and found no traces of a rat. So we released the plane.

IT'S THE REAL THING

Every month after the Tet Offensive (Jan. 1968), we had unannounced drills to respond to an attack on the base. The base siren would sound the alarm, and everybody would go to their response stations. Mine was the hospital. It was getting close to the end of July 1968 and we had not had a drill. Then on the night of 29ᵗʰ the base siren went off. I jumped out of my bunk, dressed, and put on my .38 pistol and helmet. I didn't have the truck that night, so I started walking to the hospital. A security police staff sergeant stopped and asked, "Where you going, Doc?"

I replied, "The hospital." (We called it hospital even though it was a dispensary.

He said, "Get in, I'll take you there."

As he drove, I could see smoke billowing up from the flight line. "Is this some simulation?"

The staff sergeant shook his head. "This is for real. We have been attacked."

Some Viet Cong sappers had gotten to the flight line and put demolition charges in two C-130's from 39ᵗʰ ARS and five C-130 cargo craft. The ARS craft were used for air refueling helicopters and were fully loaded with aviation gas and were destroyed. That was the source of all the smoke. The revetments kept the other four ARS planes from being damaged. The cargo C-130s were only moderately damaged. The enemy also damaged an F-100 Super Sabre jet by putting a grenade in the engine intake. The base C-47 gooney bird suffered slight damage from shrapnel.

A second group of Viet Cong tried to attack the west side of the base. They were engaged by security police in a firefight, and all were killed. Fortunately our only causalities were a fireman with heat exhaustion and an airman in the laundry with a slight wound.

The base services officer was drunk again. He entered the command post and asked what was going on. The response was, "There are VC on the base."

He asked, "Do you want me to open a dining hall?" Colonel Evans had him shipped back to the states the next day!!

THE SOLUTION TO POLLUTION IS DILUTION

The base sewage plant at Tuy Hoa was fifty yards south of the kennels. The base was diverting raw sewage into the South China Sea. I think it had to do with the deep hole in front of the kennels with the ends of two sewer pipes and no collection between them. The new wing commander wanted the clinic commander to open the beach for swimming. Captain Will Sappington started culturing seawater samples. The fecal coliform counts were extremely high. The clinic CO decided that if the fecal coliform counts dropped below a certain level two tests in a row, then the beach could be opened. Will and I advised against that because the test took about twenty-four hours for results and only showed what the condition was at the time of sampling. Since raw sewage was going into the water every day, there was no way to determine when it was safe by testing until the pollution stopped. The plan was put in place anyway, but the results never reached a level we could open the beach for swimming.

The 7th AF had a competition for best base award. A few days before the big inspection an airman drove a big, front-end loader up to the kennels. I was on my way to the hospital.

I asked, "What are you here for?"

He explained, "I'm supposed to push that big pile of sand into that hole."

"You can't do that. CE has to fix that joint in the sewer pipe. If you fill in the hole, they may have to dig a bigger hole to find it."

He went into the kennel office and made a phone call. I drove off, hoping common sense would prevail. When I got back the front-end loader was gone and so was the sand pile. I walked over to the hole. It was still there. The airman had spread the pile of sand down the beach.

I saw Will Sappington at Brooks AFB, TX, several years later. He said after I left Tuy Hoa, CE received the joint and fixed the pipe. They had to scrape sand off the beach to fill the hole. The sewage plant was operational again, and the beach was opened.

56

TUY HOA CITY

Tuy Hoa City is the capital of Phu Yen province and is located ten kilometers north of Tuy Hoa Air Base. The Da Rang River separated the base from the city. Highway 1 crossed the river over a one-lane railroad bridge that had been planked to accommodate vehicle traffic. Both the AF and Army wanted to open the town for day excursions by airmen and soldiers.

I was given a list of restaurants to inspect for approval as safe places to eat. TSgt Charles McGuire, Miss Lynn, our interpreter, and I went to check them out. We had to pay some kids to watch our Jeep to keep it from being vandalized. The first restaurant was operated by Koreans. The kitchen was clean, and the food was served hot. The next place was located in the ice plant which was used as their refrigeration. It was operated by a Chinese family. The last place was in a brothel. The food preparation area was unsanitary, and they served only cold food. I approved the first two. Word got back to me that the district commander was unhappy because I did not approve his establishment. My rejection had nothing to do with it being a brothel.

Barry Morrison, hospital administrator, Will Sappington, the new male nurse, and I, all captains, were going into Tuy Hoa in an International Harvester Scout. Barry was driving. I was in the front passenger seat. Will and the nurse were in the back seat. We arrived at the Ba River Bridge just as the traffic flow changed. We were first in line to cross the bridge with the next change. The road at that point was on an embankment with steep slopes down to the river. Vehicles were lined up behind us. We were boxed in.

The ARVN soldier from the guard hut came to the driver's side of the IH Scout. He had a carbine slung over his shoulder. He looked into the vehicle and said, "*Dai uy, dai uy, dai uy, dai uy, beaucoup* money, aye." Translation: four captains, make a lot of money. All four of us had the same thought. This could be a hold up or bid for a bribe. My .38 was holstered on my right hip out of sight of the soldier. I unlatched the hammer strap and had my right hand on the pistol grip ready if he brought the carbine off his shoulder. Just then the traffic reversed and the way forward was clear. Barry mashed on the accelerator and we left the ARVN soldier in our dust.

SEVENTH AIR FORCE
MEDICAL CONFERENCE

The Seventh Air Force Medical Conference was held at Vung Tau where the Saigon River empties into the South China Sea. It was a resort town build up by the French. Our clinic delegation consisted of Major Carl J. Sheusi, the CO, Captain Barry Morrison, Captain Will Sappington, and me. We caught a C-130 to Tan Son Nhut AB at Saigon where we had to change planes. We waited on the tarmac in the shade of the wing of our next ride. When the crew arrived they were Air National Guard as where a lot of C-130 crews in Vietnam. The pilot, a captain, invited us to board.

Major Sheusi asked, "Aren't you going to give us a safety briefing?"

The captain replied with another question. "Have you flown in one of these before?"

Major Sheusi assured him, "Yes."

The captain, seeing Major Shensi's flight surgeon insignia, "Then you must have heard the briefing many times. Please get aboard if you want to fly with us."

We all got aboard.

As we road from the airfield at Vung Tau to the Grand Hotel, we noticed all the restaurants had a wire mesh on the windows.

Major Sheusi asked, "Has someone checked this place out?"

I replied, "I am sure Colonel Anderson (Seventh AF Command Veterinarian) did."

We had dinner at one of the local restaurants without incident. The next morning at breakfast Major Sheusi asked, "I know the tap water is not safe, but is the bottled water in our room safe to drink?"

Will Sappington replied, "Did you see those ceramic water filters in the hallway and the maids pouring water in the top and filling the bottles at the bottom? Well, all those filters do is removed the mud."

Major Sheusi said, "Then what are you guys brushing your teeth with?"

Barry Morrison explained, "We use the Australian beer we bought last night."

After breakfast we all went to a separate corps meetings and met again for lunch.

Major Sheusi asked, "Is this chicken soup safe?"

I replied, "It's hot, so it's safe. Just spoon the broth from the top. Don't stir it."

Major Sheusi stirred it anyway and a chicken foot came up. He left the table and returned about ten minutes later. Major Sheusi said, "I spoke to the command surgeon, and I'm returning to Tuy Hoa on a flight this afternoon. You boys are welcome to stay for the rest of the conference."

Dr. Sheusi was a flight surgeon with the Air National Guard squadron that deployed from Niagara Falls, NY. He was an internal medicine specialist. Dr. Sheusi was a great commander - a lot better than his predecessor. We all liked him and in no way would we try to scare him. We were just being honest about the way things were in Vietnam. Dr. Sheusi recommended me for the Bronze Star.

I returned to Vung Tau in June 2013 with my long-time buddy Colonel Doug Braendel, USA, MSC, Ret. who served with the Army evacuation hospital there. We were with Vets With a Mission doing a medical mission. We had two days off in Saigon before going to Da Nang. We took the hydrofoil to Vung Tau. The Grand Hotel was still there, even grander as it now had five stars. We explained to the manager why we were there, and he showed us to the conference room maintained the same as it was in 1968.

Colonel Donald L. Anderson was wounded during the Tet Offensive in January 1968. A rocket exploded on the roof of his quarters in Saigon and a piece of shrapnel took a chunk of flesh out of his upper arm. He was treated in Japan and was returned to duty before the conference. He was awarded the Purple Heart. He retired in November 1973.

PROMOTION PARTY

When Barry Morrison and I passed through Cam Ranh returning from R&R in Hawaii, we stayed overnight with Major Wood and Captain Eason. We learned that they had both been promoted along with many of the officers in the hospital. They invited us to the hospital promotion party in three weeks. It was easy to travel from base to base. Once one got permission from one's commander, you just go to the passenger terminal tell the airman there you're traveling on verbal orders of the commander. Barry and I got the CO's permission and we caught a C-130 to Cam Ranh on Friday afternoon. As we were walking from the passenger terminal, the newly promoted Major Eason drove by, stopped, and asked, "What are you guys doing here?"

We replied, "You invited us to a party." We had a great time Saturday and caught a flight back to Tuy Hoa on Sunday.

Major Eason and I met again when I was stationed in Charleston, SC. He was assigned to the Navy unit researching infectious diseases at Camp Jejeune, NC. We spent the 4th of July weekend and stayed with his family in their base quarters. We had a great time shrimping in the New River from his boat followed by a shrimp fest.

ANONYMOUS?

I wrote the following article in July 1968. It was submitted by my commander on August 2 through HQ Seventh AF to be considered for publication in the Pacific Air Force (PACAF) Surgeon's Newsletter. On August 16, the PACAF Command Veterinarian acknowledged receipt of the article and considered it to be "interesting, well-written, and excellent in content and with enough humor to provide for easy reading."

Next I received a letter from the Chief of Veterinary Services, Office of the Surgeon General (OSG) stating, "Your humor was appreciated. Although we all know that at a particular time and place, it may not be so funny. We would like to publish your article in the *Medical Service Digest*…anonymously as to the author and place." (Meaning I was still at Tuy Hoa and some people might be offended and could affect my performance report)

On September 4, I replied to OSG that PACAF was publishing it with my byline, which they did. OSG published it anonymously in December. A number of people in the veterinary service said they recognized my writing style. Meanwhile the *US Medicine*, published by AMSUS, The Society of Federal Health Professionals, contacted my wife asking for my photograph. They published my article in their newspaper in the November 15 edition with my byline, location, and photograph. The base commander saw the article and said it was one of the funniest things he ever read.

THE TRIALS AND TRIBULATIONS OF A VETERINARIAN IN VIETNAM

Being a member of the Air Force Veterinary Corps is not particularly conducive to winning any popularity contest due to the inspection nature of the position. The veterinary officer is constantly walking a thin line, and if he steps on either side he is walking on someone's toes or compromising his position. This situation is more exaggerated in Vietnam because the problems encountered in sanitation, subsistence, and zoonoses control are more complicated than in other areas of the world. Some of the situations created by these problems have been both humorous and disappointing to me.

It has been my pleasure as a veterinary officer of only eighteen months service to be an advisor to three wing commanders, two base commanders, two deputy base commanders, two security police chiefs, two dispensary commanders, and three food service officers while stationed in Vietnam. All these positions changed personnel as a result of normal rotation except for the food service officers. When they write letters referring to "portable water" and "Typhoid Annie" one can understand why they do not last long. I have sympathy for any man who has to serve in that capacity because everybody in the Air Force is a "food expert."

My main goal after first observing the dining facilities was to improve them. I expressed this goal to my first base commander, and then started one of my many crusades to obtain that objective. I began by conducting the weekly sanitation inspections strictly according to the manual. Two months later I was ordered to report to the base commander. He had received "bleeding" copies of my reports from the wing commander. "Clean up or close up" were written across them. In almost a pleading voice he said, "Doctor, I thought you were going to cooperate with us in improving our dining facilities?"

My reply was "Sir, that is what I said, but I haven't seen any improvement in two months." Well, as usual, I blurted out an undiplomatic reply and stepped on both sides of that thin line at the same time. My "harassment" techniques continued. I became more and more unpopular. However the general food sanitation began to improve. Some techniques used were to have the club officer accompany me while inspecting the clubs, as requested by the wing commander, and pointing out to him cockroaches and maggots in the kitchen. One particularly embarrassing incident took place in the officers dining hall. A visiting Army veterinarian found a long black hair in his soup while in the company of the food services officer and the deputy base commander. To top it off, a cockroach walked across the table.

Two incidents almost resulted in me being completely alienated from my superiors. The first was the inspection of the officers club on the day of a dining-in. The general rating was marginal. The second was reporting lobsters from an unapproved source in a dining hall, and then finding out that they belonged to the base commander. I was requested by the wing commander to run finger cultures on the Vietnamese working in the dining halls. After two months of reporting that the results of cultures indicated waste contamination on the Vietnamese, I was accused of culturing mostly the personnel handling garbage. A lot of animosity developed just from my attempt to do my job. There were snide comments about "Sanitary Sam's mustache," requests that I defect to the enemy, threats to transfer me to Saigon or move me from air conditioned quarters to a tent. There was even an offer made to the dispensary sergeant major to assassinate me in consideration for a private room for him.

Under such circumstances I began to fear for my life. My salvation was a Seventh Air Force Veterinary Conference at Cam Ranh Bay shortly after the incident with the officers' club. The meeting lasted two days, but I managed to stay five. With a little foresight on my part, I avoided the pre-IG jitters that plague veterinarians throughout the service by returning to the base on the same day as the Seventh Air Force IG. Upon my return, I learned that there had actually been a plan to tar and feather me.

Much to my surprise, my superiors and subordinates spoke very favorably of me during discussions with the inspectors concerning my efforts to improve food sanitation. The dining facilities earned and received a satisfactory rating. Now there is talk of the possibility that I may be human after all. That sort of talk will last only until the beginning of my next crusade.

The veterinary care of a forty-seven-dog kennel has not been without its trials either. I was baptized by the sudden death of one of the beasts on my first day as sentry dog doctor. I began to check the medical records and found to my horror that I had inherited a group of dogs that were deteriorating with old age. My first protective measure was to ship three of the senile dogs to Saigon for destruction. But this proved to a bad decision. During the same month another dog died during surgery, resulting in four deaths in one month and depleting my supply of death certificates. To compound the stigma, it was printed in the consolidated activities report that this base contributed fifty percent of the dogs lost in Seventh AF for one month. The comment made by the sheriff was, "We never had all these problems when the last vet was here."

I was able to redeem my professional reputation when one of the sentry dogs was shot through the neck and shoulder. My sergeant and I worked for forty-two continuous hours to repair the extensive damage. Even though I was able to save my reputation, I was unable to save the dog. It died by aspirating vomit into the lungs.

Whatever traumatic events that I experience during the day, I can sleep at night confident that the sergeant major will find some discrepancies in my uniform in the morning to start my day off right.

MEDICAL CIVIC ACTION PROGRAM (MEDCAP)

The veterinary service contribution to MEDCAP was conducting rabies vaccinations in the villages around Tuy Hoa AB. Our program was highlighted in the base newspaper.

SAND BLAST

- *Information Division*
- *31st Tactical Fighter Wing*
- *Tuy Hoa Air Base, RVN*
- *November 2, 1968*

AIR FORCE VET SETS NEW CANINE FASHION

The canine population of Tuy Hoa area has a new status symbol – collars made from thin brass chain. More than five hundred dogs throughout this district are sporting the gleaming chain collars, and if an Air Force and an Army veterinarian have their way, all the dogs will soon be wearing them.

"We use the chain collars to identify dogs which have been vaccinated against rabies," commented Air Force Doctor (Captain) Samuel W. Tate, 31ˢᵗ USAF Dispensary. "We've found that the collars are pretty good drawing cards. A man sees his neighbor's dog wearing one, and he wants his dog to have one too, so he brings the dog in for vaccination."

Tate, the wing veterinarian, and Army Doctor (Captain) Ronald C. Olsen, veterinarian at nearby Phu Heip Army Base began the first large-scale rabies vaccination in the history of the Phu Yen province more than a month ago. Setting aside three days every week, the doctors visit villages, hamlets, and refugee centers to vaccinate the residents' dogs.

"We work very closely with the local Vietnamese animal husbandry officials," Tate pointed out. "We're teaching them what has to be done so that after we leave they'll be able to carry on the program without us."

Cooperation from both dog owners and the Vietnamese public health officials has been good, Tate said.

"They realize that this is a worthwhile program that will have a definite effect on the health of the people of the province," he concluded.

"They know how much damage rabies epidemic could cause."

When Captain Olsen and I set up the rabies vaccination program we scheduled to visit each hamlet two days in a row. In spite of the possible security issue of setting a predictable pattern it would insure maximum participation by the locals. Those who held back on the first day would come the second.

There were two incidents that touched our hearts that made us feel the whole effort was appreciated by the Vietnamese.

Our first vaccination clinic was north of the air base in a village on the bank of the Da Rang River. The villagers there build fishing boats about fifteen feet in length. The first day there was a big crowd, more curious seekers than dog owners and lots of children pressing in. On the way back to the base, CPT Olsen noticed his baby dial thermometer was missing from his jungle shirt pocket. He assumed it fell out somewhere. When we arrived the second day we were met by the village chief and a little boy who returned the thermometer to Captain Olsen. Through our interrupter the chief explained that the boy found it on the ground.

A week or so later we were in a hamlet west of the base. It was monsoon season and raining cats and dogs. We set up operation on the covered porch of the chief's house. We were just about to finish when two men came out of the tree line with a large dog hung from a pole they carried on their shoulders. We vaccinated the dog hung there and placed the brass chain around its neck. The men carried it off.

In 2013, I tried to find the boat builders' village. They had moved from the bank of the Da Rang River east to a beach on the South China Sea. They were building the larger Ha Long Bay Square Head fishing boats.

RETURN TO THE WORLD

I met with personnel about my next assignment. I was told that with my date of return from overseas in November 1968 I would have served nineteen months of my two-year commitment and that with twelve months of it in a combat zone I qualified for early separation from the AF upon return to CONUS. I figured the AF could not send me to any place worse than Vietnam, so I asked them to see what was available. They called me back and said there was an accompanied tour to London available. I said I would take it and signed up for another three years.

I was able to mail my stereo, tape deck, and other large items home. I knew letter mail and audio cassettes were postage free, but I don't remember about large packages. In any case, that was the best way to send those things home. I got a C-130 flight to Cam Ranh where I boarded the Freedom Bird back to the world. I landed at Seattle-Tacoma Airport. I changed to civilian clothes and booked a flight to Norfolk via Chicago and Washington, D.C. We were delayed landing in Chicago, and I had to take a later flight to Washington, DC, which put me there after the last flight to Norfolk. I got a cab from the DC Airport to the Greyhound bus terminal. I bought a ticket to Norfolk and called Shirley that I was arriving about four in the morning. I then sat down and waited for the departure of the bus. I woke up as my bus left the terminal. I ran to the ticket window and was told there was a Trailways bus to Norfolk leaving from across the street in ten minutes. I got a refund, dashed across the street, and was able to board at the last minute. I had no time to call Shirley. The two bus terminals are about six blocks apart in Norfolk. So Shirley was at the Greyhound terminal wondering where I was when she received the page that I was at Trailways. It was a joyous reunion after thirty-six straight hours of travel.

BILL WHEELER

Bill Wheeler and I are best friends. We both came from Navy families. He was a year behind me at Princess Anne High School. We were in church youth group and Boy Scouts together. The two of us did a fifty-mile bike ride around Virginia Beach in one day to complete our Biking Merit Badge. I attended Old Dominion University (College at the time) for three years before going to the College of Veterinary Medicine at Michigan State University in East Lansing. Bill went directly from high school to the University of Michigan in Ann Arbor for a five-year Naval Architecture Degree. So we had a two-year overlap of being only sixty-five miles apart in Michigan. When the two universities played each other in football we would travel to the respective home game site. In the fall of 1965 the game was played at MSU. Bill came up, but we were not able to get him a ticket. So Shirley and I went to the game and left Bill in our apartment to listen on the radio. MSU won. When we got back, Bill had locked us out of our apartment.

Bill graduated and was commissioned in the US Navy in 1966. I was commissioned in the US Air Force Reserves, Medical Service Corps, in 1966 and graduated in March 1967. While I was in Vietnam in '67-'68, Bill was an engineering officer on the fleet oiler, *USS Waccamaw*, home ported in Norfolk, VA (fleet oilers have the ability to transfer liquid petroleum products ship to ship to sea.) Shirley and Sam were living in VA Beach while I was in Vietnam. Bill would check in on them from time to time. He became "Uncle Bill" to Sam.

When I returned from Vietnam in November '67, Bill invited me for a tour of his ship and lunch in the officers' mess. The traditions of the officers' mess go all the way back to the British Royal Navy. If the ship's captain is not aboard or is taking his meal in the captain's mess then the executive officer (XO) presides, sitting at the head of the table. Each officer has an engraved napkin ring placed at his designated place, usually arranged by rank. I noticed that a napkin ring engraved "Guest" was at the opposite end of the table from the XO. When Bill and I entered the mess we placed our flight caps on a table by the door. My captain (03) bars were showing when Bill introduced me to his fellow officers.

The XO arrived, saw my hat on the table, and asked, "Who is the captain?" The mess attendants immediately rearranged the napkin rings to place the "Guest" at the right hand of the XO (this is where it should have been in the first place). We then sat down to a scrumptious meal of hot dogs and baked beans.

When I completed my Master in Public Health at University of North Carolina in May 1972, we drove across country to California to catch a flight at Travis AFB for Guam. It was over one hundred degrees Fahrenheit at Travis. I called Bill, who was attending the Naval Postgraduate School at Monterey. He invited us to spend the weekend with him and his wife, Vera, a Navy nurse. The boys enjoyed games with "Uncle Bill," playing with his Dalmatian, going to the beach, and rolling down the sand dunes. It was a balmy seventy degrees in Monterey.

In 1979 while stationed at NAVFSSO, I made a trip to visit the west coast naval bases and attend the AVMA National Conference in Seattle, Washington. Bill was stationed at the Bremerton Navy Yard where he was in charge of the overhaul of the first nuclear aircraft carrier, *USS Enterprise*. This huge ship was in dry dock. Bill took me down into the dock, and we walked all the way around the hull of the *Enterprise*. There were gigantic holes cut in the hull of the ship where large equipment was replaced. Bill said they would weld a patch over the holes. We entered the "island" from the flight deck. Embedded in the floor of the entry was the *Starship Enterprise*.

Bill Wheeler, Captain USN, was the engineering officer on the staff at San Diego at the same time as my son Sam, Lieutenant, USN, was the weapons officer on the cruiser *USS Chancellorsville*. He became Sam's mentor and "Great Uncle" to my grandson Joe.

ENGLAND

In December 1968, my next assignment was to Operation Location F, 7520 USAF Hospital, High Wycombe Air Station, England. The hospital was located at South Ruislip Air Station on the outskirts of London. My duty was Chief Veterinary Service for the United Kingdom Subsistence Center (UKSC) with its offices and mine at High Wycombe, which was forty miles northwest of London. UKSC had a cold storage on the London docks and a dry storage at Greenford near South Ruislip. I had technicians at both warehouses. My NCOIC lived in a village near High Wycombe while my family lived on base. We were responsible for inspection of all food entering the UK for US forces. I had additional duties as base veterinarian for High Wycombe AS. I was also the Scoutmaster of the Boy Scout troop there.

High Wycombe Air Station is located on Daws Hill above the town of High Wycombe, Buckinghamshire. The Wycombe Abbey School for Girls was used as the headquarters of Eighth Air Force during WWII. In late 1941 the RAF began construction of a 23,358 square foot bunker inside Daws Hill. The "Block," as the RAF called it, was completed in 1942 and Eighth AF moved in. US Bomber Command remained at the Abbey.

When I lived at High Wycombe the bunker was called the "Hole" and was the underground command post of Joint Coordination Center, Europe (JCCE). I performed one inspection of their meal combat individual (MCI) to extend their shelf life.

The station was home to the elementary school and the London Central High School operated from 1970 to 2007.

The USAF vacated the station in 1994 returning it to RAF. Since 1994 it has served as HQ Allied Forces North Western Europe (AFNORTHWEST) of NATO.

We visited the station in 2000 when our son Rob did a semester abroad in London.

HAGGLING

My first AF boss, Colonel William P. Hayman, was on vacation with his wife Maude, who was English. They were accompanied by another colonel who was in the surgeon general's office (I don't remember his name) and his wife. Colonel Hayman wanted me to show the colonel the cold storage operation, and I think to give me some exposure.

From the roof of cold storage, I showed them an excellent view of the River Thames, Tower Bridge, the Tower of London, and other sites. I then drove them to a shop in Central London where the colonel wanted to look for Delft ceramic tiles that he collected. He found several he wanted and asked the price. The shopkeeper stated the price. The colonel made a counteroffer, stating he did not have that many English pounds. I blurted out, "I can loan you the money, Colonel." I felt a sharp jab in my ribs from Colonel Hayman.

LUNCH IS ON ME

The UKSC had a visit by a logistics brigadier general from Washington. After his tour of the cold storage we planned to go to lunch at a seventeenth century pub across the River Thames that had been frequented by the English author, Samuel Johnson. It's also where many seamen were "pressed" into the Royal Navy. Before the general arrived, the UKSC Commander, Captain Huston, gathered his NCO's and mine and said lunch would be Dutch treat. We were not going to have the general pay for all of us, about ten. We had a wonderful meal. The general was very engaging with the NCOs. The waiter brought the bill, and we all got out our English pounds. The general didn't have any pounds and asked the waiter, "Do you take American Express?"

"Yes," replied the waiter as he took the general's card. The waiter returned with the general's card and gave him the receipt. The entire bill was charged to the general's card. He looked up and saw all of us with money in our hands and said, "Lunch is on me."

HIGH WYCOMBE VOLLEYBALL

I played a lot of sand lot volleyball at Tuy Hoa, so I joined the base team at High Wycombe. I was the only officer on the team. We defeated three of the four base teams in Third AF and the fourth team forfeited, so we became the UK Champions. That earned us a spot in the USAFE tournament. We flew by C-130 from RAF North Holt, near South Ruislip, to Rhine Main AFB at Frankfurt, Germany. We rented a van and checked in at the Moral, Welfare, and Recreation (MWR) office where we found out that the enlisted would be billeted at Rhine Main and officers at the Amelia Earhart Hotel in Wiesbaden about an hour away. We went to billeting and our team captain, a master sergeant, said he would handle it. Bud, the Office Special Investigations (OSI) agent on our team could not make the trip. The MSgt checked me into the enlisted billeting in Bud's place. He told the clerk that Captain Tate could not make the trip. Instead of special agent, Bud was listed in our group travel orders as secret agent.

Our team drew a bye for the first match. We watched the team from Crete defeat their first opponent by a wide margin. They devastated us in short order as well and went on to win the tournament.

CLEANERS

Colonel Nave said, "Captain Tate, I want you to investigate complaints about the elementary classrooms not being properly cleaned and give me a report tomorrow."

I did my first inspection that afternoon just after school was let out and before the cleaners arrived. I found papers and schoolbooks on the floors and desks placed haphazardly around the rooms. I gave my written report the next morning citing problems by room number. Colonel Nave called the school principal and asked him to come to his office. When the principal arrived Colonel Nave gave him my report and said, "One reason the classrooms are not being cleaned is that the students are leaving them in a mess. I'll give you two days to make corrections, and Dr. Tate will do another inspection. Any classroom that is not ready to be cleaned, I will bar the teacher from the base."

70

The principal replied, "You can't do that."

Colonel Nave said, "You don't want to try me. After Dr. Tate's next inspection, I'll deal with the cleaning contractor."

On my next inspection all the classrooms were orderly and ready to be cleaned. I went back after the cleaners left and found the floors were not adequately cleaned and lots of surfaces were dusty. I also thought it odd that the blinds in all the rooms were at the top of the high windows. I let some of the blinds down and found them to be very dusty. The cleaning contract specified that all surface up to six feet were to be dusted. The cleaners were raising the blinds to the top so they technically didn't have to dust them.

The next morning I presented my report to Colonel Nave. He called the cleaning contractor and requested he come to his office that afternoon.

Colonel Nave presented him with my report. "You have forty-eight hours to correct these deficiencies or I will have your contract terminated with cause.

We had no more cleaning problem in the school.

TENTS

I was the Scoutmaster of the Boy Scout Troop at High Wycombe, and First Lieutenant Regie Price of UKSC was my assistant. Colonel Nave, by virtue of being the base commander, was the Scout Commissioner. The umbrella tents that were passed on to us were torn, and poles were either broken or missing. I went to Colonel Nave to ask if we could get new tents.

He called the supply sergeant and said, "I'm sending Captain Tate over with a catalog for you to locally purchase some tents using the MWR account (Scouting was part of the USAFE Youth Program).

The tents arrived, and I signed for them on a temporary hand receipt. Regie and I took them down to the scout hut and unpacked them. Regie questioned me, "Why are you not throwing away the packaging and the old tents?"

I replied, "We might need them."

Our Scouts got a lot of use out of those tents, and we kept them in excellent condition.

Third AF started preparing High Wycombe AS for the move of the America High School in Bushy Park, London, to High Wycombe. UKSC was moved to South Ruislip. The commutations squadron moved to Upper Hey-ford. The station clinic was downsized to a two-man aid station. Colonel Nave was moved to South Ruislip to become Chief of Staff, Third AF. The UK Branch of NATO in the 'Hole' was deactivated. The enlisted barracks were to be converted to student dormitories. The chapel and adjoining BX were to be converted to a school library.

MWR supply was to be moved to RAF Greenham Common in Berkshire about eighty miles south west of High Wycombe. The seventy housing units were to remain open and we were to maintain the Scout troop.

The MWR supply sergeant called, "Captain Tate, you need to return those tents. I have to take them to Greenham Common."

"But we need them for the Scout troop. It's not closing?"

The sergeant said, "Sorry, you can check them out each time you need to use them. I need them within two days."

Regie and I went to the scout hut and packed the old tents in the new tent wrappings. Regie was very leery. I said, "We'll be okay as long as the sergeant doesn't open the wrapping. If not, we'll just have to turn in the good tents."

We took the bundles to the warehouse. The sergeant did not open the bundles nor ask any questions and annotated my hand receipt as returned.

About two months later Colonel Nave called, "Captain Tate, did you turn in those tents?

I asked, "Do you really want to know sir?"

Colonel Nave said, "I'll reframe my question. Do your Scouts have adequate tentage for camping?"

"Yes, sir." That was the last inquiry about the tents.

About this same time Third AF consolidated the operation of two bases in East Anglia, RAF Bentwaters, and Woodbridge into one. New housing had recently been built on the one that was downsized. The same master sergeant, who was the captain of the High Wycombe volleyball team, was made the Housing NCOIC on that base. There were a lot of low ranking married airmen living on the economy because they didn't have command sponsorship for their wives, many of whom were English. The master sergeant had all these fairly new family quarters empty, so he allowed these young couples to move on base. Somehow Colonel Nave heard about it. He said, "Master Sergeant, I understand you have unsponsored couples in base housing."

He said, "Yes sir, they were really struggling off base."

Colonel Nave asked, "Do you have enough furniture for them?"

"Yes, sir."

COMPUTER KAPUT

Regie and I decided to attend the Transatlantic Council Boy Scout Conference in Garmisch, Germany. We drove my VW hatchback because it was newer then Regie's car. We took Regie's wife, Brenda, and Shirley with us. We took the hovercraft from Dover to Calais, France. We crossed the border into Germany at Aachen. I kept seeing these signs on the Autobahn reading, *"Ausfahrt."* I thought that must be a really big city until Brenda said *"Ausfahrt"* was German for "exit." We reached a point on the Autobahn where there was no speed limit, and I decided to see how fast the VW would go. I was doing about eighty-five or ninety MPH when we came upon a construction zone at the merger of two Autobahns. As I was slowing down to the speed limit, I was flagged over by the *polizei*. He could see that I had British plates on a left hand drive VW with an USA sticker.

He asked, *"Sprechen Deutsche?"*

"Nein."

"You American, *ja?*"

"Ja."

"You go too fast, *ja?*"

"Ja."

"You no do it again, *ja?*" as he wagged his finger at me.

"Ja."

He said, "Go."

Further along the Autobahn we stopped to take pictures of Hops fields. When we exited the Autobahn at Munich the VW just stopped. We called the ADAC, the German AAA, for road assistance. They towed the VW to a local garage where the mechanic repeatedly said, "Computer kaput." We then had ADAC tow us to the VW dealership, which was closed until Monday. We left the VW there and spent the weekend in the American R&R hotel in Munich, which meant we had to scrap our plan to return to Calais via Paris. It was also at this point I realized that I had lost my glasses, most likely at the hops fields. I spent the rest of the trip wearing my prescription sunglasses day and night. On Monday we got the VW checked into the dealership. The problem was with the fuel injectors and would take a couple of days to fix. We left it there, rented a car, and proceeded to Garmisch for the last two days of the training conference. The return trip was without any sightseeing stops in order to keep our reservation on the hovercraft.

Regie and I would serve together on two Scout Wood Badge courses when I was stationed in Charleston, SC, 1974-1977. I had the privilege to attend the ceremony in Lexington, SC, where he was awarded the Silver Beaver. General William C. Westmoreland, USA, Ret. was the guest speaker, and Webelos Scout Sam got to meet the general.

Since I was the inspector at the UKSC, Regie presented me with the following tribute:

THE INSPECTOR

Bring back again the happy days of Caesar, Brutus, and Hector.
They bought and sold, lived and died with never an Inspector.
In cave man days to get a wife, upon the bean you cracked her
Then dragged her home, but nowadays, both first must see an Inspector.
In Eden's garden Mother Eve, with a few leaves bedecked her.
They ate the fruit, that now waits, till passed by an Inspector.
In other days out in the dark, we loved our girl and necked her.
Today you try it in the car and quickly comes an Inspector.
The little hen once laid her eggs as nature did expect her
But now each step from nest to nest is checked by an Inspector.
Her coop, her rooster, everything with which we can connect her.
The farmer, dealer, grower, all are bossed by an Inspector.
The cow must not give up her milk, for beef you can't discut her
Unless the smell of all her parts suits some darn fool Inspector.
When all is ended and Old Nick has got each Malefactor
We hope in each hot spot in H——, there sizzles an Inspector.

HIGH WYCOMBE CATS

The base was heated by a central steam plant. The steam pipes ran in channels to each building. The channels were covered by concrete squares with hand holes and formed the sidewalks. They didn't need snow removal in the winter. Security Police requested that I help them remove the feral cats from the channels. They had tried live traps, but that didn't work because the cats had too many food sources. So I had the idea of sedating the cats so they could be removed from the steam channels. I got some phenobarbital tablets from the clinic (it was not a controlled narcotic then), mixed it with cat food, and placed in several channels around the base. The next day I got a call from a hysterical woman who said there are cats flopping around and the Security Police were running round bashing cats with shovels. I put a stop to that. We collected the cats humanely and turned them over to the RSPCA.

BRAINS

I could see four-year-old Sam was playing in the backyard with Chaplain Dickey's son. Sam was pushed into a wooden fence. He came to the door crying. I said, "Don't come in here crying unless you're bleeding."

He took his hand away from the back of his head and said, "But I am bleeding". I looked, and he had a laceration in his scalp that was going to require sutures to close it. I walked him over to our small outpatient clinic. One of our two doctors, Captain J. L. Stinnett, a pediatrician, examined Sam and agreed he needed sutures. While I held Sam in my lap, Dr. Stinnett clipped the hair, flushed the wound, and injected a topical anesthetic. Dr. Stinnett began to place the sutures. Sam asked, "What are you doing to me?"

Dr. Stinnett said, "I'm sewing your skin back together."

"Why?"

I interjected, "So your brains won't fall out."

Sam was calm during the whole procedure. Ten days later I took Sam back to have the sutures removed.

Sam asked again, "What are you doing to me?

Dr. Stinnett said, "We are taking your stitches out."

Sam yelled, "NO! NO! My brains will fall out!"

TRANSITION

In October 1969, big changes were made at UKSC. Its offices were moved to South Ruislip. I became Medical Director, Veterinary Service for the 7520 USAF Hospital. Captain Robert Cordts, who was junior to me, took the position at UKSC. I was able to remain in quarters at High Wycombe. I was now responsible for six operational locations: South Ruislip, High Wycombe; poultry inspection in Ludlow, Shropshire; and Naval Communications Station (NAVCOMSTA), Thurso, near Aberdeen, Scotland. Technical Sergeant Smith was stationed at Thurso and performed food plant inspection for the submarine base in Holy Lock, Scotland, and the NAVCOMSTA Londonderry, Northern Ireland.

In the hospital, I had the addition duty as disaster control officer and took my turn as officer of the day.

DISASTER CONTROL OFFICER

I had the additional duty of disaster control officer (DCO) for the hospital. The staff was dispersed throughout the local communities, and some of the enlisted did not have phones. The recall pyramid was set up so that those with phones were responsible to contact staff who lived near them that didn't have phones. The plan stipulated that the CO, XO, duty officer, and DCO could iniciate a recall exercise. Staff were required to report the times they were contacted but not to physically report for duty. The hospital had a history of poor responses to the telephone recall system.

The hospital commander, Colonel C. T. Anderson, MC, wanted improvement in the response time and percent of staff contacted. On the nights that I was the duty officer, I would initiate a recall exercise at one or two in the morning when I figured most staff would be home. People complained but the response times and rates improved to the point where we met the Third Air Force standard.

I reviewed the disaster response plan and found that the veterinary technicians were all assigned as litter bearers while the surgical technicians were assigned to central sterilization. I thought the vet techs could run central sterilization, freeing up the surgical techs to assist in patient care and surgery.

The chief nurse, a lieutenant colonel, didn't like the idea. "Central sterilization and packing instruments is a highly skilled position."

I explained, "I ran autoclaves as a veterinary student in a pathology lab, and I could teach a chimpanzee to do it."

Colonel Anderson liked that the surgical techs would be freed up for patient care.

I was required to attend a meeting of all the units' DCOs in the base command post. When I arrived, I found out I couldn't enter because I didn't have top secret clearance. My clearance expired when I left Vietnam. I completed the form, but it was denied. I submitted again, and it was denied two more times. I told Colonel Anderson I could no longer be the DCO because I didn't have the clearance for the position. He said to apply again. I said I had already applied three times and was denied three times. If he wanted me to continue in the position, he would have to intercede. He called me back and said I was relieved.

I never did find out why I couldn't get my top secret clearance reinstated other than the Security Police captain who was in charge of that was on the opposing volleyball team that we beat very badly. The Navy had no problem reinstating my clearance on Guam.

OFFICER OF THE DAY

The officer of the day (OOD) acts directly under the commanding officer and is responsible for overseeing the security of the hospital, maintaining order, and protecting property mainly after duty hours. One morning the hospital administrator, a lieutenant colonel, called. "The NCO of the day reported that you did not check in as OOD last night. Colonel Anderson wants to see you right away."

I replied, "I was not notified initially nor reminded that I was OOD."

He said, "The duty roster is posted on the bulletin boards and sent to all offices daily, and a reminder call is only a courtesy."

On the way to the Colonel Anderson's office, I passed two bulletin boards. The duty rosters were three days old. I showed them to him, and I was excused.

LUDLOW

The South Ruislip office had a technician assigned to the Craven Arms poultry plant outside of Ludlow, Shropshire, about one hundred and seventy-five miles northwest of London. When the plant processed chicken for US government contracts, a veterinarian was required to perform the anti mortem and post mortem inspection on the processing line with the technician. Captain Cordts performed this duty before we switched positions. He accompanied me on my first trip to show me the routine. We stayed in the half-timbered Feathers Hotel and Pub. We socialized with the innkeeper in the pub. When we were ready to go to our room, she asked, "What time do you want me to knock you up?" (English for knock on your door in the morning).

Bob replied, "Six, and we will get breakfast at the plant."

There was a knock on our door at six in the morning.

Bob said, "I'll get a shower first. You let her in with the tea tray," which I did. There were two pots on the tray, one with hot water and one with tea. I poured a cup of tea, drank it, took my turn in the shower, dressed, and off we went to the plant. Halfway to the plant, I felt a slight pain in my stomach. I wasn't sure why, and I didn't mention it. We worked all day, went back to the Feathers, and repeated the same routine. The second morning I had the stomach pain again. This time I mentioned to Bob that two days in a row I had this stomach pains.

Bob said, "There were two pots on the tray - one with hot water and the other with tea, right?"

I nodded. "Yes"

Bob explained, "You were supposed to dilute the tea with the hot water; you are having a tannic acid attack."

When I went to Ludlow in the winter I would stay at the Bull across the street from the Feathers. I would call Mrs. Black to make a reservation for the room over the pub's water storage tank. The tank room was heated to keep the water from freezing. Therefore the room above it was always warm without having to put shillings in the room heater.

During the remainder of time in England, we inspected over two and a half million pounds of poultry valued at $1.2 million.

Ludlow is where the Rivers Corve and Teme meet. The Norman Castle (c 1075) was one of the first stone castles built in England. English Kings periodically lived there until 1650. It was also the capital of Wales in 1461. It was severally damaged in the English Civil War in 1660.

ANDREW J. TATE

Shirley woke me early one October morning 1969 and said it was time to go the hospital. We drove the forty miles from High Wycombe to South Ruislip. We waited all day and no baby. She rested that night, and the doctor induced labor the next morning. Since I was hospital staff, they were going to allow me to be in the delivery room, which was not the common practice then. The OB nurse checked her repeated and at four in the afternoon, she was dilated only two centimeters. I had been holding it long enough and had to go to the men's room. I was gone about twenty minutes. When I got back Shirley was gone. Shortly after I left the room she completely dilated, the baby's head started to appear, and they rushed her to the delivery room. When asked where I was when Andrew was born I say, "I was on the toilet."

GOLD FLOW vs. SAVINGS

The Johnson Administration was concerned with the balance of trade and preventing the gold flow out of the US supporting the military in Europe. Therefore practically all of the subsistence was shipped from CONUS, especially beef. It may also have involved supporting the American beef industry. The policy shifted with the Nixon Administration in 1969 which was more concerned with the total cost of product plus transportation. US forces in Europe were then allowed to purchase beef locally.

The Third AF contracting officer at South Ruislip had in his mind that Scottish beef was the best money could buy, so he wrote the contract specifying that the cattle had to be born and raised in Scotland. Those of us who had inspected plants in both Scotland and Ireland tried to convince him there was no difference.

He didn't even change his mind when it was all over the news that a ship from Ireland transporting cattle to Scotland for processing ran aground in a storm on the Scottish Coast.

The AF veterinary staff at Lakenheath was enlarged to handle the increase in procurement inspection in the meat packing plants. Reality eventually took hold, and procurement expanded to include plants in Ireland.

The Lakenheath veterinary unit would play a significant role in 1981 with the transfer of veterinary services to the Army.

COLUMBIA HOUSE

The Columbia House was an AF operated hotel and officers' club on Lancaster Gate across from Hyde Park in downtown London. It was used as a temporary lodging facility (TLA) for military officers. It was another facility I had to inspect when I took over the South Ruislip office. There were repeated sanitary discrepancies in the kitchen. One was the use of wooden cutting blocks, which could not be adequately sanitized due to the many grooves in them. The kitchen manager told me he had ordered neoprene cutting boards but they had not arrived. He stated that the boards still had not arrived when I did the next monthly inspection. I noticed brown, primordial goo seeping from under one of the refrigerators that was elevated off the floor. I shined my flashlight under there and could see some kind of package. We removed it with a broom handle. Wrapped in water soaked brown paper were two brand new neoprene cutting boards.

Columbia House was built in 1856-'57 originally as five Victorian town houses. It was used as a Red Cross Hospital in WWI. The AF operated it from 1956 until it was sold in 1975 and is now operated as the Columbia Hotel.

IRELAND

Another responsibility of our office was the annual inspection of the 144 food processing plants in the UK and Ireland that were on the *Armed Forces Approved Source List*. Most of the facilities in England were tea plants and large commercial bakeries. In Scotland it was meat packing plants and poultry plants that were already under routine inspection because US forces were purchasing local chicken for commissary sales. This was due to the British restriction on imported US poultry products for any purpose other than troop feeding to prevent the introduction of New Castle disease.

The sources to be inspected in Ireland were mainly meat packing and powdered milk plants. The Navy wanted to have sources for canned powered milk for its ships and submarines. I was told that it would take two weeks to complete all the inspections. So with the Automobile Association's "*Illustrated Road Book of Ireland*" in hand, Shirley and I set off to catch the Liverpool to Belfast ferry. After inspecting a plant in Belfast we drove to Bushmills. Giant's Causeway is located on the north coast of Northern Ireland near the town of Bushmills. It is an area of about forty thousand interlocking basalt columns, the result of an ancient volcanic eruption. The tops of the columns form stepping stones that lead from the cliff and into the sea. According to legend, the columns are the remains of a causeway built by a giant to do battle with a giant in Scotland.

Next we went onto NAVCOMSTA at Londonderry. The Supply Corps officer was LCDR Holland, who was the older brother of my classmate at Princess Anne H.S. in VA Beach, Virginia. We stayed two days with his family. He and I toured the station facilities while the wives went shopping in town. Shirley reported there were armed British soldiers patrolling the streets and sandbag bunkers at major intersections. I was supposed to inspect a local bakery shop. Although the wives felt safe, I didn't. I called Technical Sergeant Smith at NAVCOMSTA Thurso who said he had inspected the bakery three months ago and found no discrepancies. I skipped it. We then followed the routine of driving to the next town, checking into our hotel, doing some sightseeing, and inspecting the plant in the morning. Then we would drive to the next town.

Onto Donegal Highlands, described by Oliver Cromwell as "So desolate that there were no trees tall enough to hang a man, no water deep enough to drown him and the ground too rocky to bury him."

There I inspected a lobster "farm." It had a series of concrete troughs. Fresh sea water circulated through the tanks full of lobsters. The manager selected two for me to hold for a photo. I held the lobsters by the antennae at my waist and their tails extended to below my knees. Those two were for show; the ones he shipped by air all over the world were smaller.

Enniskillen was our next stop. In addition to performing the plant inspection, we toured the castle built in 1428. The day after we left, the Irish Republican Army (IRA) blew up the A32 motorway bridge over the River Erne. President Obama attended the 29th G8 Summit there at the Lough Erne Resort in 2013.

Next stops were Sligo and Galway. From Galway we drove along the west coast stopping at the Cliffs of Moher. The 509-foot cliffs were featured in *Ryan's Daughter* (1970) starring Robert Mitchum and more recently in *The Princess Bride* (1987) and two *Harry Potter* movies in 2009 and 2010. I crawled to the edge of the cliffs to get a picture of the beach and surf below. The exposure to the grass activated my hay fever, which plagued me the rest of the trip.

At Limerick we attended the Bunratty Castle (1426) Medieval Banquet near Shannon Airport. The next two towns were powered milk plants to inspect. At Cork we went to Blarney Castle (1425). Yes, I kissed the Blarney Stone. One has to lie on their back and hang over the edge to reach it, making sure one empties their pockets first. In Waterford we toured the world famous glass works, which started mid-eighteenth century.

After inspections in Dublin we drove up the east coast to take the ferry back to Liverpool. On board we were given British customs forms. I selected the green "Nothing to Declare" sign and put it on the dash of our VW hatch back with British licenses plates and USA sticker on the back window. When we drove off the ferry a customs agent waved us into the Declare line.

I said, "But we have nothing to declare."

The agent asked, "Where did you buy this car?"

"In England." I showed him the registration.

He said, "Ok, proceed."

We stopped for gas in Liverpool and tried to pay with some Irish shillings I had. The attendant said, "We don't take that funny money here."

I turned in my travel voucher at South Ruislip.

The finance sergeant said "Sir, we can pay for your passage on the ferry but not for your personal vehicle."

I said, "It was cheaper for the government for me to drive my own car and take the ferry than it would have been to fly over and rent a car."

He countered, "In that case you should have requested POV on your orders."

I was right. It was cheaper for the government for me to drive my POV.

HOBART DISHWASHER

Food-stained dishes on the serving line usually indicated improper operation and cleaning of the Hobart dishwasher. Dishes were supposed to be scraped to remove the food scraps and any trash. They would then be placed in a rack and sprayed with water depending on the set up. The rack was then placed at the opening of the Hobart so the conveyor would catch it and pull it through the machine. There are three sections in the dishwasher, - wash, rinse, and sanitizing hot rinse (180 degrees Fahrenheit), each having its own compartment, heating coils, and spray arms. The wash and rinse temperature could only be checked with the machine running. If I found toothpicks, straws, or other trash clogging the nozzles of the spray arms, it indicated the dirty dishes were not being adequately scraped and/or the strainers were not in the proper position.

My favorite inspection technique when I found a dirty Hobart would be to totally disassemble it, pulling the spray arms out, removing the end caps, taking out the tank strainers, and removing the curtains that separated the compartments. I would place it all out on a table and leave. If the supervisor called me back to help reassemble the Hobart then I knew they needed instruction on how to maintain the machine. If they managed to get it reassembled, I would check the next day to see if they got it right. I never had to use this technique more than once in a facility.

UNC

Near the end of my tour in England, I was selected for the AF Institute of Technology Program to attend the University of North Carolina, School of Public Health for a Masters in Public Health Degree. The first day in our health education class the professor had the class, about thirty of us, sit in a large circle. We were to introduce ourselves, say what agency we represented, where we were from, and something significant about ourselves. As introductions went around the room, we learned that many of us represented federal or state agencies as opposed to being right out of undergraduate school. Also, a lot of them were from the Northeast. Halfway around the class was a very immaculately dressed young woman. Her significant statement was, "I'm a native Tar Heel." This elicited laughter. She responded, "Well, no one has said that."

When it came my turn after several others, I said, "Although I'm not a native Tar Heel, my ancestors settled this county, and my great-great grand-father was one of the founders of the medical college at this university."

I was elected president of the student council of the health administration de-partment of the School of Public Health. However, my AF training report credited me as "President of the Student Council at University of North Carolina."

MPH FIELD WORK

A very significant part of my MPH program was the field work in community health administration in June and July 1972. I chose to study the interagency interaction between the North Carolina Departments of Agriculture and Pub-lic Health. Both agencies had veterinarians, operated diagnostic laboratories, and dealt with certain aspects of the same issues. The purpose of my study was to see if relationships outside of official duties, such as participation in the same professional, service, or religious organizations, contributed to how the agency members interacted with each other.

One issue that had been very contentious between the two agencies was the unrestricted availability of the pesticide parathion. Parathion is an organic phosphate chemical that was developed during WWII as a nerve agent chem-ical weapon. It replaced DDT to control pests on tobacco. It was sold at farm supply stores in North Carolina by the local trade name of "Big Bad John." In the summer of 1970, there were several dozen cases of serious parathion poi-sonings and at least five fatalities reported to Duke University's Poison Control Center. Dr. Martin P. Hines, director of the epidemiology division of the North Carolina Board of Health, who investigated the deaths, advocated for state and national control on the distribution and use of parathion.[7] The res-

---

[7] Willford, John Moble, "Death from DDT Successor Stir Concern." The New York Times, Aug. 21, 1970.

olution was the passage of the North Carolina Pesticide Law of 1971 and the establishment of the North Carolina Pesticide Board that required the registration of pesticide products, the licensing and certification of commercial and private applicators and pest control consultants, the proper handling, transportation, storage, and disposal of pesticides, and the licensing of dealers selling restricted use pesticides.[8]

My field work involved driving from Durham to Raleigh daily, a distance of twenty-five miles. Dr. Hines was my preceptor. He had served in the Army Veterinary Corps and was a colonel in the Army Reserve. He earned his MPH at Harvard University in 1949 and was a visiting associate professor in the School of Public Health at the University of North Carolina. In 1972, he was already a legend in the field of veterinary public health. After I explained the purpose of my study, he provided me with a list of health department staff who had interactions with the staff at the agriculture department. He introduced me to Dr. John I. Freeman, the state public health veterinarian, who invited me along on an investigation of a salmonella outbreak. Salmonella is bacterium that lives in the intestinal track of many animal species and cause severe diarrhea in humans; the most common source is food contaminated during processing, such as poultry. It can also be contracted by handling chickens, turtles, and reptiles kept as pets.

The focus of our investigation was Lumberton in Robeson County. A hatchery had sold dyed baby chicks as Easter gifts. We spent several days in the schools asking the children if they had received dyed chicks for Easter. We found a few, but no cases of illness.

I completed all the interviews at the health department at the midpoint of the program and moved to the agriculture department. Dr. Thomas F. Zweigart, the State Veterinarian, was my contact there. He set me up with a workspace on the top floor of the building. It was a room adjacent to the museum featuring the species of snakes native to NC; some had swallowed foreign material such as a marble stone egg. Prior to becoming state veterinarian, Dr. Zweigart was director of the NC diagnostic laboratories. He took me on a tour of the main pathology lab, which was on the campus of NC State University. He arranged for me to spend several days there assisting in performing necropsies.

---

[8] G.S. 143-434, Article 52

I started writing my paper in between interviews of the staff. I left the interview of Commissioner James A. Graham to the last. Dr. Zweigart took me to "Big Jim's" office and introduced me. I explained the study. He asked why as a veterinarian was I not studying some disease instead of this sociology stuff. He insinuated that Dr. Hines had sent me to spy on his department but allowed me to ask my questions. I asked if he had any social interaction with the staff of the health department, if so who, and in what setting. Mr. Graham then accused me again of being a spy for Dr. Hines and told me to leave his office.

I did not find any social connections between the staff of the two departments in spite of all the commonalities. However, I did find that there was a lot of collaboration between the agencies at the low and middle management levels. If a matter became contentious, as it did in the pesticide case, it was elevated up the hierarchy, which is usually what happens in most organizations. My field work paper passed.

I met Dr. Hines again at the AVMA convention in Baltimore in August 1998. He had served in the NC Public Health Department starting in 1951 and as State Epidemiologist from 1964 to 1983. I was saddened to learn that he died April 20, 2020, at the age of ninety-five. The obituary of this distinguished veterinarian covered two columns in the JAVMA.

Dr. Freeman succeeded Dr. Hines as Director, Division of Epidemiology, North Carolina Department of Health and Human Services in 1982. He was President of the NC Veterinary Medical Association, 1979-1980. I met him again in 1998 also at the AVMA convention in Baltimore.

Dr. Zweigart joined the NCDA in 1959 and served as State Veterinarian from 1966 to 1988. He died December 9, 2004.

James A. "Big Jim" Graham served as Commissioner of Agriculture from 1964 to 2001. He died in November 2003.

ASSIGNMENT GUAM

The AF Veterinary Corps consisted of about two hundred active duty officers. Their assignments were managed by a colonel in the surgeon general's office at Bolling AFB, Washington, DC. In 1972 it was Col Ed Menning. There was an AF Form 90 for assignment request commonly called the dream sheet. One would indicate their preference by major air command, area of the world, and specific base. Because the Vet Corps was relatively small, it did not make sense to request a base that would not be vacant when one was due to move.

I was two-thirds of the way through my masters program at UNC when I received a letter from Colonel Menning. He instructed me to rank choices of about eight continental US (CONUS) bases in order of preference. Below that list were three overseas bases, including Guam. Well, I had passed through Guam twice back and forth to Vietnam, so I ignored it. A couple of weeks later I received another letter from Colonel Menning with a different list of CONUS bases and three overseas bases including Guam and South Ruislip, UK (which was my assignment before UNC.) Again, I ignored Guam. A couple of weeks later I came home from class and Shirley said, "Colonel Menning called."

I asked, "What did he want?"

She said, "He wanted to know if I was willing to go to Guam."

Pondering, I asked, "What did you say?"

"I said I would go wherever they sent you. He wants you to call him."

So I did. I asked Colonel Menning about South Ruislip. He said it would not be good for my career to go back to an assignment I had just left and that the Navy really needed someone who had some familiarity with the Navy. My dad was a retired chief petty officer (CPO). So Colonel Menning sent Shirley and me to Guam with our two sons.

POTS AND PANS

It came time to pack our household goods for Guam. Shirley always got anxious with the packers, so I sent her and the boys off for the day. The process went very smoothly, so I thought. Shirley returned just as the truck was leaving. She asked if the movers got everything. I said yes. She opened the bottom kitchen cabinets and there were all the pots and pans. I called the moving company and they said to bring them to Goldsboro, which I did the next day.

AIR FORCE CAPTAIN WITH THE NAVY

For the first four years of my nine years service with the Navy I was a captain, which is equivalent to a Navy lieutenant (O3). A Navy captain is equivalent to an Air Force colonel (O6). I played the captain card to my advantage every chance I got. However, it backfired on me shortly after I arrived on Guam in the fall of 1972. Our household goods (HHG) had been trucked from North Carolina to Tinker AFB, OK. From there they were airlifted to Anderson AFB, Guam. They actually arrived on Guam before we did, but Navy transportation office (TMO) didn't have them. After six weeks living in the Earls Huts motel in Tamuning, they were finally located. When our HHG arrived at the air cargo terminal the clerk told the TMO at the naval station that HHG had arrived for Captain Tate. TMO immediately sent a tractor trailer to pick them up. Our HHG crates were stenciled "Captain Tate, USAF," but the driver said they were not what he was supposed to get so he rejected them. Air cargo then moved them to frustrated or unclaimed cargo area. There they sat for the whole time we were traveling across country and the six weeks after we arrived.

PICKUP TRUCK

The motor pool did not allow us to have spare tires on our vehicles. I guess it made no sense to them to have a perfectly good tire riding around on vehicles when one could outfit one vehicle with the spare tires from four vehicles (Michigan State University did the same thing).

My airman first class called me that he was stranded with a flat tire on the pickup truck. He had been waiting for an hour and half since he had called the motor pool to come fix it. I called the dispatcher, "This is Captain Tate. My vehicle has a flat tire and I've been waiting more than an hour for a repair truck." I gave the location. The repair truck arrived within ten minutes. They asked, "Where is the captain?"

My airman said, "He had a meeting with the admiral and he got another ride."

AUTOVON, NCS CHARLESTON

The autovon was a long distance phone network between military bases. Some offices had direct dial, and others had to request access to a line from an operator before dialing the number. Our office in the cold storage was direct dial because we needed to report discrepancies of arrival shipments to defense personnel support center office (DPSC) at Cheatham Annex, Yorktown, VA, multiple times a day. My office was in a space in the small stores building (like Office Depot) across the street from the CO NSC, and I had to request a line. I always said politely, "This is Captain Tate, may I have an autovon line?"

Most of my calls were routine precedence. If some other caller requested priority line, the operator would break in, "Captain, we have a priority request, would you mind placing your call later?" Of course I would relinquish the line. I found out from several Supply Corps offices that the operator would just cut them off.

I was promoted to major on January 29, 1976. My promotion ceremony was in the medical center commander's office, Captain B "Mickey" McMahan, MC.

I went back to my office to make an autovon call. I dialed the operator and stammered, "This is Captain…I mean…Major Tate, may I have a routine line?"

The operator said, "So you finally got promoted."

REAR ADMIRAL MORRISON HEADQUARTERS

The headquarters of Commander Naval Forces Marianas (COMNAVMAR) is located on Nimitz Hill, elevation 668 feet. It overlooks Agana Bay and Asan Beach where U.S. Marines landed in 1944 to liberate Guam. It was also the site of Admiral Chester Nimitz Pacific Headquarters beginning January 1945, thus the origin of the name.

ASSUMPTION OF COMMAND – BLACK SHOE

When I arrived on Guam in October 1972 my position was staff veterinarian COMNAVMAR. Although I would be working at Naval Supply Depot (NSD Guam), my supervisor would be Commander (05) Campanon, Deputy Chief of Staff for Logistics. A few days after my arrival, Commander Campanon directed me to come to the assumption of command ceremony for Rear Admiral George Stephen "Steve" Morrison and to wear my summer blues. When I arrived at the headquarters I was met by Commander Campanon who placed me in the formation of naval officers in summer whites. As more officers arrived, he kept moving me around. He explained, "See your black shoes? Everyone else has white shoes. That photographer is going to take a ground level photo of your black shoes in the midst of all the white shoes. The caption will be 'Some officers didn't get the word.' Now see the photographer on the roof? He will take a second photo of the entire formation. The caption will be, 'Such is not the case with Captain Tate, USAF, the new staff veterinarian.'" The photos were supposed to appear in the *Navy Times* or *Stars and Stripes*, but I never saw them.

ASSUMPTION OF COMMAND FLAG

Change of command is when both the outgoing and the incoming commanders are present. Assumption of command is when only the incoming commander is present. The chief of staff presented Rear Admiral Morrison, who then read his orders. The order was given, "Break the admiral's flag." The two white stars on blue field were folded at top of the flag pole. What was supposed to happen was the boatswain's mate was to snap the lanyard and the flag would break (unfurl). Well, it didn't break. After three tries, the boatswain's mate lowered the flag, unfurled it, and raised it to the top of the flagpole. Upon which RADM Morrison said, "Getting out of the Pentagon was as hard as it was to get that flag to break." That comment set the tone for the whole time he was in command.

POWER STRUGGLE

COMNAVMAR included liaison with the government of Guam and the trust territories of Micronesia. Within a week of Rear Admiral (two-star) Morrison assuming command, Lieutenant General (three-star) Johnson called him. Lieutenant General Johnson was Commander of the US Air Forces at Anderson AFB engaged in the bombing of North Vietnam. The general said that since he was the ranking officer, he was taking on the duties of liaison with Guam and the trust territories. Rear Admiral Morrison said that was fine with him. All the general had to do was present his orders from CINCPAC (Commander in Chief, Pacific) and he could take over. The general hadn't done his homework that the trust territory function went with the position of COMNAVMAR and not the senior officer on Guam.

I then realized the significance of what happened on the contract flight from Travis to Guam. We had crossed the International Date Line and had skipped a day ahead. It was still dark on the plane, but I could see people standing at the front in first class and a woman was pining rank insignia on an officer collar. It turns out it was General Johnson getting his third star before he arrived on Guam.

RABIES QUARANTINE

Well, that was not the end of the power struggle. The next one involved me. I served on the public health advisory committee, chaired by Dr. Hancock, public health veterinarian, and composed of the two department of agriculture veterinarians, along with the Lieutenant Commander Bill Self, Navy preventive health officer, and Captain Bill Johnson, the AF veterinarian at Anderson AFB. Guam had six-month quarantine for dogs coming to the island in order to retain "rabies free" status by the World Health Organization. AF families had been complaining about it for years, and they found a sympathetic listener in Lieutenant General Johnson. He started lobbying some of the Guam legislators until they finally submitted a bill to eliminate the quarantine or reduce it to thirty days. I had served in rabies areas, Texas and Vietnam, and in the rabies free country England. So Dr. Haddock asked me to write a point paper defending the six-month quarantine. Captain Johnson (no relation to the general other than by chain of command) called me, and we met for lunch at a restaurant in Agana. He said Lieutenant General Johnson had called and directed him to stay out of the issue and to tell me to do the same. I made an appointment to see Rear Admiral Morrison that afternoon and told him what had happened. He called Lieutenant General Johnson and told him he didn't appreciate him putting pressure on one of his staff officers and that I was not in the general's chain of command. Furthermore, I was a professional expressing a position on a public health issue. I was not called to testify in the legislature, and the bill failed to pass anyway. But it did bring to light some animal welfare issues at the quarantine kennels, which were corrected.

THIS IS MY AIR FORCE

In 1973, Lieutenant General Robert A. Patterson, Air Force Surgeon General, visited Guam. One of his staff traveling with him was Colonel Dave Rodgin, who as a major had been my second clinic commander at Tuy Hoa in 1968. Rear Admiral Morrison held a reception for Lieutenant General Patterson and his staff at the officers' club. All of the officers on Rear Admiral Morrison's staff were invited. As I went through the receiving line, Rear Admiral Morrison introduced me, "General, this is my air force, Captain Tate."

Several years later I heard two stories about Rear Admiral Morrison.

REFUGEES

In the year after I left Guam, South Vietnam fell to the North Vietnamese, April 1975. Many of the refugees that were picked up by the US Navy were transported to Guam where they were housed on the grounds of the old WWII Navy hospital at Asan and a tent city in a huge fenced parking lot near the submarine pier (it had been used for flea markets). Rear Admiral Morrison was concerned by the slow pace US Immigration had when processing the refugees. So he went to the chief immigration officer and explained that his sailors and Marines were working twelve-hour shifts around the clock taking care of all these refugees while the immigration agents were working only eight hours a day. The processing was stepped up after Rear Admiral Morrison's visit.

GOOD MORNING, ADMIRAL

CDR Beamon, a public affairs officer who served on RADM Morrison's staff the same time as I, told me this story. The occasion was Captain Bill Self's retirement ceremony at Bethesda Naval Medical Center when I was stationed at the Washington Navy Yard.

Rear Admiral Morrison retired from the Navy at the end of his tour on Guam. He moved to San Diego with his wife, Clara. She got tired of him hanging around the house all the time, so he enrolled at San Diego State University. Why he signed up for a course that started early in the morning was beyond our understanding. The course instructor was a graduate student. Well, Rear Admiral Morrison was habitually late for class, and it irritated the instructor very much. One morning he challenged the admiral.

The instructor said, "Mister Morrison, I understand you were a person of some importance in the Navy."

Rear Admiral Morrison replied, "Some people thought that."

"What would those people say to you when you came late to work?"

Rear Admiral Morrison smiled. "Why, they would say, 'Good morning, Admiral.'"

I knew Rear Admiral George Stephen 'Steve' Morrison as a very humble man. He and Clara were the parents of James 'Jim' Douglas Morrison, the lead vocalist of the rock and roll band, the Doors. Jim died of an overdose in Paris in July 1971, the year before Rear Admiral Morrison became COM-NAVMAR. Clara was a very gracious woman. One day she was planting flowers round their quarters on Nimitz Circle. Her digging exposed an unexploded mortar shell from WWII.

Previously he was commander of the US Naval Forces in the Gulf of Tonkin during the Gulf of Tonkin incident of August 1964. He was a veteran of WWII (Pearl Harbor survivor), the Korean War, and the Vietnam War. He died in November 2008, and Clara Morrison died in 2005.

TROPICAL WHITE LONG

Tropical white long is the Navy designation of the uniform to be worn for formal occasions, such as a change of command, in tropical areas or during the summer. This uniform had long sleeves, long trousers, and a high button up collar, rank shoulder boards, and large medals. The Air Force has no equivalent uniform short of full dress blues with a suit coat. When an invitation stated the uniform was tropical white long, I would wear the Air Force dark blue trousers, pale blue short sleeved shirt with rank on the collars, and ribbons on left breast.

I had met many of the naval officers either on official business or socially. I knew most of them had a sense of humor, especially the Rear Admiral Morrison. So when the change of command was announced for the Ship Repair Facility Guam (SRF), I made my move. The ceremony was held in a large hangar-like building on the main base. The reception was at the officers' club, "Top of the MAR." That arrangement gave me time to execute my plan. I slipped into the men's room at the club to change uniforms. I got out of my "summer blues" and put on my tropical white long. It consisted of my white long sleeved overalls from veterinary school. I pinned on my rank shoulder boards from my AF mess dress uniform and my miniature medals. To complete my ensemble, I hung my stethoscope around my neck and had my obstetric sleeve hanging out of my back pocket. I waited until most people had gone through the receiving line and made my move. I announced myself and explained I had finally found my tropical white long uniform. I thought the admiral would pass out with laughter, especially when he saw the OB sleeve.

TROPICAL KHAKI

The work uniform I wore in Vietnam was the green fatigues with long sleeves. Our uniform for semi-formal occasion was the AF 1505s, which is a khaki-colored long trousers and short sleeve shirt. When I arrived at Guam, I saw that naval officers wore the equivalent khaki uniform for work. I found out that the AF had a tropical khaki uniform with shorts and mid calf stockings.

After I had been on Guam several months, I had a dental problem that needed a root canal. The dental clinic was in a long modular building with a central passageway (Navy term for hall). The dental surgeon, Captain Watley, USN, DC, had his office at the front end where everyone going to the operations rooms had to pass. His office had those swinging doors like you see at the bars in the Western movies. One day as I walked by his office I heard "Tate."

I replied, "Sir?"

Captain Watley said, "Get yourself in here." I obeyed. When I arrived in front of his desk, he asked, "Who said you could wear that uniform?"

I replied, "This is an authorized Air Force uniform for this theater of operations."

He said, "That's not what I'm asking about. Open the door behind you." Doing so, I saw a full-length mirror mounted on the inside of the door. He then said, "Take a look at yourself. With knees like that, you shouldn't be wearing shorts!"

REGULAR vs. RESERVE

As I was recounting, I was having a root canal done and a crown. This required several trips to the dental clinic. On passing Captain Watley's office another day, I heard "Tate."

"Sir?"

"Get yourself in here." I obeyed. "You are spending a lot of time here. What are they doing to you back there?"

I replied, "A root canal and crown."

He then asked, "Are you a regular officer or reservist?"

I replied, "Regular officer (I entered the AF reserves in 1966 and selected for regular in 1969). What has that got to do with anything?"

Captain Watley replied, "We use gold on crowns for regular officers and amalgam on reservists."

I got a gold crown.

JESUS DUENAS

Jesus Duenas cultivated four hectares of land in Talofofo that he rented from the Guam government. He raised cucumbers, cabbages, and tomatoes, which he sold to the Navy commissary. At the time of one of his deliveries, I learned he and his brother-in-law were the two men who on January 24, 1972 captured Sergeant Yokoi, the Japanese soldier who hid for twenty-eight years in the Guam jungle. He invited me, TSgt. Smith, and our families to come visit his "ranch" (the Guamanian equivalent of a truck farm). His house was on a hill about a mile from the mouth of the Talofofo River. It was a small, corrugated metal hut with a dirt floor. A naked light bulb hung from the ceiling and there was a wood cooking fire.

Jesus said he would take us to where Yokoi had been hiding for twenty-eight years. With Jesus in the lead, myself, Sam, and TSgt. Smith, Jesus' daughter, and two sons started off. We left Shirley, Andy, and Shirley Smith to stay at the house. It was about a three to four mile hike, mostly hilly terrain covered with high grass. We came to a bamboo thicket with a small stream and high banks. In one of the banks Yokoi had dug a spider hole that descended eight feet and opened into a ten foot tunnel which was enlarged at the end and had an air shaft. [9] We didn't go in it because it was too small and too dangerous. We then hiked back to Jesus' home.

Jesus said his oldest daughter, Maria, was very reliable and a good baby-sitter. We hired her couple of times including a Thanksgiving holiday trip to Palau. I think that was the most money she ever had in her young life. Of course, she was living like a queen in a castle in our one-story, wooden, post-WWII quarters.

COLONEL DONALD RINGLEY STAFF CAR

Colonel Ringley was the commander of 1071st Medical Services Squadron, Malcolm Grau USAF Hospital, Andrews AFB, MD. As such, he was the veterinarian in charge of the administration of all veterinary personnel in

[9] 28 years in Guam Jungle: Sergeant Yokoi Home from World War II. Japan Publication, Inc. March 1972.

the operation locations supporting the Navy and Marine Corps. He would perform staff visits to those units. He visited us on Guam in 1973. Our first stop after getting him settled in temporary quarters was to call on Rear Admiral Morrison, Navy protocol for any official visitor. The admiral said the colonel could use a Navy staff car during this visit and directed the chief of staff to write an authorization for one. I drove Colonel Ringley in my private car to the motor pool on the main base. We went in the transportation office and gave the dispatcher, a Guamanian civilian, our authorization. He looked at the form, then looked at us, and looked at the form again. We were thinking that he was wondering why two Air Force officers had an authorization from the chief of staff. Colonel Ringley asked, "Is there a problem?"

The dispatcher said, "No, sir, I will get you a sedan right away." We went on our way and dropped my car at home.

CHECK

I operated the zoonosis clinic. We provided preventive veterinary services for military members' pets. I recruited female Red Cross Volunteers to assist in the clinic. That relieved my technicians to perform food inspections. I wanted Colonel Ringley to meet my volunteers and be able to express his appreciation. So I arranged for us to have lunch at the officers' club at the naval station, named The Pump Room for the underground water system. When the check came, I jokingly said I had to go to the men's room and asked if Colonel Ringley would pay it. He gave me a funny look, rightfully so, but paid the bill while I was gone.

That evening Shirley and I took Colonel Ringley and the Red Cross director to dinner at the Okura Hotel in Tumon. It was a pleasant evening of food and conversation. When the check came Colonel Ringley said, "I paid for lunch. You get this one, Sam."

I should have paid for lunch.

GOLF

I knew Colonel Ringley liked to play golf, and we had a great course operated by the Navy. I arranged ahead of time to make a foursome with him and three other staff officers. I didn't play golf. Since he had the staff car, he met them at the clubhouse. Afterwards I asked, "How did you like the course?"

He replied, "Very fast. I hit the ball; it would bounce and keep on going. I was hitting distances I never got before" (there was hard coral under the thin layer of grass).

COMMANDER CAMPANON & CHAIR

I had the standard government issued swivel chair. It was uncomfortable. Commander Campanon had a really nice high back leather chair. He was rotating back to the states, so I asked him if I could have his chair. He said that the chair was for his replacement, but he knew where I could get a really nice chair. We went to the north end of the first deck (Navy for floor) of the headquarters building. There was a metal door with a cipher lock. He put in the code and opened the door. Before us was the interior of a huge bunker. There was a concrete stairway with a single metal handrail that descended two decks. At the east end of the bunker were two armed sailors facing a radio console with their backs toward us. Commander Campanon said, "I'll go down there and talk to the radioman and distract them so they won't see you. Then you go down and get one of the chairs over by the oval table and carry it up the steps." I did as instructed. I lifted a chair over my head and carried up the stairway, the whole time hoping I would not be shot.

I wonder what Commander Campanon was saying to the sailors. When I thought about it, probably what he said, "While I'm talking to you, the Air Force captain is going to take one of those chairs. Pretend you don't see him and don't turn around."

What was so special about that table and chairs? There were used in conference room of COMNAVMAR headquarters when President Johnson met Vietnamese President Thieu in March 1967. They had been stored in the bunker ever since.

COAST GUARD CHICKEN

Lieutenant Commander Margeson was CO of a Coast Guard buoy tender home ported in Guam. We developed a friendship, and he invited me for lunch on his ship. There were four of us seated at the table in the wardroom. The cook brought a large roasted broiler chicken on a platter, like the presentation of a roast turkey at Thanksgiving. Lieutenant Commander Margeson asked the cook, "Aren't you going to carve it?"

The cook took the chicken to a cutting board and with a meat cleaver - *whack, whack* - and cleaved the chicken into four pieces, placed them back on the platter, and brought it back to the table. Lieutenant Commander Margeson said, "That's one way to carve a chicken."

ANDY'S FOOT

Four-year-old Andy was riding on the back of my bike on the way to the pool. We were in front of the medical clinic for the Marine Barracks Guam when he caught his foot in the spokes of the rear wheel. I wrapped his foot in a pool towel to stop the bleeding and carried him into the clinic. The corpsman on duty examined the laceration of Andy's heel and flushed and bandaged it. He said that he would need to be examined by a surgeon and for us to go the hospital immediately. I called Shirley to take us. Andy was calm during this whole time until we reached the "pearly gates" of the Naval Hospital Guam, then he started screaming nonstop. The emergency room doctor explained Andy's condition was that his Achilles tendon was torn and called for the orthopedic surgeon. Andy was thrashing around and screaming. They had to strap him to a papoose board to give him a sedative injection. The surgeon repaired the tendon, closed the wound, and applied a walking cast. His foot healed without complication.

ED'S FOOT

Ed Spalding was the Boy Scout district executive. He was a Marine Corps pilot during WWII and flew combat missions from Guam. I was the district commissioner, and we worked together to organize many activities. Ed always wore leather sandals with straps across the top of his feet. One day, a piece of coral got lodged under the strap. Ed did not immediately remove it, and it worked its way into the top of his foot. In a few days it had formed a fistulous tract. Ed asked me if I could remove the piece of coral imbedded in his foot. I said I would try. We went to my clinic where I had him sit on the counter with his foot on the table and me sitting at the table. I washed his foot and applied Betadine solution. I then injected Lidocaine into the wound and surrounding tissue, then inserted a large gauge needle into the tract and started flushing with sterile saline. We both started to feel faint and wondered who would pass out first. We stayed the course and after several rounds of flushing, the piece of coral floated out of the wound. I injected an antibiotic ointment into the wound and applied a sterile dressing.

Ed's foot also healed in a couple of days without any complication.

WHO HAS THE MOST RANK?

A fleet replenishment ship was due for maintenance at the Ship Repair Facility (SRF). This event would require that all the ship's cargo would need to be unloaded. There was a meeting among the ship's advance party, SRF, and NSD. They agreed upon a plan that included that the ship would provide a work party (crew members) to assist in the unloading and sorting of food items to be inspected by my veterinary technicians. We would determine what dry goods could be accepted for storage, what could be sent to dining facilities for immediate use, and what needed to be destroyed.

On the appointed day, a loaded flat bed truck arrived at the dry storage warehouse, driven by a petty officer 3rd class (E4), but no working party. The NSD store keeper 2nd Class (E5) told the driver the ship had to provide a working party so that the dry goods could be inspected and sorted. Meanwhile my team and I were watching this interaction. The PO3 went in the dry storage office and made a phone call. About fifteen minutes later a chief petty officer (E7) from the ship showed up.

He asked the NSD SK2, "Who said we had to provide a work party?

The NSD SK2 pointed in my direction and said, "Captain Tate" (I'm a 03 in the USAF, which is equivalent to a Navy lieutenant, not a Navy captain [06]).

The chief then asked the NSD SK2, "Who does this AF officer worked for?"

The NSD SK2 replied, "The admiral."

The chief said he would be back with a work party. I didn't say a word during the entire exchange in this apparent power struggle. The work party arrived and dry goods were unloaded, inspected, and sorted without any further delay.

DOLPHINS

A submarine tender was docked at the inner harbor of Apra Harbor, Guam. It provided support to nuclear submarines home ported there. Also in the harbor, near the NSD cold storage and dry storage warehouses, was a barge that was the base of operation for a dolphin unit. The dolphins were being trained to detect any threat, especially underwater swimmers, to the submarines or the tender. I was very interested in working with this unit. I approached the chief in charge and offered my services. The chief asked how I knew about the unit since it presence was classified as top secret. I replied that there was a lot of frozen whole mackerel in cold storage that was not going for human consumption. He agreed to let me work with them but that I needed a top-secret clearance. I applied to the COMNAVMAR to have my top-secret clearance reinstated since it expired five years ago when I left Vietnam. My clearance was granted within a week in time to draw blood samples from the dolphins.

There were several issues with the condition of fresh fruits and vegetables arriving from the states. My boss agreed that I should travel to Alameda, CA, to discuss these issues with the staff at the Defense Personnel Support Center (DPSC). It was also agreed that I could visit the navy marine mammal center in San Diego while I was on the West Coast. While I was at DPSC Alameda, I received a message from COMNAVMAR that the dolphin unit on Guam was being re-deployed to San Diego and that there was no need for me to go to San Diego. So I returned to Guam very disappointed in not being able to visit the US Navy Marine Mammal Center and not to be able to work with the dolphins.

The departure of the dolphin unit meant that the unit's barge was not being used. It had a bunkroom, kitchen, and other living spaces. I thought the barge would be ideal for us. It could be next to the cold storage warehouse, and my single airman could live on it. The kitchen could be used for our food testing laboratory and I could move my office aboard. So I wrote a point paper to that effect and sent it through the chain of command to the admiral.

About a week later the chief of staff called and wanted to see me in his office. When I arrived he told me the admiral said that it was a well-written point paper. I replied that the air force had a course on how to write point papers. The chief of staff said the admiral denied my request for the barge because it would not look good for the Navy to have an Air Force officer claiming to be a "Command Afloat." (Command Afloat is a designation all naval surface warfare offices aspire to have. It is to be in command of a warship and includes the command at sea insignia worn above the nametag over the right chest pocket.) I thought what a very parochial excuse for not letting me use the barge. When he saw my disappointment, he stated the real reason was that the barge had already been allocated elsewhere.

I eventually got to visit the US Navy Marine Mammal Center while I was stationed at the Navy Food Services Systems Office (NAVFSSO) in Washington, DC, and was visiting naval bases on the West Coast. My son, Sam, was also able to visit the center when he was stationed on a cruiser *USS Chancellorsville*. He sent me a book autographed by the center director, former Air Force Veterinarian Dr. Sam Ridgway.

SUBMARINE

I received a call one day that one of the submarines had experienced a freezer failure and needed an inspection of all of its frozen food. I could not pass up the opportunity to go aboard a submarine, so I decided to go myself rather than send one of my technicians. I was met on the pier by the chief of the boat (COB). I had my freezer suit and some other equipment. The COB said he would carry the equipment for me. We crossed over on the gangway, saluted the flag, and requested permission to board. The petty officer of the watch returned my salute and granted permission. The COB directed me to the hatch in the conning tower where there was a tube with a ladder leading to the deck below. The COB instructed me on how to descend the ladder while holding my freezer suit. "Hold the rung of the ladder with one hand, rest your back against the side of the tube, and alternate your feet downward on the rungs. Do not forget to move your feet as you slide down the tube."

Well, you guessed it. I forgot to move my feet before the next "slide." There I was, stuck in the squat position in the tube of a nuclear submarine. The COB reached down, clasped my hand, and pulled me back to an upright position. I started down again, this time alternating my feet on the rungs of the ladder.

The freezer had been repaired and had not been inoperable long enough for any thawing to occur. I completed the inspection and certified everything was safe for continued storage and consumption. I had no problems climbing the ladder to leave the boat.

RECEIPT FOOD INSPECTIONS

We received most of our food supplies by container ship from Alameda, CA. The containers were off loaded from the ship at the commercial port in Apra Harbor. They were placed on trailers and hauled to the NSD warehouses. The perishable products would be in refrigerated containers. Part of our inspection process was to examine the temperature recording to make sure the correct temperatures were maintained during the entire voyage. During such a check, I noticed the container was not locked at the corners to the trailer. I pointed this out as a safety issue to the NSD storage officer. We started documenting each container not properly secured to the trailer. In spite of our reporting, there was no consistent compliance.

I was in my office one day when I heard a loud crash. I ran out into the cold storage loading dock to see a container on its side. One of civilian warehouseman was crawling out of the container. He had driven his forklift into the container to remove a palate of frozen food when the container fell off the trailer. Fortunately, he was not injured. I immediately called the storage and safety officers. The cases of food had to be removed by hand before the forklift could be extracted and the container up-righted with the use of a crane. We had no more problems with containers not being locked to the trailers.

On another occasion, we checked the temperature recording on a shipping container of lettuce. We saw that there was a period of several days of warm temperature. We opened the container and saw these tiny flies that resembled the fruit flies that we grew in biology lab in college. We immediately closed the container. One of my concerns was that we not release a new species of flies to the island. I called the pest control section and we decided to fumigate the entire container with phosgene for twenty-four hours. Afterwards I collected several samples and sent them to the entomology lab in Hawaii. The container was taken to the landfill and the lettuce was immediately buried. The lab reported that they were indeed fruit flies and that we had taken the proper action.

Our other transportation of subsistence was by Navy auxiliary dry cargo ships (T-AK). Their primary mission was to carry material to the submarine tender but would often have cargo for NSD. Their cargo handling was "break bulk" which meant the cases had to hand loaded onto pallets in the cargo hold before they could be lifted by cranes onto the pier at cold storage.

I got to know the first mate. He would bring us items that we could not buy on Guam, such as large packages of raisins for making cookies.

My clinic needed a hydraulic adjustable exam table. MWR agreed to purchase one, since the proceeds of our vaccination clinic went into their account. I contacted a surgical equipment distributor in the states. MWR sent a purchase order, and we directed that the table be delivered to US Navy Transportation Office in Alameda, CA. The first mate made sure it was loaded on the T-AK and we received it the next month, saving a very expensive shipping fee.

BILL SELF

Lieutenant Commander William Self, Preventive Medicine Officer, was my sponsor when we arrived on Guam. Sponsors are assigned to help new arrivals get settled and in my case acclimated to the Navy. In addition, the zoonosis

clinic and my office were in the same spaces as his office in a building just outside of the NSD cold and dry storage compound. Later I moved my office to
cold storage but the zoonosis clinic remained there.

Bill and Carolyn had five children; the two youngest boys were the same
age as mine. Bill was also the Cub Master of the pack on the Naval Station
that my son Sam attended. I was the district Scout commissioner. We both
served on the advisory committee to the Guam Public Health Department.

We first lived in post-WWII quarters made of wood in Apra Heights.
When those started being replaced, we moved to Sumay on the Naval Station
where our backyards joined each other. Shirley and Carolyn were both active
in the officers' wives club. To say the least, we had a lot of interaction both
professionally and socially.

BUFFY ELEPHANT

In March 1974, someone in Washington, DC, decided that all of the 1071st operation locations should be attached to the naval medical center at their respective bases. That meant a transition from the COMNAVMAR staff to the Naval
Hospital Guam. However, my office remained at NSD. Thus, being new on
the hospital staff, Shirley and I were invited to the hail and farewell cookout at
the hospital pool. We were given raffle tickets for a door prize drawing. The
grand prize was in a box about the size of a dish pack the movers use. Sticking
out the end of the box was a curved piece of porcelain. I guessed it was a ceramic
Buffy elephant, which was very popular in the Pacific. People would use them
for magazine or flower stands. With a pair of them and a sheet of glass one
could make a coffee table. My ticket was drawn for the grand prize. Being new
to the hospital and not having an office there, I was unaware that the bathrooms
were being remodeled. I opened the box and instead of a Buffy elephant was a
white porcelain floor mounted urinal, much to my surprise and to everyone
else's enjoyment. Shirley said, "You are not taking that thing home."

I said I had a plan for it and that I was. I stored it temporarily behind the
house. A couple of days later after going home for lunch, Bill called me and
said I had to do something with the urinal. All the boys in the neighborhood
were in line using it, including his and my sons.

The next day I filled the urinal with dirt, planted a coconut in it, and took it to my office. The condensation from our office window air conditioner dripped onto the ramp to the cold storage loading dock, and that is where I put the urinal. The coconut sprouted and there is where I left it when I departed Guam.

OAKLAND

As I mentioned in writing about Bill Wheeler, I made a visit to West Coast naval activities. One of my stops was the Naval Medical Center Oakland, CA. Bill Self was now a commander and Chief of the Navy Preventive Medicine School there. In addition to staying with him and Carolyn, he had me give a lecture to his class of chiefs and petty officers 1st Class. At NAVFSSO I had found a monograph someone had written on food borne illness outbreaks on Navy ships. I summarized the chain of events that led to each incident on transparencies for overhead projection. I had the same presentation at the Navy Supply Corps School in Albany, GA, to both Navy Supply Corps offices and chiefs in the food management team class. The chiefs were administered by NAVFSSO.

After my lecture, Bill took me up to the tenth floor of the hospital for a courtesy call on the commanding officer, Rear Admiral Walter M. Lonergan. The admiral had been my first CO at Naval Medical Center Charleston, when he was a captain. From there he went to the Navy surgeon general's staff and was promoted to rear admiral. After a series of unexplained deaths at Medical Center Oakland, he was sent there to correct deficiencies.

He was glad to see me again and thanked me for teaching the class. He then called me to the window. "Sam, I want to show you something. Look down there. See that building with steam rising from it? That's the hospital laundry. I started there as a seaman apprentice. I've come a long way to rise to the tenth floor."

BILL SELF'S RETIREMENT

I was still at NAVFSO when Captain Bill Self retired from the Navy. His last assignment was on the Naval Board of Inspections and Survey (INSURV). It worked directly for the Chief of Naval Operations and conducted inspection of ships before they were commissioned and deployed. The commander of INSURV was Vice Admiral John D. Bulkeley. He was the PT boat skipper who evacuated General Douglas MacArthur from Corregidor. He received the Medal of Honor for that and later actions in the Pacific. He recruited John F. Kennedy for the motor torpedo boat training.

Bill had his retirement ceremony in the auditorium of the Bethesda National Naval Medical Center. In 2011, it was combined with Walter Reed Army Medical Center to become Walter Reed National Military Medical Center.

Bill introduced me to Vice Admiral Bulkeley there. The admiral lived in quarters at the Washington Navy Yard where NAVFSSO was located but I had not met him before.

Bill died in 2015. We still exchange Christmas letters with Carolyn.

COLONEL G.M. 'JINX' McCAIN, USMC

Colonel McCain was commander of Marine Barracks Guam. He fought in the Battle of Iwo Jima, Korea, and Vietnam. He was wounded four times and the legend was that was the origin of his nickname "Jinx." Actually, he got it from his 1940 Texas A & M football teammates because he fumbled the football.

Colonel McCain's secretary called and asked if I could come to his office at my convenience. So, I headed up to his office in the barracks. I thought it might have to do with my airman sliding into home plate and knocking his Marine catcher unconscious. He thanked me for coming so soon and handed me a set of X- rays. It was the cannon bone or third metacarpal of the front leg of a horse. It had a hairline fracture. The horse belonged to his daughter Debbie in California, and he wanted a second opinion on the treatment. I told him I didn't have any experience in treating horses. But since there was no displacement it probably would heal in four to six weeks in a cast designed to keep pressure off the foot. He thanked me for my opinion.

About six weeks later Colonel McCain's secretary called again. I went up to his office right away. He showed me another set of X-rays. The bone was completely healed and the horse was doing fine. It is the only horse case I consulted on from 5,974 miles away. Colonel McCain dreamed of establishing a horseback riding program on Guam like he had done at Camp Pendleton, CA, but it never materialized.

Colonel McCain and his wife lived on Nimitz Hill next to Rear Admiral Morrison. In his front yard was a four-foot high stone monument with the Marine Corps emblem: eagle, globe, and anchor. When Colonel and Mrs. McCain returned from an off island trip, the monument was gone. He had his Marines searching the entire island for it, including the jungles.

About two weeks later, Rear Admiral Morrison called Colonel McCain and said they had caught the perpetrators and for him to come to his quarters. Colonel McCain arrived to find Rear Admiral Morrison and all the unit COs watching a crane lift the monument off a flat bed truck and place it in his yard. The monument had been at the Ship Repair Facility the whole time having the bronze eagle, globe, and anchor cleaned.

Colonel McCain was in charge of thirteen Vietnamese refugee camps on Guam in 1975. He retired in 1976 after thirty-three years in the Marine Corps. He died in May 2003 at the age of eighty-two.

In 2011 the Colonel Jinx McCain Horsemanship Program for wounded veterans was dedicated in his honor at Camp Pendleton, CA. His daughter Debbie helps with the program.

SAIPAN

Captain William Smith USAF, VC was the veterinarian for the trust territories. He was assigned to the state department and was not in the chain of command of anyone in CINCPAC. His job was to help farmers on the islands in the territories to improve the health of their livestock so they could meet standards for export. His base of operation was Saipan. He approached me with a proposal to swap houses for a week. He wanted to bring his wife to the "big city" of Guam for shopping at the military exchanges and stock up at the commissary. So we worked out a plan. I took leave. Shirley, the boys, and I drove to

Agana Airport and left the car there. We flew to Saipan where Bill met us. He gave us an orientation tour of the island before going to his house for the night. The next day I drove Bill and his wife to the airport and gave him the keys to our car.

We had a great time exploring the island. There were beautiful beaches and a mountain vista. There were also sites of the severe fighting in WWII when the Marines liberated the island from the Japanese. Bill and his wife returned at the end of the week with all the supplies they bought on Guam. We left with great memories, lots of pictures, and a long stem vase Bill's neighbor gave me for treating her dog.

PRODUCE

The farmers of Northern Marianas formed a co-op to market fruits and vegetables. The agent for international development (AID) called the Navy procurement officer (PO) at NSD to arrange a meeting with the co-op to discuss the Navy buying their produce. The PO invited me to go along. I had met the AID while vacationing on Saipan a month or so before. We met in a building in the agriculture research farm, which also had a slaughterhouse. The farmers displayed samples of produce. It all was very good quality. The PO told the farmers, "We'll pay $1.25 a pound and not a penny more." The farmers looked at each other and after a pause agreed.

As we were leaving the AID agent pulled me aside, "Doc, that PO is not a very good negotiator; the farmers were willing to accept $0.75 a pound."

So about every other week, I and one of my technicians would catch the early morning commercial flight on a twelve-passenger plane to Saipan, Tinian, or Rota. We would inspect the produce that the farmers brought to the airport. We would validate the shipping documents and return to Guam. The produce would be loaded on the afternoon Air Micronesia jet and flown to Agana Airport. We would observe the unloading. When the cargo was watermelons, I would break one open to inspect it. I then would give pieces of it to the cargo handlers. Why did I do that? It cut down on the breakage and theft of the watermelons.

The ticket agents on Tinian and Rota would load the luggage on the plane, then get in the cockpit and fly the plane.

Tinian was also from where B-29s were launched for the bombing of Japan, including the atomic bombs. The runways are still there. There is a historic marker where the atomic bombs were loaded on the planes.

FIFTY-MILE HIKES

The biggest Boy Scout event ever held on Guam took place during Christmas vacation 1973. Each of the Boy Scout troops from each of the villages and the military bases, twelve in all, would simultaneously but independently hike fifty miles in one week. They were to plan their own routes. The stipulation was they had to camp one night at Liberation Park (the Statue of Liberty is still there) in Agana. Each troop was also to perform conservation and a service project.

My job was to deliver each day all the supplies and tools needed for all the service projects. As it worked out, there were two or three projects each day. I would deliver the equipment in the morning, go back to work, and retrieve the tools after work. For the service projects, the Scouts cleaned up every historical site on the island of overgrowth and trash. On the conservation projects, they planted every tree and shrub stocked in both the US forestry and Guam government plant nurseries. That included planting hundreds of fire resistant iron wood seedlings on the hills of the Navy Magazine.

RETURN TO THE STATES

My tour on Guam was for two years. After eighteen months, I called Col. Shannon, who was making assignments then. The conversation went thus: "This is Captain Samuel Tate. What openings do you have in six months?"

He asked, "Who are you again and where?"

"Captain Samuel Tate, and I'm with the Navy on Guam."

He said, "We no longer make assignments that way. Fill out an AF Form 90 (dream sheet)."

I said, "With all due respect, Colonel, my wife was asked to come to Guam, and she is ready to go back to the States. What assignment do you have for her?"

He said, "Send me your dream sheet, Captain." End of conversation.

I have no recollection of what I put on the dream sheet, but it definably was not Bolling AFB, Washington, DC, which was my assignment notification. I had two reasons for not wanting to go to Bolling. One, I didn't think I could afford to live there, and two, I had served on a headquarters base before (South Ruislip, 3rd AF) and every colonel on base was in my business.

I worked very closely with the Commander of NSD Guam, Captain Herford, both professionally and with the Boy Scouts. He was the district chairman, and I was the district commissioner. I told him about my next assignment to Bolling AFB and asked if he could use his connections in the Navy Supply Corps to get me another Navy assignment. He said he would. Two months before I was to depart Guam, I received official orders to the Naval Base in Charleston, SC. What a surprise and relief. I told Captain Herford about it and thanked him for interceding. He said he had forgotten all about my request and had no idea how it happened.

I found out later that the commander of the Naval Supply Center Charleston (NSC) was upset because there had been a series of short assignments of veterinary officers there. He complained to Colonel Menning who was now commanding of the 1071st that the Air Force apparently didn't see the importance of supporting the entire US Navy Atlantic Fleet Ballistic Submarine Force. Colonel Menning said he had a career officer returning from two years at NSD Guam who could be made available. That pleased the captain. So Colonel Menning requested Colonel Shannon to change my orders to Charleston.

TRANSIT VIA HAWAII

Captain Ray Ingles was the trust territory action officer on the COMNAV-MAR Staff. He was also on the district Scout committee. His wife had a position with Thai Airlines as vice president for Central Pacific. Ray transferred to Hawaii before I was due to leave Guam. Before he left, he told me to get a delay in route on my permanent change of station orders and spend some time in Hawaii. We talked a couple times on the phone. He said the military R&R facilities at Fort De Russy were full, but his wife made reservations for us at a hotel one block away and in Waikiki (this was before the Hole Koa Hotel Armed Forces Recreation Center was built).

My replacement arrived the day before we left Guam. We had about a two-hour overlap in his hotel room. I had prepared a briefing book for the AF captain who had no prior experience with the Navy. After about a half-hour, he asked what language I was speaking. He was not at all familiar with Navy terms or acronyms. I assured him that it was all explained in the briefing book and that the NCOs would guide him.

We left Agana, Guam the next night on a commercial flight to Honolulu. I was awakened by an announcement over the public address system, "Is there a doctor on board?" I waited and after the second request, I identified myself to a flight attendant. "I am not a medical doctor but a veterinarian. Can I be of some assistance?"

She snatched me out of my seat and took me to the rear of the aircraft. There was a small boy stretched out over several seats. The flight attendant said he was unresponsive.

I was told that he was in a group of four Vietnamese children that were being escorted by a nurse to the Mayo Clinic for heart surgery, but the airline had not been informed of that fact. I examined the child. He was not breathing, had no pulse, and was cold to the touch. I told them the child was dead. They requested I start CPR because they were required to attempt resuscitation. I started CPR. Every time, I breathed into his mouth, I heard a gurgling in his lungs. I stopped after several minutes when I got no response.

We covered the child with a blanket but left his face exposed because we did not have the authority to declare him dead. The flight attendant moved us to first class for the rest of the flight. Our plane was met in Honolulu by health officials. They declared the child dead and removed his body, along with the nurse and the other children. I was interviewed by the authorities and then allowed to deplane with Shirley and the boys.

Ray met us at the Honolulu Airport in his summer white uniform. He drove us to the hotel and helped us carry our bags into the lobby. The clerk saw that our reservation was made by the Vice President of Thai Airlines and a Navy captain was handling our bags. He assigned us the penthouse suite. We had the entire rooftop of the hotel with a balcony on all four sides and a bathroom for each of us.

NSC CHARLESTON

L. Mendel Rivers was the U.S. Representative from South Carolina and represented Charleston – base of the 1st congressional district for thirty years. He was Chairman of the House Armed Services Committees and made sure federal money poured into Charleston. After his death in 1971, the Navy named the submarine *USS L Mendel Rivers* (SSN-686) in his honor.

Naval Base Charleston stretched for miles on the west bank of the Cooper River. According to native Charlestonians, Charleston is where the Ashley and Cooper Rivers met to form the Atlantic Ocean.

Starting at the south end of the waterfront were the piers for cruisers and destroyers, home port for about one-third of the Atlantic Fleet. Proceeding north were the submarine piers, both attack and FBM submarines. Set back from the piers was the cold storage warehouse. Next was the Ship Repair Facility with all of its shops, then rows of warehouses of the Naval Supply Center with the dry subsistence warehouse at the extreme north. It had its own pier where Navy auxiliary dry cargo ships (T-AK) loaded supplies destined for the submarine tenders at Holy Lock, Scotland, and Rota, Spain. They also transported Polaris missiles. The base even had its own railroad locomotive. -

On the west of the main street were various support facilities including surface warfare and submarine schools, commissary, gym complex, NSC HQ and offices, officers' and enlisted clubs, childcare center, and barracks to name a few. The medical center and the Navy Lodge were located outside of the base perimeter.

Further north on the waterfront but not contiguous with the main base, was the Naval Weapons Station Charleston. In addition to performing maintenance on weapon systems, there were more submarine piers.

West of the cold storage was FBM warehouse specific for Polaris missiles and submarine parts. Clearly the base and NSC supported the majority of the Atlantic FBM submarine force.

Charleston was also HQ of the 6th Naval District, which covered North and South Carolina and Georgia (the naval district system no longer exists and neither does Charleston Naval Base). While I was stationed in Charleston,

Vice Admiral Samuel L. Gravely, Jr. was the commander. He was the first African American in the US Navy to serve as an officer on a fighting ship, first to command a ship, the first fleet commander and the first to become an admiral. He served in WWII, Korea, and Vietnam. The destroyer *USS Gravely* (DDG-107) commissioned in 2010 was named in his honor.

My veterinary unit in Charleston was officially designated Operating Location CO, 1071st Medical Services Squadron, HQ Command, USAF. We were attached to the Naval Regional Medical Center Charleston , but the majority of our work was for NSC and its CO considered me part of his staff as well.

COLD STORAGE

The receipt inspection of perishable subsistence was very good. My NCOIC was extremely thorough. I once had a truck driver tell me, as my technical sergeant was on the phone reporting to DPSC Cheatham Annex that his load of eggs where above the required temperature, "I can take that load to any base on the East Coast and it would be accepted. But when I deliver here, I know that nothing will be over looked."

The Defense Logistics Agency inspector general rated our receipt inspection program outstanding. However, our ability to adequately inspect stored perishables was due to a lack of a space for testing. Since there were no women working at cold storage, I got permission from the CO to have the women's bathroom converted to a food testing lab.

DRY STORAGE

Dry storage was a different story. My technician had no workspace and no testing area. There was a major insect and rodent problem. I made recommendations on establishing a pest management program, which included plugging the holes where the corrugated metal siding met the foundation. I did not get the response I anticipated. That all changed by a simple handwritten not from the CO of the submarine tender at Rota, Spain to NSC CO. "We have enough bugs, don't send anymore." Things changed rapidly. The holes were filled and a trailer was ordered to be our dry storage inspection office and lab. We were now able to detect insect infestation in products before they could spread.

OFF LOADS

The shipyard was having a problem complying with USDA requirement for disposal of garbage from foreign vessels and US vessels returning with food purchased in foreign ports. I worked with them to convert a dumpster into a garbage cooker which satisfied USDA.

We also responded to ship board refrigeration failures. On one ship we saved a hundred thousand dollars in frozen food. In two other instances we prevented destroyers from being removed from operational status. Ships coming into the shipyard for overhaul or maintenance in the food storage spaces had to off load all their food. We had to inspect it all to determine disposition: accept for storage, force issue to a dining facility for immediate use (within a week at no cost to the facility), or destruction. During the off load of one submarine tender, only one percent of the $261,424 worth of subsistence was surveyed (destroyed).

Perishable substance sorting was no problem because the cold storage and the dining facilities were close to the piers. Dry goods were more difficult. They would be trucked to dry storage to be inspected. Any force issue had to then be trucked back to the dining facilities. That didn't make any sense to me. So I implemented a program to inspect dry goods right on the pier next to the ship. It reduced multiple handling and also had the ship provide a working party to help sort the material. One summer day we were inspecting dry stores pier side to a destroyer. The working party was made up of very young sailors. During a rest and water break I overheard one of the sailors ask my sergeant, "Is he an officer?"

"Yes, he's an Air Force captain."

The sailor said, "I've never seen an officer work before."

USS SANTA BARBARA (AE-28)

The NAVMEDCEN had a program for medical officers, dentists and nurses, who had not served on ships, to go to sea on short exercise tours to get an understanding of the ship board living conditions and routines of sailors. In October 20, 1975 three medical officers and I put to sea on the ammunition ship *USS Santa Barbara* (AE-28). The mission was to conduct underway replenishment (UNREP) of the carrier, *USS America* (CV66). The *America* had just completed overhaul in Norfolk, VA, and was preparing for deployment to the Mediterranean Sea and the Persian Gulf.

During the day-long voyage to rendezvous with *America*, I volunteered my expertise in food service sanitation to the CO. I conducted a courtesy inspection of the galley and mess desk (dining area) with the senior mess management specialists (MMS) and the hospital corpsman (HM1). I observed their food preparation and conducted a class on food service sanitation. There was a cockroach infestation and the HM1 had already arranged for treating the spaces after the dinner meal. I went along and showed him some places he might have missed on his own. When female roaches are killed by a pesticide, their egg packets are released and can become a source of re-infestation if not completely cleaned up. We came back several hours later and were sweeping up dead roaches and egg packets by the dust-pan full. The MMS then washed and sanitized all the food contact surfaces in time to start preparing breakfast.

The next morning it was an amazing sight of the *America* on the horizon silhouetted by the rising sun. As *Santa Barbara* closed on the *America*, it took up position on *America*'s starboard (right) side. UNREP with carriers is always performed to the starboard side because the island with its navigation bridge is constructed on that side. We then commenced three days and two nights of UNREP.

UNREP is conducted by two methods: alongside connected replenishment (CONREP) and vertical replenishment (VERT REP), which can be performed separately or simultaneously.

In CONREP, cables are stretched between the two ships using ram tension, allowing for smooth transfers, as well as considering any movement of the ships in the water. This system is known as Standard Tensioned Replenishment Alongside Method (STREAM). The *Santa Barbara* had two STREAM stations on each side and could replenish two ships at the same time, port and starboard. Even in very calm seas the water between the ships becomes very turbulent and the smaller ship can be sucked into the larger. It requires exceptional ship handling skills by the crews on the bridge.

In VERTRREP cargo is transferred from ship to ship by helicopter. The helicopter never touched down on either ship. Cargo is lifted in slings with a cable hooked under the helicopter, flown to the receiving ship and released on the deck, then repeated.[10]

On the third day of UNREP we were offered the opportunity to visit the other ships in the formation, one of the docs chose to go to the destroyer following in the plane guard position. Its purpose is to recue downed flight crews or a man overboard. The other two docs and I chose to go to the *America*. In both instances we were transferred by helicopter. We spent the whole day touring the ship including time on the bridge and the port where the weapons were being received. I also got a tour of the three galleys onboard. We had two meals on board and flew back to the *Santa Barbara* before dark.

It was a terrific experience to appreciate both large ship board food service and material handling which paid dividends in my latter assignment to NAVFSSO, which I was selected for in 1976.

The CO of *Santa Barbara*, Captain Paul H. Bassin, wrote a letter of appreciation to both CO's NAVMEDCEN and NSC Charleston for my invaluable assistance.

The *USS Santa Barbara* was transferred to US Military Sea Lift Command 1998 and continued in service to the fleet until retired in 2005. She was sold for scrap in 2007.

The *USS America* was decommissioned in 1996. In May 2005 she was used in live fire underwater explosions tests. After four weeks of test, she was scuttled 266 miles south east of Cape Hatteras, NC, and sits upright in the bottom at 16,860 feet. The *America* is the largest warship ever sunk. The amphibious assault ship LHA-6 (landing helicopter assault) was commissioned October 2014 as the new *USS America*.

COFFEE

I first learned there was a problem with the GI ground coffee from the ladies at the childcare center. They invited me over to taste some from their percolator. It definitely had a burnt taste. We then withdrew a ten-pound can (the largest size can produced) of the same lot in the warehouse and percolated it. It tasted burnt. We then prepared coffee in the coffee makers at both cold and dry storage without telling the workers what we were doing. Their unsolicited comments were, "Who made this coffee? It's terrible, it's burnt." We also started getting complaints from the dining facilities. We stopped all distribution and notified DPSC HQ in Philadelphia. They told us to submit an unsatisfactory material report (UMR) and send some cans to US Army Labs in Natick, MA. Meanwhile there was an article in the *Virginia Pilot* that the Navy was burning coffee at its landfill in Norfolk. The coffee odor could be smelt for miles. DPSC heard about it and stopped the destruction of anymore coffee there. Natick Labs confirmed our results. DPSC put a hold on all of the company's coffee worldwide and got a contract non-compliance ruling against the company. That company appealed the ruling. I was then directed to send samples to the USDA tasting lab in Washington, DC. I hand-carried the sample cans there and watched the taste testing procedure. USDA upheld our UMR, and the company lost its appeal and had to return ten million dollars. However, they were allowed to recover all stocks stored in CONUS. Overseas stocks were destroyed. We never learned what the company did with all that burnt ground coffee. Some speculated they processed it into instant coffee.

FILLED MILK PLANT

The fresh milk being supplied to the Roosevelt Roads Naval Station, Puerto Rico was coming from cows with chronic mastitis. The milk had high bacteria counts and antibiotic residues. The Navy decided to solve the problem with a filled milk plant like the one at Rota, Spain. NSC was the contract agency for the project. I was called to consult on the sanitary and quality assurance specification for a six million dollar contract for the plant construction and product production. We got a bid from a large dairy processing cooperation. Everything was looking good until another company appealed on the basis of a government contracting provision small business set-aside, which meant a percentage of government contracts had to be awarded to small businesses. The company that won the appeal and was awarded the contract was the same company that had previously operated the plant in Rota and was not renewed when the contract expired. I knew it was going to be trouble, but there wasn't anything I could do other than voice my concerns.

True to my prediction, the contractor was having performance problems. In January, NSC sent me and a procurement officer to investigate the problem and recommend solutions. We spent three days there documenting sanitation, quality assurance, and production problems. We also found that, as a result, the Navy activities had reduced their order quantities, which directly affected the payment procedure set in the contract. We made our recommendation to the CO and corrections were implemented.

We were at our BOQ room when I said, "No one back home will believe we've been here three days and not gone to the beach." It was another way of saying they won't believe we worked the whole time. So we put on our swimsuits and drove to the beach. Just as we got in the water, it poured cats and dogs.

ICE CREAM CONES

One of the submarine tenders rotated back from Holy Lock, Scotland and was going to have a Cub Scout Pack visit before it off loaded to go into the yard. The food service was going to serve the Cubs ice cream, so the supply clerk ordered one hundred ice cream cones from NSC who had a local purchase contract with Piggly Wiggly grocery chain. A tractor trailer truck pulled to NSC receiving area and started to unload one hundred cases of ice cream cones. Each case was the size of a dish pack that commercial movers use and contained one thousand cones.

Piggly Wiggly never questioned the quantity for the requisition because they were used to large orders from NSC. However, they didn't have that much in stock so they contacted Baskin Robbins, who pulled stock from their stores all over the East Coast.

The one hundred cases were returned, and Baskin Robbins was happy to get them back. Someone went down to the local Piggly Wiggly and brought one hundred cones off the shelf.

SMOKING THE BOAT

Fire aboard a ship is very serious, especially on a submarine. (The Navy calls a submarine a boat not a ship) NSC received a TWX (electronic message) from an attack submarine at sea that had a fire in its galley originating in the deep fat fryer. The fire was stopped by the fire suppression system over the fryer, but the gallery was filled with smoke. The boat had to be brought to snorkel depth to clear the smoke. The TWX contained the product information of the deep fat fryer cooking oil. We had the same lot in dry storage. We submitted an UMR to DPSC and sent sample cans to Natick Labs. NSC issued an all ships alert to cease the use of that lot of oil.

Natick Labs tested the oil and found that its flash point was well above the temperature of the deep fat fryer. So the oil was not the cause of smoking the boat. I consulted the NAVFSSO food service management team in Charleston. Their opinion was that the deep fat fryer was not properly cleaned. As food is fried, particles break off, especially if it is battered, and sink to the bottom where they collect near the heating coils. These cracklings have a flash point lower than the cooking oil. NAVFSSO then sent an all ships TWX reminding them of the proper cleaning of the deep fat fryers, and NSC released the hold on their stocks.

CAPTAIN E.B. "MICKEY" McMAHAN, USN, MC

Captain McMahan was my second boss and Commander of Naval Regional Medical Center Charleston. He had a very friendly and easy-going personality. My mom and dad, a retired Navy chief in WWII, were coming to visit us in Charleston. Dad called me and said, "I need a gallbladder operation and can't have it until I have a stress test. I can't get an appointment for one at the Naval Medical Center Portsmouth. Can you see if I can get one there in Charleston?"

I went to Captain McMahan and explained my dad's situation. I asked if cardiology could do his stress test. Capt. McMahan replied, "Portsmouth may not accept our results." He then called for his secretary, "Jossie, please get Admiral Johnson[11] on the phone."

"The admiral is on the line, sir."

Capt. McMahan began, "Jack, this is Mickey. The father of my staff veterinarian has not been able to get a stress there. He is a retired chief."

The admiral replied, "I will look into it. What's his phone number?" I provided the number.

Captain McMahan said, "Thanks, Jack."

Shortly after I got home, Dad called. "What on earth did you do?"

I asked, "Why, what happened?"

Dad explained, "The admiral called from the naval hospital and wanted to know would it be convenient for me to have a stress test the day after tomorrow!"

"What did you say?"

Dad said, "I said that would okay and thank you."

Dad was cleared for the surgery, and I drove up to Portsmouth to be with him. He did just fine.

Captain McMahan was Chief of Obstetrics at National Naval Medical Center, Bethesda, MD, at the same time I was at NAVFSSO in the Washington Navy Yard. He said if I was ever in Bethesda to look him up. One Friday, on my way to catch the bus to work, I stepped off a curb and sprained my right ankle. I went on to work, but by noon it was badly swollen and painful. I went to the clinic in the Navy Yard, but all they could do was wrap it. They sent me to the clinic at the Navy Annex next to the Pentagon. They did an X-ray and put my foot in a shell cast (one that doesn't go completely around the leg). They gave me the phone number for orthopedics at Bethesda and said to make an appointment for next week. They gave me a pair of crutches. So I got an appointment for Wednesday. They took another X-ray, determined there were no fractures, and put an elastic support sock on. Told me to come back in two or three weeks. Nowadays they would have dispensed a boot.

So, I called Captain McMahan and told him I was in the building. He said he was on the way to the barbershop and didn't want to give up his appointment. I could come up to the top floor and wait for him in his office.

---

[11] I don't remember his name.

So Shirley pushed me, carrying the crutches and in a wheelchair, into the elevator. I was wearing my summer blue uniform. When we got off the elevator there was a Navy captain in a doctor's coat.

He asked, "May I help you, Major?"

"Yes, sir, we are looking for Captain McMahan's office."

"I'll take you there."

A few minutes later Captain McMahan arrived and was laughing.

I asked, "What's so funny?"

"That captain you met at the elevator, he is chief of orthopedics. He wanted to know how long I have been seeing his patients."

AF INTERNS

The Air Force had recruited so many graduating medical students that there weren't enough intern positions for them in AF hospitals. So in May 1977 the AF sent three of those brand new captains to do their family practice internships at the Naval Regional Medical Center Charleston. I was the only AF officer there, so the Air Force Institute of Technology (AFIT), which administers all training outside of the AF and located in Dayton, OH, assigned them to my unit for administrative purposes. Captain McMahan also made me their sponsor.

I had enough advance notice to send each one a welcome letter with instructions before they departed their medical schools.

Do not start your travel before the effective date of your orders or you will not receive your full travel pay (a mistake I made).

Hand carry all important papers, birth certificate, marriage license, military orders, etc. Do not allow them get packed in your household goods.

Be sure to arrive in Charleston by the no later than date (NLT) on your orders.

Call me when you arrive in Charleston, day or night.

When you arrive, do not try to enter the Naval Base because you will not have proper ID to do so (Charleston was a nuclear security base).

A couple of days before the expected arrival of the three doctors, base security called. "Major Tate, there is an individual who is dropping your name and trying to get on the base."

"Is he there now?"

Security said, "No, he left."

"If he shows up again, call me and hold him until I get there."

The next day the manager of the Navy Lodge called, "Major Tate, there is a guy here creating a disturbance because I won't rent a room to him and the woman he claims is his wife. Neither have military IDs but he has a set of AF orders."

"Tell them to wait there for me. I'm on my way."

The manager assigned them a room after I explained their status to him. I than took the Captain C aside. I asked, "Did you get my letter?"

"Yes."

"Why didn't you follow my instructions? You have caused a lot of unnecessary trouble for yourself."

Captain C explained, "I saw that the letter was signed by a veterinarian and didn't think it applied to me."

I said, "I'm the officer in charge of this AF unit here. You will obey my instruction."

By the next day all three officers had arrived, and I took them to the introductory briefing at the hospital for the new interns and sponsors. Captain McMahan welcomed them aboard. The director of professional training then presented an overview of their program and turned the interns over to their sponsors to get them processed and receive their uniforms. They were to be back at the end of the week to get their assignments.

All of the in-processing for my three officers had to be done at Charleston AFB. First stop was pass and ID. While I was assisting Captain A, there was a commotion in the line. Captain C was in a confrontation with an AF technical sergeant. Apparently, the wife of the technical sergeant had bumped into Captain C or the other way round, and words were exchanged. I intervened, and they calmed down. I instructed the two that were married to bring their wives back here the next day to get their ID cards. Next stop was finance. I knew that this was going to be very complicated. I asked to see the NCOIC who I had dealt with before and was aware of the men in my detachment. Sure enough, each officer's source of commissioning was different. Two had been in the early commissioning program and longevity for pay had to be calculated.

The master sergeant said, "We will process your travel vouchers and pay you the full amount for you and your dependents. Each of you will receive your three hundred dollar uniform allowance. I will estimate your base pay and allowances and pay you today. It will take a couple of days to figure out your longevity and professional pay. Until then I will maintain you in casual pay status, which means you come here and get paid every two weeks. If you have bank accounts, we can make direct deposits."

We went to the cashier who paid each officer more money than they had ever seen.

The last stop on the base was the uniform shop. I showed them what they needed and they purchased the uniforms. I gave them the next day to get dependent IDs and to meet me the day after.

When we next met, Captain C complained his wife could not yet get into the commissary. They spent the day apartment hunting instead of getting her an ID card. Friday, I turned the three uniformed captains over to the course director.

About three weeks later the course director called. "Dr. Tate, Captain C is complaining he's not getting paid."

I said, "The Finance NCOIC is handling it, and Captain C is getting paid every two weeks. It just might not be the full amount he's entitled. His total pay issue will be resolved shortly."

About two months into the program the course director called again "There's a problem with Captain C. While on pediatrics service he accused a master chief (09) of child abuse in public without proof."

"What would you do if he was Navy?"

The course director said, "I would issue a warning. If there is another incident, I would put a letter of reprimand in his training record."

I said, "He is in your internship program. You should treat him the same as the Navy interns."

A couple months later AFIT decided to transfer the administrative responsibilities for the interns from my detachment directly to the hospital. That was the last I heard of Captain C.

OFF THE SHELF
vs. MILITARY SPECIFICATIONS

During the mid 1970s there was a push in DoD to purchase off the shelf items instead of military specification for practically everything for which there was a commercial equivalent. For example, a company that canned green beans produced the same product for several grocery lines and the government, just with different labels.

The problem the Navy had when it came to food was not what was in the package but the packaging, especially when it came to submarines. FBM subs deployed for six months at a time and were not resupplied during that time. So when they loaded for deployment, every nook and cranny on the boat was used. Cans would be taken out of the cases and stored in spaces against the hull. When all spaces were full, the cases would be stored in the passageway. The crews literally ate their way down to the deck (floor). The packaging had to withstand all this traffic. Also, all the subs of that period had to be loaded case-by-case, bag-by-bag through a hatch.

I was having difficulty convincing the people at the Defense Logistic Agency (DLA) that the Navy had unique package requirement. Captain R. E. Curtis, SC, USN, CO of NSC prevailed on the vice admiral, CO of Navy Supply System Command (NAVSUP), to request the DLA send a team to Charleston to see firsthand what we were telling them. One of the team members was an army colonel who was the DLA staff veterinarian. They made the obligator call on the Captain Curtis who called the CO of an attack submarine loading up for deployment. He asked if some VIPs could visit but didn't reveal the purpose. We drove to the Weapons Station and boarded the sub. The crew was loading commercially packaged fifty-pound sacks of flour one at a time down the hatch with one sailor on the deck below. While we were observing, a sack of flour slipped and hit the deck below. Splat. Flour went everywhere. I was accused of orchestrating the whole incident. I said there was no way the crew knew why we were there. Anyway, it substantiated my point.

The problem was not just food packaging – it extended to cargo pallets. The mil spec for them stipulated oak. DLA decided the commercial standard pine was adequate. In most instances it was. The exception was Navy and Marine Corps. The Marines had a supply depot in Albany, GA. All kinds of supplies were prepositioned there in configuration for specific types of amphibious ships. So when a Marine expedition unit (MEU) deployed from Norfolk and Little Creek, VA, the cargo would be shipped by rail directly to the pier. There was a special conveyor system that caught the pallet and moved it to the storage area of the ship (like pulling a car through a car wash). Well, the first load out using pine pallets was a disaster. The pallets broke apart on the conveyor rails.

A TALE OF LOBSTER TAILS

Lobster tails were one of the morale meals for submariners. A company in Florida processed and packed them. These were not the Northeast lobster, but came from the Gulf of Mexico and the Caribbean waters, known as rock lobster. We had a lot of cases in cold storage worth about one million dollars. I'm not sure where the original complaint came from about sulphur-like odor and dark color of the cooked lobster tails. We pulled a case from storage and took it to the dining facility because we didn't have a way to cook a whole case. There were about twenty to twenty-four tails per case depending on the size of each tail. The chief baked the tails on an oven sheet. Sure enough, there was sulphur-like odor and some of the tails turned dark gray while other remained white to pink. I put a hold on the lot and called DPSC Philadelphia. They contacted the company, who was puzzled why some tails were edible and others were not, even though they appeared normal. DPSC, at the urging of the seafood company, agreed to have the AF chief master sergeant who performed the procurement inspection and an expert on lobster tails come from Florida to Charleston. He repeated the bake test and got the same results as I did.

DPSC decided that the chief master sergeant and I were to inspect every case, sort out the tails we thought were bad, and repack the apparent good ones to make full cases. Because some of the lobster tails that appeared normal when frozen were inedible when cooked during our test, I restricted their issue to shore stations only. We then weighted the bad ones and disposed of them. The company reimbursed the government several thousands of dollars for the losses. This was my last major nonconformance before being transferred to

NAVFSSO, but not the end of it. About six months later I got a call from NSC Charleston. There had been an inventory audit in cold storage, and there was a discrepancy between the weight markings on the cases and the actual weight of the lobster tails. I reminded them that all the cases were repacked after sorting, but we were not told to change the weight markings. That was the last I heard about it.

Overall, our findings of non-conformance were upheld by USDA on appeal by the contractors in nine out of ten instances. In one year alone, from July 1975 to July 1976, we reported five instances of non-conformance in canned goods, including substandard substance grades, falsifying dates of pack, and changing can codes to match USDA grading certificates. One company was investigated for fraud.

COLONEL PACE'S STAFF VISIT

In January 1977, Andrews AFB was transferred from AF Systems Command to Military Airlift Command (MAC). That change included Malcolm Grow Hospital and its tenet units. The 1071st Medical Services Squadron was renamed Air Force DOD Medical Support and its twenty-eight operation locations that supported Navy and Marine Corps bases with veterinary services were now in MAC.

I received a call from Captain Cable,[12] the base veterinarian that Colonel William E. Pace, MAC Command Veterinarian, would be performing a staff visit at Charleston AFB and planned to visit my operation for about an hour (Charleston AFB was already in MAC). I called Col. Donald Shuman, 1071st at Andrews, and requested he inform Col. Pace that I would be glad to coordinate his visit, but if its purpose was to understand the scope of the mission, Col. Pace would need more than an hour. Plus, Navy protocol necessitated that a visiting 06 call on both commanders at NAVMEDCEN and NSC, which would take at least an hour.

Colonel Pace consented to add a couple more hours to his visit in April. The base veterinarian, Captain Cable, drove him over from Charleston AFB, and I took them to call on Captain McMahan at NAVMEDCEN. At the time,

12 I don't remember his name.

I had already been selected to replace Lieutenant Colonel James A. Martin as staff veterinarian at NAVFSSO in June. Without confiding with me, Col. Pace announced to Captain Mc Mahan, "We do not have an immediate replacement for Major Tate when he leaves to go to Washington. Captain Cable will provide attending service one or two days a week. However, Captain Cable is separating from the AF in two months, and we don't have a replacement yet for him either. So it could be several months before a veterinarian would be assigned to Charleston Naval Base." Captain McMahan responded something to the effect that he sympathized with the situation.

On the way to meet NSC Commander, Captain Richard Curtis, I told Col. Pace that what he explained to Captain McMahan was not going to go over very well with Captain Curtis. Colonel Pace said, "You are the one who said that a veterinarian was not needed to do this job."

I didn't correct the colonel that what I was asked several months ago was if the mission would suffer without a veterinarian for several months. My reply had been, "No, but only if at least a master sergeant was in charge." That position had been vacant for six months.

I made the introductions and then Colonel Pace proceeded to tell Captain Curtis what he had told Captain McMahan. Captain Curtis blew a gasket. "Where did you say you are from? Don't you realize the importance of Major Tate's job and that the missions of this activity encompass worldwide support of this nation's number one strategic deterrent, the Fleet Ballistic Missile Submarine Force?" (Captain Curtis always put FBM before the AF two strategic systems.)

Captain Curtis picked up the phone and called Captain McMahan, "Mickey, this is Dick, did you understand what this colonel is saying? I won't stand for it. I'm calling Admiral Grinstead at NAVSUP, and I suggest you call the surgeon general."

With that, we left Captain Curtis' office and Colonel Pace returned to the air base without a tour of the naval base. A couple weeks later Colonel Shuman set a letter to both Captains McMahan and Curtis describing that Lieutenant Colonel William Ashby, who was returning from the Philippines, would be my replacement and would arrive in two months. I would be extended until he arrived.

My extension affected Lieutenant Colonel Martin at NAVFSSO. He was a reservist on active duty but had a "hip pocket" rank of colonel upon retirement. He proposed that he be allowed to retire and then be recalled to active duty at his reserve rank of colonel. Instead he was extended on active duty, which he was not too pleased about.

My last few months at Charleston were routine and without major incident. Captain Curtis sent a letter to Captain McMahan strongly recommending me for the Air Force Commendation Medal. Captain Curtis also bestowed on me title of "Honorary Pork Chop." The name refers the slang for the Navy Supply Corps officers' insignia.

Sadly, Colonel Pace and I would clash again.

WASHINGTON NAVY YARD

The Washington Navy Yard is a very historic and interesting place. It opened in 1799 on the bank of Anacostia River, and for many years it was the largest shipyard in the U.S. In 1814 during the War of 1812, US Militia and Marines burned it to keep it from falling into the hands of the British. After it was rebuilt, its main function was ordnance production and known as the Naval Gun Factory until 1964.

During both World Wars many large manufacturing buildings were constructed connected by railroad tracks. When I was stationed there, there was a lot of excavation for underground utilities. Invariably they would run into rail road tracks that had been covered by payment. The rails had to be removed before they could proceed. There was so much street disruption, the saying was, "As soon as traffic lines are painted on the pavement, it's time to dig it up again."

NAVY FOOD SERVICE SYSTEMS OFFICE

NAVFSSO establishes and monitors all policies, procedures, programs, and regulation concerning the management, administration, and operation of all Navy general messes and afloat private messes. This mission is accomplished by several sections. Ship habitability designs all new construction and renovation layouts of all shipboard galleys and berthing spaces.

The dietary and commodity section produces the twenty-one-day menu for all navy messes. This document is the basis for all navy subsistence requirements, procurement, and storage in the supply centers and depots. The dietitian is also the voting member on the Armed Forces Product Evaluation Committee (AFPEC) which selects food items for the military and evaluates problems with food items already within the supply system. The staff veterinarian works majority of the time with this section and acts as a technical advisor to both the Navy and Marine Corps members of AFPEC.

The finance section administers the funds appropriated by congress for the basic allowance for subsistence (BAS). Both enlisted and officers who live in their own quarters received BAS in their pay check twice a month. The BAS money for those enlisted who eat in the shore dining facility and both officers and enlisted when at sea was retained by the Navy to operate those messes. The finance section also audits the financial records of all messes.

The system changed in 2002. All personnel now get full BAS and pay for their meals al-a-cart.

The food management team section coordinated the activities of the teams that provided assistance to ship and shore station messes. They were also involved in the selection of messes for the prestigious Captain Edward F. Ney Award established by the Secretary of the Navy and the International Food Service Executives Association in 1958.

To keep the entire office running was the administration section. They assign all the typing, handle mail, and message traffic, travel orders, and reservations.

NAVFSSO was located in the Washington Navy Yard in a double winged, three story building on the corner of O Street SE and the 11th Street Bridge, where John Wilkes Booth crossed the Anacostia River after he shot President Lincoln. The O Street wing housed the offices of RADM Grace Hopper who developed the computer programming language. Her nickname was "*Amazing Grace.*" The Arleigh Burke class guided missile destroyer *USS Hopper* (DDG-70) was commissioned in his honor in 1997.

NAFSSO was in the opposite wing of the building on the water front side on the third floor above the dental clinic.

Jimmy Carter was president when I arrived in Washington. I had been excited that my office overlooked the presidential yacht, *USS Sequoia*, which was used by all the presidents from Herbert Hoover to Gerald Ford. FDR used it most frequently. Jimmy Carter thought it was too ostentatious so he had it sold at auction. Afterwards it changed owners many times. It is now in a repair yard in Belfast, Maine.

The view I now had was of the Navy dive barge. The southern border of the Navy Yard was East Capitol Street. Several of us would jog at lunch, cross the river on 11th Street Bridge, coursing south along the river bank to East Capitol Street Bridge and back. We also went down to East Capitol St. to welcome home the US Embassy personnel who were held hostage in Iran.

Years later, NAVFSSO moved to Mechanicsburg, PA, along with NAVSUP and was re-designated Navy Food Services Program.

NATIONAL MUSEUM OF THE NAVY

The Navy Museum was located just two buildings from NAVFSSO. Sometimes I would take my lunch break there. The summer before the USS *Arizona* Memorial Visitor Center opened in Pearl Harbor, a Navy artist, a reserve officer, painted a three-section mural of the USS *Arizona* at sea as it would appear in 1939-40. It was interesting to watch him work while on scaffolding. The museum was another place Sam and Andy would hang out during the summers when they rode with me to the Navy Yard. I was able to see the mural again in Pearl Harbor when I visited my son, Commander Samuel L. Tate, in 2003.

NAVY HISTORY LIBRARY

I made the acquaintance of Captain Edward L. Beach, Jr. USN, Ret. while checking out some books in the Navy History Library. He was a submarine officer 1934-1966 and was the author of the bestselling novel "*Run Silent, Run Deep*," 1955, which was also the name of a 1958 film. He wrote thirteen novels in all. In 1966 he authored "*The Wreck of the Memphis.*" The USS *Memphis* (CA-10), formerly named the USS *Tennessee*, was anchored in Santo Domingo Harbor when it was struck by one-hundred-foot wave on 29 August

1916. That and succeeding waves caused her to strike the harbor bottom, and then pushed her to the beach under cliffs a half mile away. She was a complete wreck in ninety minutes. Sixty-eight men were killed or missing, and 204 were badly injured. The CO was Captain Beach's father, Captain Edward L. Beach, Sr. One of the survivors was pharmacist mate and later Lieutenant Commander Edwin Garner Swann, my great uncle. I remember seeing a photo of a wrecked ship on a table in his home in San Diego, CA, when I visited there in the 1950s as a boy. It was the same photo in Captain Beach's book.

LEAKING MCIs

The Meal, Combat, Individual (MCI) or "C-Rations" were in US Military use 1958 to 1980. Each ration packed in a 2.6 pound cardboard carton containing four cans consisted of: "M" - unit-meat based entrée; "B" unit – dessert, usually a fruit in juice; and a spread can of jelly or cheese. Packed on top were a brown foil accessory pack and a white plastic spoon. There were twelve ration cartons of assorted meals per case weighting twenty-five to twenty-six pounds. Each case also had four P-38 can openers. The P-38 was developed in 1942. Legend was that we won WWII because US soldiers could open their cans faster with the P-38 than the German could with their bayonet. Thus, US soldier had more time to fight then the Germans.

During the early years of production of MCI, military specification (MIL-SPEC) required the cans be 0.4 mm thick and enamel coated on the inside. This was to prevent high acid content fruit juices in the dessert unit and tomato sauce in the meat unit from reacting with the metal can. When enamel linings no longer became common industrial practice the requirement was dropped from the MILSPEC. Canned goods for commercial consumption were not subjected to long supply lines and extended storage that the military experienced. The next cost reduction change to the MILSPEC was reducing the thickness of the cans. These changes set the condition for a shorter time needed for the high acid foods to react with the metal and caused the cans to leak. The leakage then damaged the other cans in the cardboard carton and spread throughout the case and eventually to other cases on the pallet. Millions of these MCIs were stored in depots in CONUS, Europe, the Pacific, and aboard some ships.

In July 1977 in my second week at NAVFSSO the CO, H.E. Hirschy, Jr., Captain SC, USN sent me to DPSC Philadelphia to be on the DoD working group to establish procedures to make disposition of the damaged MCIs. Colonel Frank Ramsey was the Army veterinarian on the working group. He was promoted to brigadier general in 1980 and became the Chief of Army Veterinary Corps until he retired in 1985.

The solution recommended was to sort and removed the damaged items and the units that were highly acidic either by contract labor or military personnel depending on the amount of material at each storage point. That is my best recollection. I may be wrong.

Jokingly, I proposed, "Do nothing in Europe, leave them where they are. When the Russians break through the Fulda Gap they are going to rely on those meals in Germany to feed their troops. Won't they be surprised to find all those rations not fit to eat?"

I thought they would tar and feather me and run me back to DC on a rail.

Turns out, there was some validity to my remarks. After five years of development of the meal ready to eat (MRE), there was a briefing in 1980 at the Pentagon for Paul H. Riley, Deputy Assistant Secretary of Defense (Supply, Maintenance, & Services.)

I was sitting behind Mr. Altizer, the assistant to Mr. Riley and Chairman of AFPEC. When the briefer stated that the procurement would be a ninety-day supply, another staff assistant leaned over to Mr. Altizer and whispered, "Dave, who are you planning on feeding all the MREs to?

Mr. Altizer asked, "Why?"

"We only have enough bullets for thirty days."

Our dog handlers in Vietnam were issued a MCI before going on night duty as their midnight rations; they could choose the menu they preferred. They did not always eat the entire contents of the carton, so we had a box in the kennel office where they could deposit the unopened cans for anyone to use. I especially liked the ham slices.

BUS OR VAN

Dale City consisted of villages arranged in alphabetical order along Dale Blvd. My mode of transportation from my home in the Hillendale section of Dale City, VA, to the Navy Yard was a commuter bus.

Everyone who rode the bus usually sat in the same seat each trip; mine was over the rear wheel well. It was an hour trip each way on the Interstate 95 express lanes. I usually slept the whole trip. On one trip home I woke up as the bus was approaching the Acredale Shopping Plaza on the way out of Dale City back to DC. I looked around, and the bus was empty except for me. No one woke me at the car pool lot in Glendale. I hailed the driver and he dropped me off. I called Shirley from a store to come pick me up.

The buses the private transit company used were secondhand. They ran late and experienced break downs too often. On one trip home I felt my seat getting warmer and warmer. Then smoke started coming up from the wheel well. I called to the driver and he pulled over. The brake lining had caught on fire. We had to wait for another bus to pick us up.

On another trip home, the bus stopped at L'Enfant Plaza on Independence Avenue SW to pick up more passengers. There was a loud "clunk." The engine stopped and wouldn't restart. The driver got out and looked under the bus. The transmission was sitting on the pavement. We waited two hours for another bus. That was the last straw.

The commuter company held a meeting in a Dale City elementary school. The room was packed. A number of riders voiced their complaints and the company made all kinds of promises to do better and buy new buses. The transportation dispatcher for the Navy Yard was there recruiting drivers and riders for a van service he was starting. I signed up to be a driver of a sixteen-passenger van. I would pick up my passengers at the Glendale carpool lot by 6:15 A.M. drop some off at Crystal City in Arlington and then onto the Navy Yard by 7:15 or 7:30 A.M. My most productive time was that half hour before others arrived in the office. In DC one's workday ended based on what time one's car or van pool left. In my case, it was 3:30 P.M. Everyone understood "car pool time," even with someone on the phone.

The dispatcher owned six vans that went from the Woodbridge-Stafford area into DC. Passengers were required to pay for a whole month to hold their place even when they were on vacation. If a driver took vacation one of the passengers would drive and not be charged. This system resulted in empty seats occasionally. When Sam and Andy were out of school they would ride with me to the Navy Yard. I would give them Metro cards and lunch money, and they would spend the day at one of the Smithsonian Museums. They would meet back at the Navy Yard by 3:30 P.M. I recently told this story in the presence of Sam and Andy, both retired military officers. Andy said, "That's what you thought we did!"

MILSPEC to IMPS

About September 1977 the US Senate committee on Government Affairs, Subcommittee of Federal Spending Practices and Open Government, Chaired by Senator Lawton Chiles, released its report in a two-year investigation of DoD's meat inspection and procurement practices. The subcommittee recommended transferring the in-plant subsistence quality assurance functions from DoD (AF & Army Veterinary Corps) to the USDA. The exception was overseas procurement such as the meat inspection done by the AF veterinary unit at Lakenheath, England. The transfer also involved converting all the MILSPECs for meat to the USDA specifications (IMPS).

I was appointed to represent Navy and Marine Corps on the working level group to do the specification conversion. In most instances the USDA had comparable requirements for the school lunch program. Where the USDA did not have an equivalent to the MILSPEC we had to write new IMPS for it. This process involved me traveling to DPSC Philadelphia every week. We completed the project about March 1978.

I received a letter of appreciation from assistant secretary of defense (MRA&L) through the Secretary of the Navy and Rear Admiral Grinstead, Commander of Naval Supply Systems, for my contribution.

PRESIDENTIAL SERVICE BADGE (PSB)

I was preparing for one of my many flights to Philadelphia when Captain Hirschy called me into his office. When he was a lieutenant, he was the food services officer of the White House naval mess facility when Kennedy was President. It was his ceremonial sword that formed the crossed swords on the catafalque for Kennedy's coffin. Mrs. Kennedy thought she could keep the swords until she was told they were the personal property of officers on the staff.

Uniformed services members who serve the president are awarded the Presidential Service Badge to be worn on either their uniform or civilian clothes. Captain Hirschy lost his badge, along with a one million dollar payroll, when he evacuated the American Embassy in Saigon in April 1975. He asked me to find out from The Army Institute of Heraldry (TIOH), which had an office at DPSC, how he could get a replacement PSB.

I found the TIOH office. It was in a room with floor to ceiling, wall to wall box drawers. I explained to the clerk why I was there. He handed me a form and said Captain Hirschy would need to complete it in triplet and submit it. He then went to the wall and pulled out a drawer and brought it to his desk. He said, "Since you have come all the way from DC and asked on behalf of your captain, you can give him this one." The PSBs have sequential serial number on the back. The number on this one was 002.

I went into Captain Hirschy's office the next day. "I found out how you can get a replacement PSB"

He asked, "How?"

I handed him the form. "All you have to do is fill out this form in triplicate and send it in."

Captain Hirschy gave me his slightly disappointed look he often displayed.

Then I handed him the PSB. "However, if you are an air force officer and ask nicely, they just give you one."

MEAL READY TO EAT (MRE)

Development of the MRE accelerated in 1975 with the efforts of Natick Research, Development, and Engineering Center concentrating on the refinement of the retort pouch to contain a wet ration with a three-to-ten year shelf life that could be easily shipped, carried in the field, opened, and consumed straight out of the package if necessary without further heat or water. The retort pouch consisted of five layers of laminated flexible plastic and metal foils in which raw or cooked food could be processed aseptically at 240-250 degrees Fahrenheit in a retort or autoclave similar to a pressure cooker the same as the canning process.

I served on two DOD committees that were evaluating various aspects of the MRE development, AFPEC and Store Product Committee (Chairman) of the Armed Forces Pest Management Board. My work on both of these committees overlapped in the issue related to packaging. We were evaluating the R&D being done at Natick, Rutgers University Packaging Engineering Department, and USDA Stored Products Pest Lab at the University of Florida, Gainesville, which involved site visits.

One of the issues was that the retort pouch was not impermeable to insect penetration. Rutgers developed the flexible plastic exterior package to contain the retort pouches and other element of the MRE.

The retort pouch was resistant to chemical reaction with acidic products, which prevented the problems of leakage experienced with MCIs. The shelf life of MRE was determined to be five years when stored at seventy-five degrees Fahrenheit. There have been many improvements in the MRE beginning in 1988 since that initial procurement in 1981.

MRE CONTENTS[13]

- Main course – meat based
- Side dish
- Dessert or snack – commercial candy
- Crackers or bread
- Spread of cheese, peanut butter or jelly
- Powdered beverage
- Utensils
- Flameless ration heater – added after 1988
- Beverage mixing bag
- Accessory Pack:
  - Xylitol chewing gum
  - Water resistant matches
  - Napkins/toilet paper

---

[13] You Tube: Comparing C Ration to MREs SGT Neil Gussman

- Seasonings – salt, pepper, sugar, creamer, and/or Tabasco sauce
- Freeze-dried coffee powder

My son Andy, USMC, still preferred Spam over MREs when was in the field. He had a portable stove to cook it. I asked if he knew what Spam was. He read the label. My point was that Spam was a WWII ration, and I spent four years working on the MREs.

R&D on other packaging and meals were simultaneous with the MRE. At an AFPEC lunch (those lunches were always the food items being evaluated) at Rutgers University was the tray pack B ration designed to be served in field kitchens. The precooked food item was packed in an aluminum tray, sealed, and processed in a retort, similar to the MRE and commercial canning. The tray fit in the steam table of the field kitchen or could be heated in an immersion heater before opening. The use of tray packs greatly reduced the need for canned food and the work in preparing hot meals in the field. The tray pack now is called unitized group ration.

The other major advance was the development of the insect resistant bag for bulk products such as flour and rice. The bag consisted of multiple layers of outer paper bag, insecticide treated paper, plastic moisture and insecticide barrier, and inner bag. This packaging prevented the insect penetration from both within and from without of the product.

AFPEC TRAVEL

AFPEC met quarterly and rotated meeting locations. At least once a year we met at Natick to review new developments. Lunch was always the food items being evaluated at that meeting, as I mentioned before. Dinner would be at one of the famous restaurants at Boston Harbor or a lobster feast at the home of one of the Natick staff. The other regular meeting site was at DPSC where we usually ate dinner at the Old Original Bookbinder's Seafood Restaurant (1898) on Walnut Street in Philadelphia. The other two meetings a year were to R&D sites Rutgers or military bases of special interest because of innovative décor such as Shaw AFB in SC. Fort Lee, VA, was also a regular site because it was headquarters of the US Army Quartermaster Corps and their culinary school.

Each service voting member on AFPEC was a dietitian. All four were women - three civilians and one Army colonel. The colonel checked out a staff car for one of our trips to Ft. Lee. Since I lived south of DC just off I-95, the four ladies picked me up on the way to Ft. Lee. One of the neighbors asked Shirley, "Who are all those women that picked up Sam?"

Shirley said, "Oh, that's his harem. He travels everywhere with them."

HELICOPTER RIDE

On another trip to Ft. Lee, Mr. Altizer decided instead of us all driving, he would arrange for us to go by helicopter. We all met at the Pentagon where waiting for us on the helipad were a UH-1 Huey and CH-47 Chinook. Mr. Altizer and the more senior members rode in the Huey and the rest of us in the Chinook. The flight south was noisy but uneventful until we reached Ft. Lee. The commanding officer was waiting at the airfield to greet us and had a bus to take us to the meeting. He waved to us as the pilot of the Huey overflew the airfield and kept going with the Chinook following. The pilot saw a likely clear field and landed. Within a few minutes a National Park ranger arrived with his blue light flashing and informed the pilot he had landed on the Petersburg Battlefield.

Shortly thereafter the CO arrived with the staff car and bus and apologized to the ranger. We loaded into the vehicles and the helicopters flew to the airfield.

LOLITS

The four female dietitians were also affectionately called "Little Old Ladies in Tennis Shoes." They were not little or old, nor did they wear tennis shoes. At my last AFPEC meeting, they made me an honorary member of LOLITS and presented me with a gold tennis shoe on a pedestal to go with my Honorary Pork Chop. They also hosted a farewell lunch and gave me a garment bag.

NAVAL TRAINING CENTER (NTC) ORLANDO, FL

Another project AFPEC was working on was the use of soy in ground beef to reduce costs. Each service selected dining facilities to test the acceptance of menu items in which ground beef was the main ingredient. NTC Orlando was one of the Navy sites. NTC San Diego and the Navy Construction Battalion Center at Port Hueneme and Point Mugu, CA, were the others. I visited them on my West Coast trip mentioned in the section "Bill Wheeler."

I arranged to visit NTC Orlando and then join the AFPEC meeting in Philadelphia. The lieutenant commander supply corps officer was the twin brother of one of the department heads at NAVFSSO. I can't remember their names.

He gave me a tour of the galley during the noon meal preparation. While we were eating lunch, his mess management chief said, "Commander, I have some bad news and some good news."

"Bad news?"

The chief continued, "One of our mess attendants has Hepatitis A" (a highly contagious virus transmitted by contaminated food or water).

That got the attention of both the commander and me. The commander asked, "And the good news?"

"He's been AWOL for two weeks." That's the period in which Hepatitis A is contagious.

BEARD

In the late 1970s the DoD was dealing with perception that the military had too much presence in DC. It has been a backlash from the Vietnam War. Whatever the cause, we were directed to wear civilian clothes. At the same time, the Navy allowed both enlisted and officers, except COs, to grow beards. I spent two weeks leave at my parents' cottage in Kill Devil Hills, NC. When I returned I had a beard. I was in my office when Captain Hirschy walked down the passageway. He did a double take as he passed my office, "What's with the beard?"

"I'm impersonating a naval officer."

He shook his head and went on.

The next day I was to attend a military veterinary symposium at Walter Reed and had to wear my uniform. That was the end of the beard.

BODY SURFING

The next summer we were again at my parents' cottage. I was body surfing. I caught a wave that pushed me to the bottom, and I felt a crack. My first thought was that I broke my neck, so I allowed myself to go limp and let the surf push me onto the beach. I realized all my limbs were working. My nose was full of water. When I blew my nose, I felt a bulging sensation on my face. I thought my left eye had popped out. I covered my face with both hands and walked up to Shirley. Spreading my fingers, I asked, "Is my eye ball popped out?"

Shirley said, "No, but the left side of your face is all puffy."

We went to the Outer Banks Emergency Clinic. A physicians' assistant examined me and said I had a pocket of air under my skin. He prescribed antibiotics, Sudafed decongestant, ice packs to bring the swelling down and to follow up with the ear, nose, and throat clinic (ENT).

I made an appointment for the next week at the ENT Clinic at Malcolm Grow Hospital, Andrews AFB. They took a wrap-around X-ray of my head. The chief of ENT, a colonel, came in with my diagnosis. "You have a crack in your ethmoid sinus which is allowing air from your nasal passage to seep out under the skin. You did this body surfing?"

"Yes sir."

The colonel said, "I did the same thing in Hawaii when I was your age."

ACTING COMMANDER NAVFSSO

The Washington DC Area Supply Corps Association has a social event every fall. There is a golf tournament, tennis matches and other sports activities followed by a banquet. Captain Sherwood called me into his office before all the supply officers left. He said I was the acting CO for the day and I could even use his office. I was sitting at his desk when the secretary answered the phone. I heard her say, "All the officers are gone for the day."

The "from" line in Navy correspondence always is indicates it is from the commander of whatever command, so all correspondence is prepared for the COs signature with their printed name only, no rank. The originator would have a draft typed and circulated to all department heads and XO. They would provide comments and initial next to their office symbol. The process was called chop. In the absence of the CO, the acting CO would sign their name under the word "acting."

The comments and initials were in a color ink specific for each department. The XO was red, finance was green, etc. I had coordinated a letter and received everyone's chop and sent it for final typing. It hit the COs inbox at a time he and the XO had duty elsewhere (TDY). The letter came back to me marked all up in green ink. I was furious. I took the final copy and the chop copy back to finance. The finance officer was a lieutenant commander (O4), equivalent to my rank of major.

I asked, "Why did you mark up my letter when you had already approved it? See your chop."

The finance officer answered, "Well I was acting CO and had more responsibility."

I had the letter retyped and waited for Captain Sherwood to return.

AF VETERINARY CORPS DISESTABLISHED

The second round of the repercussions of Senator Chile's report was that congress in 1979 made the Army the DoD executive agent for all veterinary activities and deemed the USAF Veterinary Corps redundant. The USAF was made a separate branch from the Army Air Corps in 1947. It wasn't until 1949 that the AF created its own medical service, including the Veterinary Corps, by AF General Order #35. Therefore, it was much easier to disestablish the AF Veterinary Corps on March 21, 1980 by general order than it was the Army Veterinary Corps by an Act of Congress. Effective 1 March 1980, all AF veterinarians were transferred to the Biomedical Sciences Corps.

The AF supported the Navy and Marine Corps at twenty-eight locations. The Army already supported the rest. The Installation and Support Subcommittee of the Assistant Secretary of Defense Ad Hoc Steering Committee, chaired by Major General Arginson, Deputy Assistant Secretary of Defense for Health Affairs, was formed to develop a plan to transfer the responsibility and manpower authorization for those locations to the Army. Brigadier General Thomas G. Murnane, Chief, Army Veterinary Corps represented the Army and Colonel William E. Pace, Deputy Assistant Surgeon General represented the Air Force.

The Surgeon General of the Navy appointed me as the Navy-Marine Corps representative. As a major I was going to be the lowest ranking officer on the subcommittee. I called Colonels Menning and Pace to advise them of my appointment and asked if they had any guidance to me on an AF perspective. They said I was to represent the interest of the Department of the Navy to the best of my ability and experience. I called Colonel Donald Shuman, AFELM, at Andrews and he provided me with the manpower document for all the operating locations. Major General Arginson opened our first meeting that we were to come up with a plan to phase in over two years.

Brigadier General Murnane proceeded to connect Navy and Marine bases to the nearest Army medical department activity (MEDDAC). The Army linear thought was serving very well until he got to the Naval Station Guantanamo Bay, and the Naval Air Station Keflavik, Iceland. The Army proposed to support Guantanamo from Ft. Stewart, GA, and Keflavik from Ft. Devens, MA.

I spoke up. "You can't get to either one of those naval bases from those forts without going through Norfolk, VA. Their military air, logistics support, and chain of command all originates in Norfolk. Also, it's Navy protocol to in brief and out brief the command, which would also have to occur in Norfolk. The Norfolk Naval Base and Naval Supply Center are already supported by MEDDAC Ft. Eustis."

They all understood my point. In 1990 I was in an Officers Christian Fellowship Bible study with Colonel Lumpkin, MEDDAC, Ft. Eustis Veterinarian. Someone asked him what the scope of his position was. He named the locations but said he didn't know how he ended up with Guantanamo Bay and Keflavik. I said, "I can tell you how."

Major General Arginson announced at the opening of the next meeting that the phase in time line would be one year instead of two.

Brigadier General Murnane said, "I don't remember us voting on that."

Major General Arginson shot back, "Whatever gave you the idea this is a democracy, general?"

Major General Aginson asked, "How many manpower authorizations are we dealing with?"

Colonel Pace said, "Forty-two."

I spoke up. "I believe it is forty-eight, sir."[14]

Colonel Pace looked startled. "Where did you get that number from?"

"Colonel Sherman gave me a copy of the manpower document."

Colonel Pace asked brusquely, "Well, it is wrong?"

I then realized two things. One, I had embarrassed Colonel Pace in front of two general officers and the other staff in the room. Two, I suspected the AF surgeon general's office was playing a shell game with manpower authorizations. In other words, they had sequestered the additional slots in the AFELM where they were not being filled and using them somewhere else in the AF, and I had just unwittingly revealed it. This may or may not have been true, but the perception was there.

Colonel Shuman called me the next day. "Colonel Pace wants to see you in his office and wants an apology."

"I realized I embarrassed him, but I had asked if he had any guidance for me. He could have warned me to stay away from certain issues."

Colonel Shuman said, "You need to give him an unequivocal apology. I'll try to shield you from any repercussions." These were maybe not his exact words, but I understood his meaning.

I made an appointment, drove over to Bolling AFB, and gave my unequivocal apology to Colonel Pace. I don't remember his exact words, but he accepted my apology after some expression of his embarrassment and that I was to confine my comments to Navy matters only.

Officer effectiveness reports (OERs) are written by the rater, commented on by addition rater, and commented on by an endorser. The ratings inflated over time and practically every officer receives the highest rating for evaluation of potential. One way to give an officer more promotion potential is to have the endorser to be a general officer at a numbered AF, major air command, or Headquarters Air Force.

---

[14] I don't remember the exact number but there was a difference.

My next annual OER covered 1 Aug 1979 to 30 July 1980, the period in which this event occurred. I received all top ratings from Captain William Sherwood, CO NAVFSSO. Colonel Shuman chose to be the endorser by virtues of "Additional Rater Qualifies as Endorser," thus by passing the AF surgeon general's office, the next level of command. While providing me some cover, it also eliminated a general officer endorsement that my contemporaries in AF assignments were getting. The end result was my OER was not as competitive as others for promotion. I was not selected for lieutenant colonel.

Brigadier General Murnane retired as Chief of US Army Veterinary Corps June 1980 and died July 2017.

Colonel Pace retired from the AF 1 June 1980. He served in the Florida Dept. of Agriculture and retied as the State Veterinarian. He died in May 2008.

Colonel Menning retired as Chief of the AF Veterinary Corps Sept 1, 1980. He died October 25, 2021.

Colonel Shuman retired 28 Feb 1981.

THE ARMY WANTS YOU

The School of Aerospace Medicine at Brooks, AFB, San Antonio, TX, every two years hosted the Current Veterinary Service Problems and Programs. The main issue on everyone's mind in May 1981 was our new status in the Biomedical Sciences Corps. We also had a presentation by the Army Veterinary Corps from Ft. Sam Houston. They explained how we could transfer to the Army and be integrated into their promotion system. There was an open window of two years. Then there was no guarantee that one would keep their date of rank. They set aside a time in which any interested officer could speak to them privately.

The AF lieutenant colonel in charge of the Lakenheath office doing all the meat inspection in Ireland and Scotland had a wife who was English. The Army made him an offer he could not refuse, a guaranteed assignment in place for another three years. Thus, he became the first AF veterinarian to transfer to the Army. That also meant the support for NAVCOMSTA's Thurso, Scotland, and Londonderry, Northern Ireland, and the submarine base in Holy Lock, Scotland transferred to the Army veterinary unit at Lakenheath.

LOST IN THE PENTAGON

After Brigadier General Murnane retired, Colonel Frank Ramsey was promoted and became the Chief of US Army Veterinary Corps in July 1980. I convinced Captain Sherwood that we should attend the promotion ceremony because he would be working with Brigadier General Ramsey after the AF was replaced by the Army. I had attended more meetings at the Pentagon than anybody in NAVFSSO, and Captain Sherwood had never been there. The above ground floors are numbered one to five. The concentric rings from the center out are designated as "A" through "E." On each ring there are five corridor entryways, which split into two corridors. Thus, there are ten corridors running from the "A" ring to "E" ring.

We entered the Pentagon by the southeast concourse, which put us on the second floor of "A" ring. The ceremony was in the auditorium of the third floor. My intention was to go to the correct corridor and take the stairs up one flight to the auditorium. I got confused because a food kiosk had been built in the corridor entryway, and I went right past the corridor I wanted. Instead of turning around and going back, I took Captain Sherwood to the escalator at the next set of corridors and backtracked on the third floor.

Captain Sherwood said, "Sam, you were lost!"

After the ceremony I introduced Captain Sherwood to Brigadier General Ramsey and to some of the other people I knew, and we went back to the Navy Yard.

NAVY COMMENDATION MEDAL

I asked Captain Sherwood if he was considering nominating me for an award. He said he was. In that case, I requested the Navy Commendation Medal as the culmination of my nine consecutive years serving the Navy. He agreed. A couple of weeks later he told me he might have to downgrade it to the Navy Achievement Medal because two other officers were leaving at the same time and SECNAV may not approve three Navy Commendations from the same command at the same time. I expressed my disappointment in that the

Achievement Medal was usually awarded to enlisted personnel and junior officers. And as an Air Force officer I should not count against his quota. He also had the option to submit through AF channels for a second AF Commendation Medal.

On 2 July 1981 the SECNAV approved the Navy Commendation Medal. To my knowledge I was the only AF veterinarian to receive it.

RAMSTEIN AFB, GERMANY

Ramstein is HQ USAF Europe (USAFE) and home of the 86th Tactical Fighter Wing (TFW) a part of which was the USAF Clinic. Shirley, Andy, and I arrived at Ramstein in late July 1981. Sam had stayed behind to attend the Boy Scout National Jamboree at Camp AP Hill, VA, with his troop. We stayed in a local hotel for about a week until we could move into a house in Schrollbach about four miles west of the base. Our house was new construction, built on the site of a previous barn on a farm belonging to the Ohlingers. The house consisted of an unfinished basement and attic. Our living quarters were on the first floor, and we had access to the other two floors until they were completed a couple years later.

RED FLAG

On August 25, 1981, I was in the first half of professional staff of USAF Clinic to go to Munich for medical Red Flag. The four-day course, wartime casualty management, was held at Bunderswehr Medical Academy. There were medics from all USAFE bases in attendance. There was a social in the officers' club the first night. I was speaking with Colonel James P. "Paul" Jensen, USAFE Command Veterinarian. We had worked on projects together when he was at DPSC and I at NAVFSSO. Although we had been transferred to BSC, our job titles did not change until 1982. He said he wanted me to meet his boss, Major General Max B. Bralliar, the USAFE and US European Command Surgeon.

Colonel Jensen said, "General Bralliar, this is Major Tate the new Chief of Veterinary Service at Ramstein."

Major General Bralliar said, "Glad to meet you, Dr. Tate. Do you still operate the clinic or has it been turned over to the Army yet?"

"Yes I do. It's scheduled to transfer in 1982."

"Good. I have this stray cat my wife took in. It seems to have some difficulty breathing, and I'm sure it needs a rabies shot. I would like for you to take a look at it when we get back."

I said, "I'll be glad to."

The next day we started our training in earnest. There were lectures from noted trauma surgeons such as the ER chief of Cook County Hospital, Chicago, who treated gunshot wounds every night. Other speakers had served in combat hospitals in Vietnam. We had exercises in triage, hemorrhage control, preparing patients for evacuation, and loading into various ambulances and medevac helicopters.

Our class returned to Ramstein on August 29. The second half of the clinic staff arrived in Munich on Sunday, August 30. Major General Bralliar stayed in Munich for the second four-day class. I was not to see his cat for a couple of weeks because of what happened next.

USAFEE HEADQUARTERS

I had just arrived at my office just inside the East Gate at seven in the morning on Monday, August 31. I was on the toilet when about 7:20 there was a loud BOOM and the whole building shook. The base sirens went off to sound the alarm. I went to the clinic four blocks away. Some of the minor casualties started to arrive and were being treated, and I wasn't needed. I went back to my office.

The scene at the USAFEE HQ building, a half mile from my office, was entirely different. A car bomb consisting of propane tanks packed with explosives detonated in the parking lot in front of the building. Fortunately, the dental clinic was just across the street and the dentists had just returned from Red Flag. Two of the dentists and four enlisted staff rushed to the site. One dentist started searching the parking lot for survivors while the other and staff entered the bombed building and helped move victims to safety. The main entrance to the building had two sets of glass doors. In the space between the doors, they found Brigadier General Joseph D. Moore, Assistant Deputy Chief of Staff for Operations, lying in a pool of blood. A glass shard had severed the femoral artery in his leg. The immediate action taken by that dentist saved his life. The dental clinic became the main triage and casualty collection point. The two most severe casualties were taken to US Army Landstuhl Regional Medical Center about five miles from the base on Landstuhl Hill. The thirteen minor casualties were taken to the USAF Clinic.

Explosive ordnance disposal (EOD) inspection of the building found an unexploded propane tank in a third floor office in the front of the building. Photos of the scene showed a hole in the wall between the second and third floor windows where the tank penetrated the wall being propelled by the initial explosion of the other two bombs. The anti-American terrorist group, Red Army, was responsible.

THE GENERAL'S CAT #2

Major General Bralliar finally found time to bring in his "wife's cat." Technical Sergeant Labrandy was with him. Labrandy was a vet tech on "loan" from my office to serve as assistant to Colonel Jenson. It was common practice to "loan" techs to the command veterinarian because there was no manpower authorization for such a position. The cat was in a carrier. As Labrandy carried it into the exam room, I offered for the general to be present. He declined and said he would just sit in the waiting area.

Labrandy opened the carrier door, and the cat shot out and tore around the room. We knocked over a stainless steel bucket hanging from under the drain on the exam table with a clang. I said to Labrandy, "With all this commotion, the general might think we are killing his cat." The cat went under the medicine cabinet, which gave us time to plan our next move.

Labrandy was already wearing large leather gloves. I gave him a towel to throw over the cat as I moved the medicine cabinet. He caught the cat in the towel and just as he placed it on the table there was a "T-U-R-R-P-P" sound. The cat was motionless. We uncovered the cat.

"Labrandy, you killed the general's cat!" I exclaimed.

Labrandy panicked. "What are we going to do?"

"I will go tell the general." I walked out to face him. "General Bralliar, unfortunately there was a struggle to capture your cat after it got out of the carrier. During the struggle, your cat died. I think I know why it had a breathing problem, but I need to perform a necropsy to be sure."

Major General Bralliar said, "Yes, please do. I will need an explanation for Mrs. Bralliar."

"Would you like to observe the necropsy?"

Major General Bralliar said, "No, I'll just wait."

I performed the necropsy and found just what I expected. The cat had a tear in the diaphragm, and the chest cavity was about seventy-five percent occupied by the liver and intestines, causing a severe reduction in lung capacity. The slightest amount of exertion exceeded the cat's respirator reserve. The tear was probably caused by some previous impact trauma. I explained my findings to Major General Bralliar and asked, "Do you want to see the abnormality?"

Major General Bralliar shook his head. "No, I accept your diagnosis. Will you take care of the remains? Thank you for your efforts."

Major General Bralliar had a reputation for being eccentric. The building his office was in was located a couple blocks from my office on the way to the clinic. Reserve parking for generals on base had signs marked "Any General." The command surgeon's building had its own parking lot, and Major General Bralliar had a reserved sign with two stars on it. Everyone knew that was his parking space. One weekend while the general was out of the country, the surgeon duty officer, a lieutenant colonel, parked in the general's parking spot. Major General Bralliar heard about it and fired him.

EGGS

Colonel Jenson called one day to say Major General Bralliar wanted to know why the commissary did not have grade "AA" extra-large eggs. I called the commissary officer who informed me that the contract specified a minimum of grade A large. The extra large were more expensive and not in demand by customers. He said he would order some and they would be in next week. I passed the information to Colonel Jenson. The next week Colonel Jenson called again. Major General Bralliar went to the commissary to buy eggs and there was a sign stating, "Ring the bell for extra-large eggs." I called the commissary officer again. He said if he put the extra-large eggs out on display, they might sell out before the general got there. He held some back to make sure he had some for the general. I passed that onto Colonel Jenson, and I heard no more about the eggs.

Colonel Jenson rotated back to the states without an immediate replacement, so Major Mark Stokes was appointed as "acting." The incoming lieutenant colonel came over on permissive TDY to look for accommodations. He completed his house-hunting. When he found out that a general was flying to the states on a VIP aircraft, the lieutenant colonel used Major General Bralliar's name when asking the general if he could hitch a ride. Major General Bralliar notified the Assistant Deputy Surgeon General for Environmental Health that the lieutenant colonel was not acceptable for his staff. The lieutenant colonel's orders were cancelled, and Mark Stokes was made permanent Command Environmental Health Officer.

There was a gracious side to Major General Bralliar as well. Mrs. Bralliar was driving Shirley and Katie Buethe, wife of Colonel Buethe, Major General Bralliar's deputy, when they were involved in an accident on Landstuhl Hill. Security Police called Major General Bralliar who immediately came to the scene. He made sure everyone was all right. He made arrangements for Mrs. Bralliar's car to be towed, assisted the ladies into his car, and drove them back to Ramstein. Shirley said he was extremely caring.

Major General Bralliar left Ramstein in June 1982 to become Surgeon General of the Air Force with the rank of lieutenant general.

VETERINARY SERVICE TO ENVIRONMENTAL HEALTH

Ramstein had the largest base veterinary service in USAFE. I supervised thirteen enlisted personnel who inspected three to three and a half million dollars of food per month, sixty-five food services facilities, and trained more than nine hundred food handlers annually. I was appointed veterinary public health consultant to the USAFE Surgeon General. I was also a member of USAF

Clinic committees: Executive, Health Care Provider Utilization, Aerospace Medicine Council, Rabies Advisory Council, Infection Control, Clinic Library Board, and Local Purchase Review Board.

I initially had responsibility for the veterinary care of the military working dogs but that was transferred to the Army in January 1982, and we were designated as the environmental health section, still the largest in USAFE.

EXCERISES

The bombing of USAFE HQ made it evident that the already robust readiness training and Salty Nation exercises would be ramped up. I was appointed Assistant Chief of Medical Exercise Evaluation Team and became chief in one year. Our team was part of the 86th Tactical Fighter Wing (TFW) Exercise Team, which planned the quarterly exercises.

Our mission was to prepare moulage causalities for the exercises, evaluate the body care (combat first aid) and evacuation procedures provided by the participants, and evaluate medical triage and treatment at a field hospital.

I accompanied the clinic CO, Colonel William Palmer, during my first exercise. We observed a female second lieutenant holding the hand of a moulage casualty, apparently not knowing what else to do.

I asked, "Captain, what is that ensign doing?"

Colonel Palmer said, "Boy, you really did spend a long time with the Navy!"

It was always a problem to get units to give us airmen to be casualties. So, in one exercise I used my sons' Boy Scout troops who were on spring break. Sam and Andy played casualty roles during the exercise. One time they were radiation victims and were dropped off in a base parking lot. They were picked up for triage with Sam carrying Andy piggyback across the parking lot. Another time, Sam was fitted with a moulage kit that had a pump simulating an arterial wound. He really enjoyed squeezing the pump to make the "blood" fly out of his arm wound. However, the staff in the triage was not too happy about the mess it was making and took it away from him. Andy had a sucking chest wound and at age thirteen, became the youngest first lieutenant in the Air Force.

I had a lot of experiences in the Boy Scouts of setting up tents, so I was assigned to help the chief nurse in instructing our medics, officers, and enlisted in how to set up a field hospital. Ramstein Clinic was the USAFE test site for the new temper tents, which replaced the WWII general purpose large and medium tents (GPL and GPM). These new tents consisted of a series of aluminum "A" frames with extension legs connected by spacer bars. Two "A" frames made a section, three frames made two sections. The length of the tent was expanded by the number of "A" frames added. Each section was covered by a blanket which formed the roof and sides. The blankets were interlocking at the edges so they allowed for expansion. The end panels were separate and attached to the edges of the end sections. The "A" frames were assembled and each section covered in the down position with the grasshopper legs spread on the ground. All the legs on one side then were fully extended and locked in place. The tent now went from being level to on a slant. The process was repeated on the other side, and the tent was fully up and level. The feet of the legs had holes to anchor them with iron pegs. There were insulated liners with built-in mosquito nets for use in all climates. Heating and AC units could be hooked to the ducts in the liners. There also were rubberized canvas blankets for the floor.

The other equipment to be tested was modules. There were two one-sided fold outs and one double-sided fold out. They could be connected to the temper tents by a canvas vestibule. The package had the flexibility of being set up in any configuration needed.

We set up this field hospital on the edge of the flight line for a Salty Nation exercise in December 1981. I actually performed minor surgery on a military working dog in the surgical module. It snowed, and we were snug as bugs in a rug. We transported the whole thing to a field on Landstuhl Hill in March 1982.

Our chief nurse presented a report with slides of the two exercises at the USAFE Medical Services Training Symposium in Garmisch, Germany in April 1982.

Ramstein had the only base level animal model training in USAFFE. We used anesthetized sheep to teach non-surgically-trained medical doctors, dentists, and nurses life saving skills in treating combat casualties. I assisted the surgeon in the course for two years.

I also provided training to our two hundred Prime Beef and Prime Rib team members in advanced concepts of field hygiene and sanitation (much of which I learned in the Boy Scouts). This training improved the quality of their engineering support to deployed units.

EXPERT MARKSMAN

The Geneva Convention allows medics to have side arms to protect their patients. We were not issued pistols in Germany like we were in Vietnam. However, we had to periodically re-qualify with the weapons. This involved a firearms safety class and live fire at the shooting range. All the medics went through the process twenty at a time. On the range we were given ten practice rounds to sight in the weapons. Then we fired ten rounds each from various positions for a total of forty rounds for a score. At the end of the firing, the instructors scored our targets. I had forty-three holes in my target. Major Brubaker, the environmental health nurse, was firing next to me. She had only thirty holes in her target. I was awarded the expert marksman ribbon, and she failed and had to repeat the course.

ENVIRONMENTAL HEALTH

While all the medical readiness training and exercises were going on, we still had to perform our primary mission in public health, food inspection, and food service sanitation. I was one of only two veterinarians in Germany; the other was Army, qualified to instruct the week-long National Institute for the Food Service Industry Course in Applied Food Service Sanitation. The participants in the course were managers and supervisors of the sixty-five food service facilities we inspected. I incorporated my slides of navy foodborne illness into the material the Institute provided.

I developed and presented a course on childhood diseases for workers at the child care center. They videotaped it so I could be repeated after I rotated back to CONUS.

I made recommendations on construction and remodeling plans for the childcare center, elementary and high school, Ramstein German Kantine, and the officers' open mess.

The Vogelweh Exchange cafeteria had a few positive TB tests among the food handlers. I investigated and found that some of the Turkish nationals had severe reaction because they had been vaccinated against TB with bacilli Chalmette-Guerin (BCG) vaccine, which was a common practice in Europe. They should have never been tested, and I explained that through an interpreter. The other positives were followed with chest-X-rays and sputum cultures. There were no active cases.

Christine was the younger of my two German secretaries. She often wore very short mini-skirts and flimsy blouses. She was always braless. I asked Lilo, who was slightly older but mature secretary, to speak to Christine about wearing clothing more appropriate for a professional office. Christine took the matter to the on-base German Employee Grievance Committee, which sided with her. So I told her it was mainly a safety issue because our office was the first building inside the gate and that people often came in to ask directions, sometimes when the secretaries were alone in the office. She understood and started wearing more appropriate clothes. She came to me one morning shortly after our discussion and asked, "Dr. Tate, do you know what measles look like?"

"Yes."

Christine asked, "Does it look like this?" while lifting her blouse and exposing her bare torso.

"Yes, Christine, you have the measles."

The environmental health office remained in the veterinary clinic building for several months after the Army took over the animal care. There was talk of repurposing the building for security police because it was just inside the front gate. I advocated for the building to remain a veterinary clinic because it was fully equipped for that purpose. The cost involved in relocating the clinic to another building was the deciding factor, and the Army got the veterinary clinic. We moved to the second floor of the main clinic.

One of our functions was contact tracing. We interviewed patients referred to us by the medical section who had communicable diseases to determine who they had been in contact with. We then called those contacts to make appointments for testing. If the contacts were foreign nations, we communicated their information to the local health department. Shortly after we moved to the main clinic, there was an audit conducted for the allocation of office space. The auditor interviewed me (we called them bean counters) and wanted to know how many patients we saw per month in the last year. I provided the number and said, "There were two offices in the clinic that you could not base space on the number of patients seen. One was environmental health because our mission was preventive and not individual treatments like the other sections. The other office is the clinic commander. Although he was a medical doctor, he infrequently saw patients but always in a treatment room not his office."

We were able to keep our office space.

FRONT SEAT

German law stipulates that children under twelve years old are not allowed in the front passenger seat of automobiles. Andy would turn twelve in October 1981. We drove to Frankfurt in August 1981 to pick up Sam and our dog Cubby. We loaded everything into the car, and Sam jumped into the front seat.

Andy said, "You are not allowed to ride in the front seat until you are sixteen years old."

Sam would not be sixteen until May 1982. Shirley and I played along and said nothing. We were going somewhere on Andy's twelfth birthday, and he jumped into the front seat.

Sam said, "I thought you had to be sixteen to ride in the front seat."

Andy laughed, "Ha ha, I fooled you. It's twelve."

CASTLE de RIBAUCOURT

Sam's Boy Scout troop went to Belgium in the spring of 1982 to tour Brussels and Waterloo. Our base of operation was the Chateau (Castle) de Ribaucourt. We spent the first night in the rooms over the stables where German soldiers lived during the occupation. The next night we moved to a stone building that had a single great room with a bottom floor two stories high and an attic above. It was called the Orange Hall because it housed orange trees in the winter. We had to move to the attic the next night because a Belgium Cub Pack occupied the great room.

Our host was Count Daniel Christyn de Ribaucourt (1922-2007). He served as Mayor of Perk, the adjoining village, as did his father Victor (1882-

1961) before him. He held a very prominent position in the Belgium Boy Scouts and frequently hosted scout units and events. He gave us a tour of the Round Tower (c. 1196) and some of the chateau, which was the headquarters of British Lt General Dempsey during the Battle of Arnhem, also known as Operation Market Garden. Cornelius Ryan chronicled it in *A Bridge Too Far* in 1974, which was made into the epic WWII film in 1977 by the same name. The Count posed for a photograph with Sam and the entire troop. He told us a little about the German occupation.

It was not until 2019 that I learned the entire story of heroics of his parents during the war. I had visited Yad Vashem in Jerusalem in 2014 and was very familiar with the distinction *Righteous Among The Nations*.

Christyn De Ribaucourt, Victor Christyn De Ribaucourt - Van Eyll, Elisabeth Victor Christyn De Ribaucourt (mayor of Serville Onhaye, west of Dinant, from 1939 until 1976) lived most of his life in his castle Ostemerée (in the community of Anthée, but closer to the village Serville). During the war, Count Victor and Countess Elisabeth Christyn De Ribaucourt founded in their castle a home for needy children named the 'Home Prince Baudouin'. As many as 90 children between 7 and 12 years of age were there at any given time, and they stayed between one to three months. They were mostly children whose parents were too poor to feed them properly. Hidden among them were close to 40 Jewish children. When they arrived, Count Victor made them take off their yellow stars and provided them with forged identities. The Count and the Countess also hid weapons and took in Resistance activists and young men who refused to work in Germany. The Count and Countess did everything they could to help the daily functioning of the Home by providing all the means to make the children as happy as possible. The Home was administered by the Baroness Henriette De Jamblinne* de Meux and its director Commander Max Housiaux* as well as Father Jean Lefebvre*. Moreover there was a full staff of educators, some of them former boy scouts, so that games, songs, courses, hikes, and campfires filled the children's days. The Count and Countess did not hesitate to endanger their lives and that of their eight children by giving shelter to Jewish children and Resistance fighters.

In 1943, just after the birth of the family Christyn De Ribaucourt's youngest child, the Germans searched the castle for English parachutists who, by that time, had already left. The following day the Germans arrested Count Victor and imprisoned him at St. Gilles where he remained for three weeks. He managed to be released after he and his wife continuously insisted that they had never hidden any parachutists. On yet another occasion, the count's family was denounced and had to go into hiding. They drove away on a cart and horses to a little village called Vodelée where they remained for several weeks under forged names. On July 25, 1999, Yad Vashem recognized Count Victor Christyn De Ribaucourt and Countess Elisabeth Christyn De Ribaucourt-Van Eyll as Righteous Among the Nations.[15]

BERCHTESGADEN

I mentioned in *Uniform Snafu* that we attended the USAEUR Veterinary Conference in Berchtesgaden in 1982. We left Sam and Andy at home with one of my technicians and his wife child sitting them. The plan was for them to put the boys on the train at Landstuhl on Friday morning, and we would meet them in Berchtesgaden and have dinner at the bahnholf (train station). Our friends said we were crazy to allow a sixteen and twelve-year-old travel that far on a train by themselves. My response was that if they could navigate around on the Metro in Washington, DC, they could certainly make the transfers in Mannheim and Munich. The train from Munich arrived at five in the afternoon, right on schedule. The boys were not on it. We checked with the station master who said that if they missed that train in Munich there was another one arriving at eight that evening.

So Shirley and I ate dinner at the bahnholf and waited for the eight o'clock train. The boys were not on that one either. I was worried, and Shirley was very worried. The station master told us there was one more train from Munich at midnight. We went to the hotel to wait and returned to the bahnholf. To our relief, we greeted the boys on the midnight train. Andy's account: "The train from Landstuhl was late, and we missed our connections in Mannheim

---

[15] Yad Vashem website

for Munich. We took the next train to Munich where we caught the last train of the night to Berchtesgaden."

One of the places I wanted to take the boys was to Hitler's mountain top retreat, The Eagle's Nest. It was foggy and raining. We wouldn't be able to experience the view from the top, but we went anyway. At least they got to see the interior. We went out on to the large porch where you couldn't see more than several feet.

We also toured the Salzbergwerk Berchtesgaden (Salt Mine), founded in 1517. It is the oldest active salt mine in Germany. Tourists put on black miners coveralls and caps and straddle the train cars like riding a horse. The ride took about an hour and travels 1400 meters into the mountain.

RAMSTEIN CHAPEL

We were very active in the Ramstein Chapel. Colonel Lee Reavis was the head usher and recruited both Sam and I to usher. The names of the ushers were listed in the bulletin on the Sunday that we served. Sam and I were listed as "Sam the Taller and Sam the Elder." Sam was six feet, six inches tall. Our installation staff chaplain was Colonel Samuel D. Nelson. The ushers counted the offering in a locked office that had a large glass window to the outer reception area. Chaplain Sam, as he liked to be called, would tap on the glass and want the attendance number. He did this on Easter Sunday. Colonel Reavis told me, "Hold that thousand dollar check up to the window." We finished the count, secured the funds, and opened the door.

Chaplain Sam said, "Someone was moved by a very powerful sermon."

Colonel Reavis replied, "Chaplain Sam, we collected the offering before the sermon."

The Protestant men of the chapel had a cook out for all the base and headquarters chaplains at Ramstein. Since the chaplains were our guests, we decided to sing the *Doxology* instead of asking one of them to bless the meal.

Praise God, from whom all blessings flow;
Praise Him, all creatures here below;
Praise Him above, ye heavenly host;
Praise Father, Son, and Holy Ghost. Amen.

159

There was an awkward silence as we looked towards the rabbi as a concern we had been insensitive to his faith.

The rabbi asked, "What? You think I didn't know the hymn?"

It was confirmation that in the military the chaplain is your chaplain no matter the faith background.

Colonel Reavis called me one day in 1981. "Major Tate, you and your wife will attend a meeting in the basement recreation room of building such and such at 19:30 hours (7:30 P.M.) on Thursday." That was our invitation to attend our first Officers' Christian Fellowship (OCF) meeting. The speaker was Lieutenant Colonel Ward Graham, USAF, Ret. Ward was OCF Field Staff for the East Coast and Europe. He flew U-2s during the Cuban Missile Crisis. We joined OCF that night and have been members ever since. Ward became my mentor when I became an OCF leader at Seymour Johnson AFB, NC, and Langley AFB, VA. He lived in Manns Choice, PA, the site of the OCF Conference Center, White Sulphur Springs. We would see him and his wife Bobbie often when we attended events there. Ward developed esophageal cancer, the same as my father, and died in 2005.

There were two OCF groups at Ramstein. We were in the one led by Colonel Reavis. We rotated weekly meetings at member's homes. Bill and Gretchen Housely were civilian newlyweds and missionaries with Young Life. They had the contract to conduct the youth programs for the chapel. They had been in our OCF group for about a month when we hosted the meeting at our home. As we were starting the meeting, Bill spoke, "We have not had any prior association with the military and are not sure how to address you officers."

Colonel Reavis, in his fake crusty attitude, said "It's colonel to you, boy, and don't forget it!"

My turn was next. "I am not as formal as Colonel Reavis. You can address me as doctor."

Colonel Bob Segars set Bill at ease. "We are on a first name basis here."

Colonel Radford Lee Reavis retired to College Station, TX, home of his alma mater, Texas A & M where he died of Alzheimer's June 2016.

Colonel Judson Robert Segars was awarded the Silver Star (the military's second highest award for bravery) for action in Vietnam. He transferred from

Ramstein to the Joint Forces Staff College, Norfolk, VA, where he was an instructor and became the deputy commandant. We had a lot of interaction in OCF after I moved to Yorktown in 1988. He died in November 2001 of brain cancer.

I last saw Bill Housley at Colonel Segars' funeral at Arlington National Cemetery.

CHRISTMAS VACATIONS

The Europe Region of Officers Christian Fellowship held retreats during Thanksgiving and Christmas holidays. The 1982 Christmas retreat was in Flims, Switzerland in the Glarus Alps. Colonels Reavis and Segars also attended with their families. We rented all our ski equipment from Landstuhl MWR. The first skiing day I went to beginner's school while Sam and Andy went to the slope in town. The next day I graduated to that slope. The following day I went with the boys on the cable car to ski on a slope half way up Piz Dolf. We got on a black trail (advanced), and I slid all the way down on my bottom.

The fog finally cleared on the glacier at the very top of Piz Dolf, Crap Sogn Gion. It was Shirley's birthday, and we were going sightseeing to the village of Falera. To get there we took the same bus as the boys to the cable car station. We changed buses to Falera, and they went up the mountain to ski. Falera was very tranquil and picturesque in the snow. We took the bus back to the cable car station. Shirley could see that the cars were very big, holding about twenty people. She said she would like to ride that, so we got tickets and got on. That car only went to the first level where the boys and I skied the day before.

Shirley asked, "Where are the boys skiing?"

"Over on the glacier"

"How do we get there?"

I said, "On the next two lifts"

The first one was a six-passenger gondola, which was not very scary. But the next were four passenger gondolas over a gorge between the two peaks and very terrifying.

Shirley said, "We've come this far, we might as well go all the way."

Now the boys had no way of knowing we were coming. Our gondola arrived at Crap Sogn Gion and there was Andy asking, "Can I have some money for goulash soup?"

During one of the evening fellowships, I expressed my hurt at not being selected for promotion to lieutenant colonel. Colonel Uno, US Army, who was recently not selected for brigadier general put my disappointment in perspective. "When we were commissioned as second lieutenants, we realized that not all of us would be the chief of staff. It is just that some of us would find that out sooner than others."

We decided to go to England for Christmas 1983. A good friend of ours from chapel, Sue Sorger's father, was the Queen's Warden of Great Windsor Park. He made reservations for us at a bed and breakfast in Ascot and gave us a tour of Windsor Castle. We had a great visit with Paul Barber and his mother Marge at Bourne End, Buckinghamshire. Paul was one of my assistant Scoutmasters at High Wycombe in 1968-71. We sponsored him to work at the National Capital Council Scout Reservation in Goshen, VA, the summer of 1972. We visited Paul at Goshen on way to Travis AFB, CA, for our flight to Guam.

Also in Bourne End we stopped by to see Mrs. Wiltshire, Sam's kindergarten teacher. She was in her late seventies when Sam was there as a student in 1969. Her husband was killed at Dunkirk. She invited us to stay for tea. She asked Sam to help her and asked what his sister would like. Andy had shoulder length hair. We had tea, toast, and jam. As we were leaving, Sam stopped on the porch, turned around, and said. "Thank you for my lessons, Mrs. Wiltshire," just as he was expected to do fourteen years before. We toured the sites in London, Piccadilly and Trafalgar Square, and the Tower of London. A special treat was the Boy Scout Training Center at Gilwell Park where Sam and Andy again put their feet in the foot print of Lord Baden Powell, the founder of the Boy Scouts.

CHRISTMAS TREES

I was the Boy Scout Assistant District Commissioner. The wing commander, by virtue of his position, was the District Commissioner. When Brigadier General Robert C. Oaks served in that position I would ride with him to council meetings in Heidelberg. He became USAFE Commander in 1990 as a four-star general.

The major fundraising project for all the Boy and Girl Scout Units was a Christmas tree sale. We arranged to obtain trees from a local *forest- meister*. The older scouts would cut the trees and bring them to the outdoor tennis courts. They cut trees every couple of days so we always had fresh trees. The Brownies, Cubs, and Scouts would work the tree lots one unit at a time.

The money from sales would be deposited each day in the district bank account. We distributed the money to each of the thirteen units according to the number of man hours worked.

One year we got a request to donate six trees to a unit in Riyadh, Saudi Arabia. The person making the request came and picked out six trees and took them to the cargo terminal for airlift to Riyadh.

In April I got a bill from Military Airlift Command for a thousand dollars for airlift of cargo from Ramstein to Riyadh. I called my friend Colonel Lee Reavis, USAFE Deputy Assistant Chief of Staff for Logistics. He said to bring the bill to him at the underground HQ and tell the sentry to call him, which I did. He looked the bill over and said he would take care of it. That was the end of it.

PSYCH EVALUATION

A young female airman in our office was having a difficult time adjusting to being new to the AF, in a foreign country, and away from home. The clinic commander referred her to the psychiatric clinic at Wiesbaden Hospital. My superintendent and Staff Sergeant Jim Hines offered to drive her to the appointment. The patient and superintendent were in uniform, and Jim was in Western attire - boots, hat, and all. The medic at the psych evaluation assumed Jim was the patient.

Jim was promoted to technical sergeant and served with me again at Seymour Johnson AFB, NC.

SITE SURVEYS

I was tasked by HQ USAFE to be the medical representative on three site survey teams in 1983.

I was to access the condition at each site as to sanitary food service, water sources, and waste disposal, on site medical capabilities, evacuation routes, and local disease threats.

MOROCCO, JANUARY 1983

We were instructed that our trip would be conducted in entirely in civilian clothing. We were not to bring any military clothing whatsoever, so Sunday after chapel service we went to the base exchange (BX) to buy a London Fog overcoat. One of Andy's friends asked what we were doing. He replied, "We're buying my dad a spy coat."

I was told the deployment was to be an F-4 squadron from the 86TH TFW of about fifty airmen. The deployment scenario was that the AF was to be the defenders against an air attack for Navy aircraft from a carrier in the Atlantic on its way to the Mediterranean Sea. I started talking to a team member on the flight to Rabat. I asked, "What unit do you represent?"

He said, "Air traffic control"

"How many people and when do they arrive?"

"Ten and a week before the main body."

The next officer answered, "Civil engineering, fifty, and ten days before."

The response was like that as I went around the cabin finding representatives from aircraft maintenance, services, security police, etc. I totaled about four hundred people deploying, with most arriving before the air squadron, which would include the medics. I recommended sending some of the medics with the advance party to give some medical capability.

The American Embassy hosted a reception for us the first night. We received a briefing on shopping and the medina (walled old town). We were told that the merchants already gave the embassy their lowest price and there was no need to bargain as was the custom. The embassy provided us with four-passenger white Fiats. We had some time over the weekend to go site seeing and shopping in Rabat. The carpet pavilion is on a plateau above the Qued Bau Regreg (river). Next to the pavilion is a large field where sheep skins are laid out to dry in the sun.

It was very interesting to watch the carpet sales process. First the carpets were certified in the pavilion. The maker then hired a porter to carry the rolled carpet up the hill to the main street of the medina. There the owner would speak to the first merchant, and the porter would unroll the carpet. A price would be discussed. The porter would roll up the carpet, and the pair moved to the next merchant. The porter unrolled the carpet even though the second merchant was only feet away from the first merchant and had already seen the carpet. The process was repeated up the street merchant by merchant, even returning to some until the carpet owner got the price he wanted.

Our team leader was a civil engineer colonel. He bought a leather jacket and told his captain where and how much he paid for it. The captain went to the shop and picked out an identical jacket and offered the merchant one birham below what the colonel had paid.

The merchant said, "No, No, I give you embassy price."

The captain said, "You don't understand. I have to pay less than the colonel did."

The captain got the coat for ten cents less than the colonel.

We stayed in the Moroccan Army officers' quarters. It was like a multi-story hotel and overlooked the mausoleum of Mohammed V (1906-1961) who was the first King of Moroccan independence. His son Hassan II was also entombed there in 1999.

Another main attraction was the Kasbah (Citadel) of Udayas with its Bab Qudaia Gate with its many steps. The gate and steps have been featured in car and motorcycle chases in several movies.

We got down to business the next day. The 117 km ride east of Rabat to the Royal Moroccan Air Base at Sidi Slimane took about an hour and a half. The US built the base in 1951 for Strategic Air Command (SAC) B-47 and B-50 bombers. The USAF left in 1963. The team met with Moroccan AF officials in the conference room of the old base operations building before dividing into our specialty groups. I went with the engineers because I would see the water system with them. Many of the buildings abandoned by the USAF had been vandalized and were of no practical use for our deployment.

As we did our walking tour of the base we observed holes dug adjacent to the street intersections. The Moroccan engineer made no mention of them. I noticed a Moroccan civilian in a tweed overcoat holding back from the main group. I asked, "Do you speak English?"

Tweed coat said, "Yes."

"Did you work here with the Americans?"

Tweet Coat replied, "Yes, I was the base engineer."

I pressed, "So all these holes in the ground are they where the water pipes have been removed?"

Tweed coat nodded. "Yes."

I got more useful information from the man in the tweed coat than the Moroccan engineer captain who told us the water chlorination system was fully operational while I could see the testing equipment rusting in the corner.

Our services officer and I toured the dining facility which had been the NCO Club. The kitchen was absolutely a mess and the food hygiene practices were deplorable.

The team reconvened at base ops for our briefing with the Moroccan Brigadier Wing Commander. Our team chief pulled me aside, "Doc, be diplomatic. We don't want to offend the brigadier."

When it came my turn to brief I said, "General, your staff have been most gracious in offering the use of your facilities for our airmen. I have discussed the deployment with other team members and determined that our service units need extensive bare base experience. This deployment will offer that opportunity." I could see the colonel's thumbs-up.

We drove back to Rabat and turned in the cars at the Embassy. The next day, we were informed our 707 was down for maintenance at Ramstein. We went back to the embassy and checked out the cars again. Some of us wanted to go to Casablanca about an hour south, eighty-eight kilometers away. Our driver was an F-4 pilot and drove like he was in afterburner. We arrived in Casablanca to get caught in the middle of a multi-lane traffic jam. We had no option but to follow it around a traffic circle. The next thing we knew we were headed back out of town. The only photo I got was the rooftop sign of a hotel through the rear window. We ate dinner at a seaside pizzeria almost to Rabat. The 707 arrived the next day to take us back to Ramstein.

ESKISEHIR, TURKEY, JUNE 1983

The Operation Distant Drum was a deployment of an 86th TFW squadron to Eskisehir, Turkey to participate in a NATO exercise. Eskisehir (old city) located in northwestern Turkey, is the fifth largest city, the provincial capital and home of the Turkish 1st Main Jet Base Command.

Lieutenant Colonel Melvin Q. Antonio, Chief of Aeromedical Services and my boss, was also on the team. I don't recall all the specifics of this inspection as I do for the Morocco trip. We in briefed the Turkish Brigadier Wing Commander in his conference room. He had tea, chai, served in tiny cups, and every time we took a sip a chai boy would top off our cup. There was already an AF detachment on the base. They had a building that served as their office, living quarters, and kitchen adjacent to a large field. They informed us that all previous deployments set up a tent city in that field. They said they were self contained and did not rely on the Turks for anything other than utilities. It was dusk when we left the base. There were armed sentries placed about every one hundred feet on both sides of the base main boulevard. I thought they must have a lot of enlisted men to be able to do that.

The next day Dr. Antonio and I visited the TAF General Hospital in the city. It was an old structure with ceramic tile floors and walls throughout. We saw the directory and noted all the doctors were AMA board certified specialists who had completed their specialty training in the US. Dr. Antonio was impressed and confident that our airmen would get excellent treatment if needed.

The team was billeted in military hotel off base. Dr. Antonio and I left the hotel to do some sightseeing and shopping. A Turk in a tweed coat approached us and said, "You are on the American survey team." We both thought this guy was some kind of foreign agent. He continued, "I work on the base and I saw you there. I offer you my services as a guide and an ally. What are you looking for? I can help you."

We replied, "Jewelry, leather goods, and meerschaum pipes."

The Turk said, "My cousin has a jewelry store just around the corner."

Dr. Antonio purchased some pieces for his wife.

The Turk now said "Now I take you to my cousin's leather shop."

I bought a multi-pocket bag that was about six by six inches that opened into over the shoulder bag, about eighteen by eighteen inches. A mosque was on the way to the meerschaum factory. He offered to take us in. We took off our shoes and entered. The interior was beautifully decorated with colored tiles. He got permission for me to take photographs. He introduced us to his cousin at the meerschaum factory. The stone is mined in Eskisehir. We got to observe the carvers and see many masterpieces. I had given up pipe smoking in 1969, but I bought a pipe as a souvenir. We walked along the streets a few blocks from the main street and noticed a lot of doctors' shingles on the doors. Eskisehir has the highest ratio of doctors per capita than any other city in Turkey. Our guide refused payment. We assumed he was paid by his cousins.

Our return flight included a refueling stop in Ankara. We were waiting in a hanger when we saw about twenty Turkish airmen pushing an F-4 jet. Nearby was a tug by which a crew of two usually did the same job.

I wrote a draft of my report in long hand and had my secretary Lilo typed it. Colonel James Calene the clinic CO called a couple days later and wanted to know who typed my report. I said my secretary. He said German nationals were not cleared for that information. OSI Agents came and confiscated the typewriter ribbon. The next day the *Stars and Stripes* carried a press release from USAFE HQ about Operation Distant Drum.

NORWAY, OCTOBER 1983

The first base on our Norway site survey was on the island of Andoya for a deployment of a fighter squadron of Iowa Air Nation Guard 132nd Wing. The passenger terminal and hangar were adjacent to the fishing village of Andenes on the north end of the island. The commercial side flew helicopters to ferry passengers and supplies to oil platforms in the North Sea. The Royal Norwegian Air Force (RNoAF) flew P-3C Orion aircraft for surveillance of Russia submarines and to assist the Coast Guard with Search and Rescue.

The base HQ and support facilities were in an alcove in the ridge of Mount Royken about four miles across very flat terrain from the hangers. The 132nd pilots on our team said the winds were so strong in the winter that cars were blown off the Kong Hans Gate road. The food service facilities were top notch. Fish was served at every meal. The medical clinic was typical for one squadron with one flight surgeon. The clinic administrator drove me along the ground excavation route south along the east coast to the village of Bjornskinn where a ferry went to the mainland. There is a bridge at Risoyhamn now.

Mount Royken dominates the northwest end of Andoya. A cavern was dug into it and served as the base fuel storage. The mountain range extended along the west coast. We took a ski chair lift to the top of the ridge. The ski slope had trees ten to twelve feet tall. I asked how one could ski with all those trees. The answer was that they are covered with snow in the winter.

We stayed in the village of Andenes. We used the sauna at the community center. At night I took some great photographs of the Northern Lights (aurora borealis) over the Andenes Church.

Colonel Odd Hafnor CO Andoya Air Station presented our team members with an Arctic certificate that we had been north of the Arctic Circle, 66 33' N.

Our next site was Bodo Main Air Station, also north of the Arctic Circle. I don't remember much about our visit there. The RNoAF flew F-16s from there. I think this is the base that has the underground multi-level hangar the size of an aircraft carrier built into the side of a mountain. I didn't get to see it but other team members did. Wikipedia confirms that there is an underground hanger in Norway but doesn't state where. I do remember purchasing Norwegian wool sweaters for the whole family in Bodo City.

Our last base was Trondheim. We were eating breakfast in the RNoAF officers mess, and I noticed about a dozen US Marines seated across the room. I introduced myself and stated our mission. They said they were the site survey team for the Marine Corps Prepositioning Program Norway during the same time as the Iowa Nation Guard deployment. That is when I found out the Norwegians were promising the same resources at the same time to both the AF and USMC.

We had a one day and a night layover in Oslo. I toured the Norwegian Armed Forces Museum and Norway's Resistance Museum in the Akershus Castle and Fortress (c. 1290) on the bank of Oslofjord. Our return commercial flight to Frankfurt was via Copenhagen.

NORMANDY

Memorial Day Weekend 1984 preceding the 40th anniversary of D-Day, Shirley and I took a camping trip to Normandy. We left Sam and Andy with one of my airman couples because the boys had already been to Normandy with the Boy Scouts. We made a campground outside of Caen as our base.

Our first stop was Pegasus Bridge on the Orne Canal. It is the site where D Company of the Ox and Bucks, British Parachute Regiment (Paras), 6th Airborne Division was the first company to go into action as a unit on D-Day. The story of D Company's capture of the bridge was featured in Darryl Zanuck's 1962 epic movie *The Longest Day*. Major John Howard, CO of D Company served as a consultant on the movie. Richard Todd, a captain in D Company, played Major Howard in the movie. Stephen E. Ambrose, author and historian, met Major Howard in June 7, 1981 at Pegasus Bridge while Ambrose was leading a group of American veterans on a tour of WWII battlefields. Major Howard proceeded to give them the account of D Company's capture of the bridge. Ambrose and Howard became close friends. Ambrose was able to interview all the surviving members of D Company and published in 1985 *Pegasus Bridge, June 6, 1944*.

That is a lot of background to get to my story. While we were at the bridge a tour bus arrived with British veterans and their wives. All the men were wearing maroon berets. They were Paras of D Company. They invited us to accompany them into the Gondree Café where we heard firsthand accounts of the action around a table model of the battle.

Next we visited Merville where the Paras captured four guns in casemates that were aimed at Sword Beach. From there we visited all the invasion beaches east to west: Sword, Juno, Gold, port of Arromanches, Omaha, and the cemetery at Colleville-sur-mer, Pointe du Hoc, Utah, and the town of St. Mere Eglise. We also visited La Cambe German war cemetery with its distinctive black crosses.

After sightseeing in Cherbourg we traveled along the coast to Avranches and set up camp. We spent the next day at Mont-Saint-Michel, the eighth-century, castle-like abbey on the tidal island. The sea rises forty-six feet from low to high tide. We headed back home from there.

Lieutenant Colonel Carl Kyzar, USA Vet Corps at Landstuhl stopped by my office on June 1. "You just got back from Normandy. Did you travel on the autobahn?"

I nodded. He continued, "Did you happen to see if they took Americans Express at the toll booths?"

"As a matter of fact I did see the American Express sign. Why?"

Kyzar said, "I am the convoy commander for forty medical vehicles going to Normandy for D-Day anniversary. I was told to pay the tolls for all of them with my American Express card and I would get reimbursed when I got back."

I remarked, "You would think the French would be thankful for the medical support and waive the tolls."

GOODBYE, RAMSTEIN

All large events at Ramstein such as change of commands, Christmas markets, and graduations were held in an air craft hangar. Sam graduated from Ramstein High School in June 1984. He had started his second year of preschool at the Little Red School House on Guam. He chose as his senior essay the title *Hut to Hangar*. His essay was one of two selected to be printed in the graduation program.

HUT TO HANGAR

From hut to hangar sums up my education. I started the first grade in a Quonset hut at Agana, Guam, and I am graduating as a senior in a flight hangar at Ramstein, West Germany.

This hut-to-hangar experience has involved not only twelve years of education but all of the hardships of living through some of life's most difficult times as well. It represents the good and bad influences of peer pressure and emotional troubles emanating from clashes with friends, parents, and teachers. It represents an infinite amount of reflection about school work, essays, poetry, sex, friendships, careers, and pleasures. It covers the athletics I have taken part in, the summer jobs I have worked, and the sacrifices made to cram all of those activities into each day. It represents all of the far-off

171

places I have visited, all of the pain of losing friends in a move, and the agony of making new ones.

If first through twelfth grade represents all of this, then what will college be? A four-year cram course encompassing the same?

Sam Tate

Colonel James G. Calene was the clinic commander my last two years at Ramstein. He nominated me for my second Air Force Commendation Medal.

This time we left both Sam and Andy behind to serve as Boy Scout camp staff. Both were at the high adventure camp in Garmisch. Shirley, Cubby, and I packed up for our journey to Seymour Johnson AFB, Goldsboro, NC. I told Shirley to take a good look at the mountains because the highest elevations in eastern North Carolina are overpasses.

SEYMOUR JOHNSON AFB ENVIRONMENTAL HEALTH

Seymour Johnson (SJ) is the only US Air Force base named for a naval officer. He died in a plane crash March 5, 1941. The base hosts four F-15 squadrons of the 4th Fighter Wing and 916th Air Refueling Wing all supported by the USAF Hospital. My duties as chief of environmental health services were very similar to those at Ramstein. I served on six hospital committees and the base childcare advisory committee. I was also the medical intelligence officer and senior medical representative to the wing command center. I supervised eleven technicians and one secretary. Technical Sergeant Jim Hines from Ramstein served with me again. We moved offices from the veterinary building about three months after I arrived to a deactivated patient section of the hospital, D wing. I was known as *D'e Wing Commander*, pun intended. I told my staff that if they found patients wondering in our hallway, it was because other sections did not know where to send them. My staff was to find out where they were supposed to be and escort them there. Our motto was, "We do everything no one else wants to do, and we do it better than they could ever do".

Public health wise, we had a lot going on. We managed two programs mandated by the AF Surgeon General. First was that all AF and civilian hospital staff had to be antibody tested for measles or be vaccinated. The second was that all active duty personnel had to be tested for HIV. It was my job to call the people who tested positive for HIV and make an appointment with the flight surgeon who would inform them of the test results and counsel them. The hard part was that the patient surmised the results just because I was calling and the anxiety that caused.

We were having a problem with personnel not returned in forty-eight to seventy-two hours to have their TB tine test read. I prepared a slide for the wing commander's weekly staff meeting that showed the no-show numbers per organization. The no-show rate dropped by thirty-eight percent.

The North Carolina Health Department contacted me on December 17, 1986 with notification that an index case of measles had been in the base childcare center. MSgt Tucker and I screened 644 records and found forty-six children had been exposed to the index case. We did contact tracing on all forty-six and found no additional cases. We also arranged follow up serological testing. The health department did an immunization audit three months later of the childcare center and preschool and found one hundred percent compliance with the North Carolina Immunization Law.

The director of the childcare center held the position in 1971-72 when I was attending University of North Carolina. We would place the boys there while we attended to hospital appointments and shopped at the commissary and BX. They would write the child's name on a piece of tape and place it on their back. We got back to Durham, and Sam still had the name tape on his back. I removed and he explained, "My name, my name!" like he had just lost his identity.

The director was pleased to see her six-foot-six former student.

VIRGINIA MILITARY INSTITUTE

Sam was accepted to VMI while in his senior year at Ramstein. He had never seen the campus, so after he arrived from Germany we took him to Lexington,

VA, two days before matriculation. He got a tour of the barracks. We met Colonel Chaplain Charley Caudill, USAF, Ret, and Colonel Leroy Hammond, US Army Ret, who hosted the Officers Christian Fellowship. The NROTC at VMI more oriented to the Marine Corps, and the professor of naval science is always a Marine colonel. We met with the XO who was a Marine major aviator. There was a large charcoal painting of General Stonewall Jackson on the wall behind the major's desk. General Jackson was depicted as a WWII Marine aviator with the leather helmet of that era.

The major asked Sam, "Have you seen the barracks?"

Sam said, "Yes, sir."

"I guess you found them to be very Spartan?" he asked.

Sam replied, "Sir, I just spent three months in a two-man tent on a mountain in Germany. I don't think there is anything here that Spartan."

The Major said, "You will do very well here, Midshipman."

The next day we went to the field house for matriculation. Sam signed the book. There was a sign there that stated, "Mothers, kiss your sons goodbye."

A couple weeks later I was on my way to work and a VW Beetle followed me into the parking lot. It was the deputy base commander, a lieutenant colonel.

I saluted him. "Good morning, sir,"

The Lieutenant Colonel said, "I noticed the VMI sicker. I know you went to Old Dominion, Michigan State, and University of North Carolina. When did you go to VMI?"

I explained, "I didn't go to VMI. My son is a rat (freshman) there now."

The Lieutenant Colonel explained, "I went to VMI. The next time your son is home bring him over and I'll get him an orientation ride." He arranged for Sam to fly in a KC-10 tanker on a refueling mission.

In fact, Sam did so well his rat year that he was offered the choice of an appointment to the US Naval Academy or a three-year NROTC scholarship. He chose the scholarship because he didn't want to repeat the first year. He played in the regimental band and was the second class (junior) drum major. He also spent a summer semester at Oxford, England, where he connected again with Paul Barber.

OCCUPATIONAL HEALTH

The base occupational health program was administered by the Aeromedical Council chaired by the flight surgeon and had three sections. The bioenvironmental engineering (BEE) did all the shop inspections for chemical and physical hazard and determined protective equipment and practices in accordance with *Air Force Occupational Health Standards*. Their findings would be presented to the council who would determine what physicals and tests were needed based on the exposures. The physical examination section performed the physicals and lab test and recorded the results in the individual medical records. Environment health then reviewed the medical records of all the personnel in that shop, looking for trends, and reported them to the council. If the trends indicted exposures, then the BEE would evaluate the shop for noncompliance with preventive measures.

When I did the medical records review of all the instructors at the firing range I found several that had abnormally high blood lead results. I interviewed them and found no lead exposures outside of their range duties. The BEE and I inspected the range. It was enclosed on three sides. The end of the structure behind the firing position had two built in exhaust fans. There was a protective roof over the firing positions, but the rest was open. The instructors would stand behind the shooters with the fans behind the instructors. We examined the original plans and found that the roof had been extended forward to give shooters more protection when it rained.

The BEE performed air flow tests that showed the roof extension interfered with the exhaust of airborne lead. Corrections were made to the exhaust system. This case was presented by the BEE and me at the Tactical Air Command (TAC) Environmental Health/Bioenvironmental Engineering Management Seminar in March 1987.

Another huge project was preparation of vehicles for prepositioning at Diego Garcia in the Indian Ocean; all had to be painted desert sand color and preservatives applied to all the rubber parts. The paint in spray form was moderately toxic. Fortunately, there were no problems with the painters wearing respirations. These vehicles were eventually used in Desert Storm.

SAM'S SEA BAG

Sam came to Goldsboro after his junior year at VMI. He had a week before he had to report to the Norfolk Naval Air Station, VA, for NROTC summer training. He asked me to help him pack his sea bag. I got out his grandfather's *Blue Jacket Manual,* the navy handbook for recruits. We turned to the chapter on sea bags. We rolled all his clothes and laid them out on the bed as described and pictured in the book. We turned the page to find, "Now your chief will show you how to pack the sea bag." Well, Sam's grandfather, Chief Petty Officer Tate, USN, wasn't there, so Sam stuffed the clothes in the bag. We drove to Norfolk, and Sam reported in wearing civilian clothes. The lieutenant commander instructed him to change to khaki uniform and do it quickly because he needed to get to the clinic for a flight physical. Sam changed in the men's room but came out in his loafers, which I pointed out. His uniform shoes were in the bottom of the sea bag. With proper shoes on he reported back to the lieutenant commander who said, "Aviators don't wear that hat" referring to the "wheel hat." Sam had to dig in the sea bag again to find his flight cap. The next day he was in the copilot's seat of SH-2 Seasprite helicopter.

EXERCISES II

Combat readiness training was just as intense at SJ as it was at Ramstein. The AF was getting very serious about chemical warfare defense, so I trained my technicians as the patient decontamination team. I also provided field sanitation and hygiene to the 4th Civil Engineering Squadron during one of their deployment exercises.

The fighter squadrons were required to generate combat sorties while all personnel were in full protective gear (MOP). These exercises ran twenty-four hours a day for two to three days. All the support personnel, maintenance, weapons, flight line, etc. were housed in the hangars when off shift.

We anticipated a lot of heat stress casualties when these exercises were conducted in the summer. We disseminated information on hydration and avoiding caffeinated drinks, coffee, and tea. I also designed a survey to be conducted on flight line personnel in various jobs to identify the risk factors and those positions at highest risk for heat-related illness. We also gathered data from heat illness patients to track their jobs and behaviors.

January 1986 the AF Surgeon General directed that all AF medical units conduct annual deployment exercises, Red Flag II. Plans called for the medical staff of 4th Wing to deploy with the 1st USAF Hospital at Langley who had all the equipment for the air transportable hospital (ATH), so we were left with two WWII era GPL tents to practice with.

The hospital administrator, a captain, was cadre leader and I was the assistant and primary instructor. We chose Fort Bragg because it was away from SJ, seventy miles, but close to Pope AFB from where we would obtain a field kitchen and staff. We borrowed GPL and GPM tents from two Army National Guard armories near Goldsboro. We selected a site in the woods opposite drop zone X-ray and near the Army Recondo training area. The trees were just beginning to bud.

The hospital staff was divided into three sections. Each section would deploy for three days in sequence with one day in-between. We wanted to add some realism to the exercises. Major Gold, a scouting friend of mine from Germany, was stationed at Ft. Bragg, and he cleared it for EOD to issue us some smoke grenades, flares, and noise simulators. I had to hold the captain back from getting any real explosives. We got back to camp and he wanted to try a slap flare, which shoots into the air and deploys a parachute to prolong its illumination. A breeze caught the chute and it drifted away from us. We ran through the woods chasing it until it hit the ground and set the pine needles on fire. Fortunately, we got the fire out before it spread. No more slap flares.

The field kitchen crew set up and provided two hot meals per day. Lunch was MREs - by the way, the freeze-dried strawberries make great daiquiris. Everyone used the standard WWII mess kits and they were instructed how to operate immersion heaters for hot water to wash, rinse, and sanitize (SWT method). We also trained the BEE and EH technicians in mosquito and tick surveillance. The captain wanted the stretcher bearer course to be an obstacle race with smoke and noise. We had to change that to instruction on how to negotiate obstacles and vehicle loading without smoke and noise when one of our female medics wrenched her knee. When all three sections were completed, they were confident they could live and operate in a deployed site, but probably less austere than the one we set up. The Army National Guard was not too happy when we returned their green tents all yellow with pine pollen, but we had no way to clean them.

Colonel Robert H. Scott, Dental Corps, became our hospital commander after having been acting CO when the two previous MDs had been relieved. He was the first non-medical officer to command after the policy change that medical treatment facilities could be commanded by other then medical officers.

Colonel Scott appointed me cadre leader for the 1987 Red Flag II. I received approval to use the Boy Scout camp about ten miles from the base, which reduced travel time. There were cabins for sleeping; eliminating the need for tents except the two we had for training. We could use the dining hall staffed by cooks from SJ, thus eliminating the need for a field kitchen. The camp would benefit from the first aid supplies we would donate. The three training sessions went very well without a hitch. Colonel Scott attended the last night's meal. Since this was my last exercise before retirement, they secured me on a stretcher, carried me down to the lake, and dumped me in from the boat dock. I swam under the dock and waited long enough for them to begin to worry that I had drowned. I emerged from the water and gave Colonel Scott a soaking wet bear hug.

PLANS FOR RETIREMENT

We were on vacation in VA Beach in the summer of 1986. I went over to Hampton to see Dr. John Freed. I was his Big Brother at MSU, and I passed several of my student jobs to him when I graduated. He served the minimum two years in the AF Veterinary Corps. He then started a small animal practice in Hampton. I told him I wanted to go into private practice when I left the AF. He said my clinical skills would be rusty after twenty years of public health. He suggested I try to take a refresher program somewhere. I had maintained my veterinary license in Virginia and was a Virginia resident, so Virginia-Maryland College of Veterinary Medicine (VMCVM) was a logical choice. I made an appointment with the assistant dean for admissions and explained what I wanted to do. Both he and the Dean were excited about this novel approach to transition a veterinarian to another career path. The plan was for me to start in August 1987.

My mandatory retirement day was April of 1988. We did not want Andy to change high schools during his senior year. So selected September 1, 1987 as the date to retire, which put our move in July when accounting for terminal leave. Going to a new high school for his senior year was better than moving during it.

Andy is a planner and, even more, a schemer. The assistant soccer coach and family lived in the other end of our building. Andy's scheme was to live with them his senior year. He had already convinced the coach before presenting the plan to us.

He presented his plan to us thinking it was fool proof until I said, "Great idea, Andy, but we are not leaving you a car." That was the end of that.

RETIREMENT CEREMONY

The base held a retirement ceremony at wing HQ the last Friday of every month. Colonel Scott insisted I participate. I was due to start terminal leave on July 14th so I would do the ceremony on June 26th. I was the only officer along with three NCOs were being honored. Our spouses were escorted to their seats. A flight of airmen paraded up the driveway. The wing commander presented us with medals. Mine was the Meritorious Service Medal. Each of us received a retirement certificate and a flag. Our spouses were presented with Certificates of Appreciation from the Chief of Staff of the Air Force. My office staff held a retirement lunch for us at one of the local restaurants.

There was a medical IG inspection scheduled in late July, but my replacement wasn't scheduled to arrive until September. Since my terminal leave didn't start until July 14th I was back in the office on Monday June 29th. I wanted to make sure everything was ready for the IG. Colonel Scott came over to D wing.

Colonel Scott said, "I thought we got rid of you on Friday."

I packed up my things and left. We went to my parents' beach cottage in Kill Devil Hills, North Carolina. We returned in time for the movers to pack our household goods and leave for the Virginia-Maryland College of Veterinary Medicine, Blacksburg, VA.

First Lieutenant Samuel Tate, USAF, VC, Lackland AFB, Texas.

Veterinary Staff (from left to right, front row) Sgts. Payne and Peterson, A1C. Peters, MSgt. Balsik; (2nd row) TSgt Travers, Billie Walker, SSgt Diaz; Lt Col Hayman; (3rd row) Grover and Crosset. May 1967.

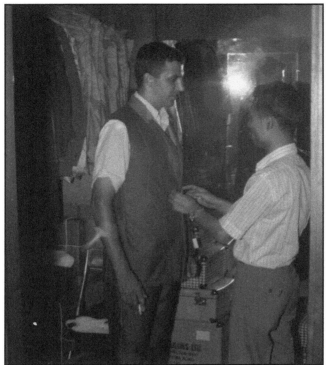

Capt. Don Adona fitted for new suit, R&R Hong Kong, 1968.

BG. Frank Ramsey and wife.   Maj Tate and Shirley with Pauline and
                                  Brigadier John Clifton, RAVC. US Army
                                  Europe Veterinary Conference, Berchtes-
                                  gaden, Germany 1982.

Capt. Barry Morrison, wife Betty, Shirley Tate and Capt. Samuel Tate,
R&R, Hawaii 1968.

Capt. Sam Tate, Cam Ranh Bay, Vietnam 1967.

Capt. Robert Eason, Maj. David Woods, Capt. Sam Tate, Cam Ranh AFB, Dec 1967.

Pres. LB Johnson, Gen. Ky, Pres. of Vietnam 12th USAF Hospital, Cam Ranh AFB, December 1967. Note small Christmas tree in sand lot.

31st Security Police K-9 Kennels, Tuy Hoa AB,1967.
Note sewerage treatment plant beyond kennels.

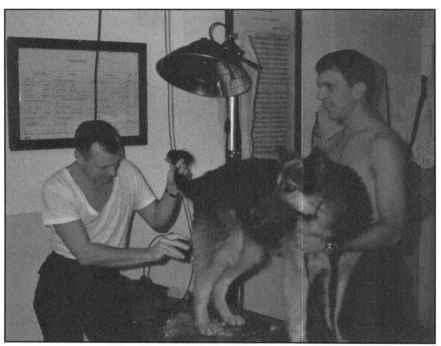

TSgt. Kenney, NCOIC, Veterinary Service;
Rusty 881F, A1C Sourwine, kennel attendant, 1968.

Wounded Rusty 881F, MSgt. Watkins and handler, April 1968

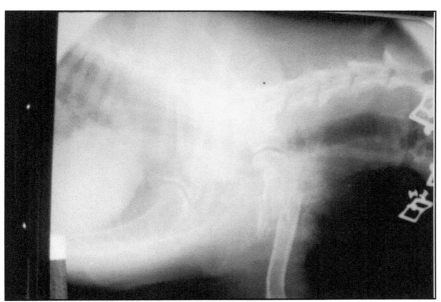

Rusty's X-ray, fractured humorous.

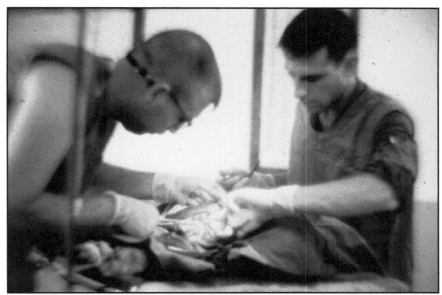

Capt's Tate and Sorkin performing surgery on Rusty.

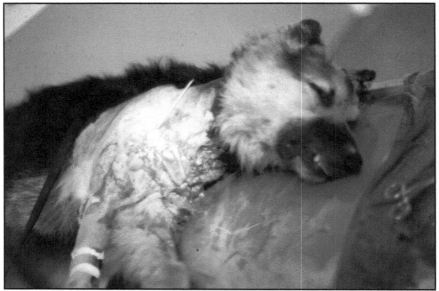

Surgery complete, bone pin in place.

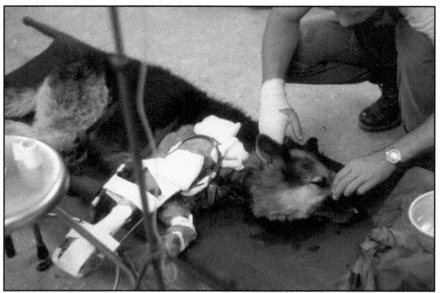

Above: Wounded handler strokes Rusty, Thomas splint applied.

Sgt. Andy Sirabyn keeps watch while Capt. Tate naps after all night surgery.

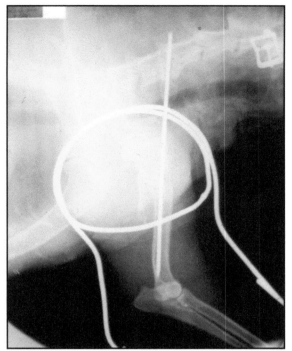

Post Operative X-ray.

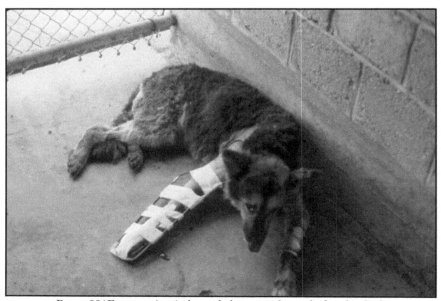

Rusty 881F recovering in kennel about two hours before he died.

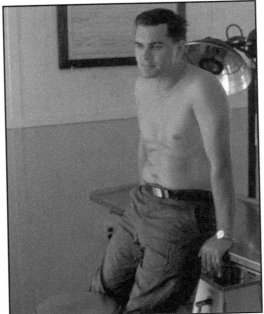

MSgt. Watkins, NCOIC, Security Police K-9 Kennels.

The Baboon army mascot.

189

39th Air Rescue Squadron C-130's destroyed in Viet Cong sapper attack
Tuy Hoa AB, July 30, 1968. It was the real thing.

Capt. Tate and Vietnamese interpreter, Miss Lynn, inspecting food in Korean restaurant for Approved List, Tuy Hoa City.

Highway 1 Ba River Railroad Bridge, Tuy Hoa.

The Grand Hotel, site of 7th AF Medial Conference, Vung Tau, September 1968.

Dr. Tate in front of Grand Hotel, Vung Tau, June 2013.

CPT. Ronald C. Olsen, USA, VC holds a dog for Capt. Samuel W. Tate, USAF, VC as vaccinates it for rabies at a MEDCAP clinic in the Vietnamese village on the bank of the Da Rang River, Oct 1968.

Two Vietnamese boys carry their dog on a pole to get it vaccinated for rabies.

The High Wycombe Air Station volleyball team, 1969 United Kingdom Champions. Capt. Tate is number 20 on back row.

Scoutmaster Sam Tate and Assistant Scoutmaster Regie Price on the top of Zugspitze, highest mountain in Germany, while attending the Transatlantic Council (TAC) Boy Scout Conference in Garmisch, May 1969.

Scoutmaster Sam Tate, Scouter Pete and Assistant Scoutmaster Paul Barber in their camp blankets, Camp Mohawk, England July 1969.

Col Nave, Base Commander and District Scout Commissioner receives TAC certificate of appreciation from the Cub and Boy Scouts of High Wycombe Air Station, winter 1969.

Capt. Tate inspects a lobster farm in Donegal, Northern Ireland
for the Approved Sources List.

The Blarney Stone, Blarney Castle (1425), County Cork, Republic of Ireland. Spring 1971.

Sam and Andy Tate with LT. Bill Wheeler. We were in-transit to Guam. Bill was attending the Navy Post Graduate School, Monterey, CA. June 1972.

LCDR. Bill Wheeler and wife, Vera, Bremerton, WA. 1979

Inner Apra Harbor, Guam viewed from Mount Tenjo, Guam.

Assumption of command by RADM Morrison, Commander Naval Forces Marianas.
Note the Boatswain mate at the flag pole to the right behind the admiral.
October 1972. (libweb.hawaii.edu)

TSgt. Smith, wife Shirley, Jesus Duenas, Shirley and Sam Tate at Duenas Ranch, Talofofo, Guam.

Sam, Jesus Duenas, daughter Maria, and sons on the way to Sgt. Yokoi's cave. 1973.

Andy, Sam and Shirley Tate with Capt. Bill Smith and wife at Banzai Cliff.

Capt. Tate, Andy and Sam on Japanese tank, Last Command Post, Saipan. 1973.

District Commissioner Capt. Sam Tate and Andy, Liberation Day Parade, Agana, Guam. July 21, 1973.

Andy and Sam supervise scouts spreading   crushed coral at the Libugon Vista Point, Hwy 6, during the "50 Mile Hike Around   Guam", December 1973.

Underway Replenishment of USS Theodore Roosevelt CV 71 by USS Santa Barbara AE 28. (US Navy photo by Michael Tuemler, US National Archives)

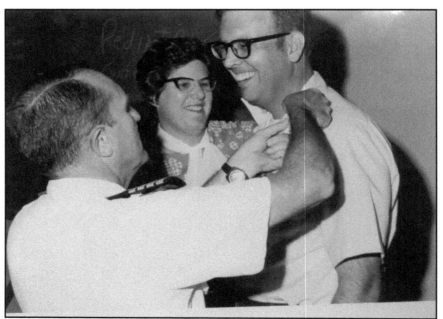

CAPT. McMahan and Shirley Tate pin oak leaves on Maj. Sam Tate, Naval Regional Medical Center, Charleston, SC. January 29, 1976.

CAPT. Hirschy, Commander Navy Food Service Systems Office, presents Maj. Tate the Air Force Commendation Medal, Washington, DC. July 1977.

USS Arizona as it would appear 1939-1940 painted at the National Museum of the Navy, summer 1978.

Maj. Tate writing navy manuals at the Navy Food Service Systems Office.

The services' dieticians on the Armed Forces Product Evaluation Committee induct
Maj .Tate as an honorary member of the Little Old Ladies in Tennis Shoes
(LOLITS). June 1981.

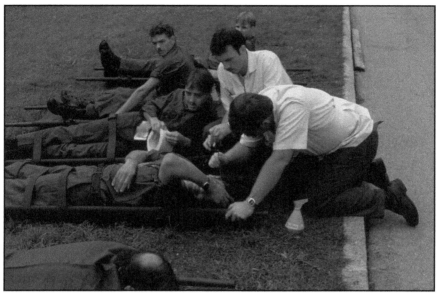

Moulage causalities, Medical Red flag, Bundeswehr Medical Academy, Munich, Germany. August 25, 1981.

Car bombing of USAFE HQ building, Ramstein AFB, Germany. Left: Front entrance, note hole in the wall between 2nd and 3rd story windows. Right: parking lot. August 31, 1981. (USAF Police.org photos)

Buddy care of moulage casualty during Salty Nation exercise, Ramstein AB.

Set up of Air Transportable Hospital (ATH) using general purpose tents,
Landstuhl Hill. 1982.

Castle de Ribaucourt. Below left: Count Daniel de Ribaucourt and Sam Tate.

Scouts from Ramstein. Sgt Luc Janssens and Count de Ribaucourt are far left, Sam Tate is in far right. Belgium Oct. 1982.

Shirley Tate at St. Remigius
Church, Falera near Flims,
Switzerland.

Shirley Tate at St. Johns Stone,
Craps Sougn Gion in background.

Andy Tate, hot-dogging moguls, Flims, Switzerland. December 1982.

Sam and Andy Tate, Silver
Buffalo, Feb. 1971.

Sam and Andy Tate, Silver Buffalo.

Andy Tate in the footprint of Lord
Badden Powell, Gillwell Park.

"Feed the birds" Andy Tate in Trafalgar
Square, London, England Dec. 1983

Sheep skins drying in the sun.

Qudaia Gate, Bab Kasbah of Udayas, Rabat, Morocco. January 1983.

Mount Royken, Royal Norwegian Air Force Base.

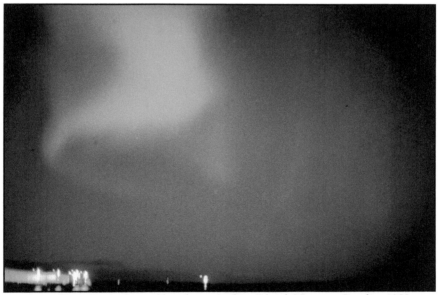

Auroa Borealis, Andenes Church, on Andoya Island, Norway. October 1983.

40th Anniversary of D-Day Invasion of Normandy
Shirley Tate at Pegasus Bridge over the Caen Canal, Benouville, France.

Gold Beach & Mulberry Harbor "B" at Arromanches, France. May 1984

Omaha Beach at low tide.

The Spirit of American Youth Rising from the Waves,
American Cemetery Colleville-sur- mer.

Three generations, Scout Sam, Maj. Sam & Claude Tate, Bayern High Adventure Camp, Garmisch, Germany. June 1984.

Cadet Tate (Rat), Virginia Military Institute.

Andy, Cadet Sam, Shirley and Maj. Sam Tate. Parents Weekend. October 1984.

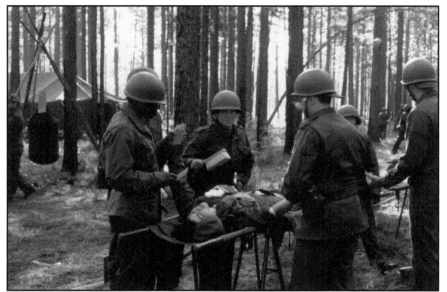

Causality Decontamination, Medical Red Flag training, Fort Bragg, NC. 1985.

Maj. Tate's Retirement Ceremony, 4th TFW, Seymour Johnson AFB, NC. June 1987.

PART 3

VET SQUARED

VMCVM

We found a townhouse to rent in Blacksburg, but it wasn't available until September and my classes started in August. Cubby and I set up the VW camper at the New River Campground while Shirley and Andy stayed in VA Beach. The owner also rented inner tubes for tubing on the New River. It was a very popular activity for the college crowd. I started helping him in the evenings, patching inner tubes in exchange for free camping spot. He also watched Cubby while I was in class, and I drove the shuttle van for him on weekends.

My refresher program consisted of auditing lectures with the junior class and clinic rotations with the senior class. There was a schedule of lectures for the entire year indicating which one pertained to small animals and with the large animals (livestock). That made it easy to choose the ones I wanted to attend. I chose for the senior clinic rotation radiology, anesthesiology, medicine, surgery, and emergency medicine. I took the opportunity to do a second rotation in medicine. In order to collect my GI Bill benefits I had to take graduate level courses for credit outside of the vet college. I chose virology, accounting for non-MBA majors, and sociology.

The first hour of radiology involved reviewing X-rays (rounds) by body systems. Then patients started arriving from the other services to be X-rayed. They would be accompanied by the primary student assigned to their case and a student to administer and monitor anesthesia. The radiology student would determine the positioning and measurements for the X-ray machine settings. The processing was automatic - no more hand dipping film (now it's all digital, no films at all.) We then read the X-rays. The large animal ward had its own X-ray area, so students assigned to those cases worked there. Towards the end of the rotation we were doing rounds and the seniors wanted me to go first. The obvious feature was a stag horn calculus in the kidney. However, I followed protocol and started at the edges of the film and worked my way to the center, describing the findings as I went. The professor pointed to a small, soft tissue mass that I omitted and was superimposed on the ureter (the tube from the kidney to the bladder). "What is that?"

Before I could answer, the seniors asked in unison, "Have you been to the beach lately?"

I explained, "They are nipples." It was a set up.

Anesthesiology was the most intense rotation. The students had to devise an anesthesia regimen for their specific case, defend each element before getting approval, and drawing the elements from the pharmacy. Once the pre-anesthesia was administered and maintained on a gas anesthetic machine, the animal had to be constantly monitored. I was the anesthetist on a long surgical case. Suddenly the body temperature started dropping. I called the technician and showed her the monitor screen. She took one look and asked, "Dr. Tate, where is the temperature probe?" I looked and it was on the floor.

One of the seniors asked why I wasn't assigned to any large animal cases. I said, "I have better sense than to be kicked in the head by a cow." I went on to small animal medicine rotation while he went to large animal ambulatory. I saw him a couple weeks later at a party. He had a bandage on his head. I asked, "What happened to you?"

He said, "I got kicked by a cow!"

I did my emergency medicine rotation at a clinic in Vienna, VA. I stayed with Bill and Vera Wheeler in Fairfax, VA. Bill was stationed at Navy Sea Systems Command and Vera was working at the NIH. I was working nights seven days a week, so we rarely saw each other in the four weeks I was there. The head veterinary technician (vet tech) at the emergency clinic tried to intimidate me the first night the way she did senior students.

She said, "You need to bring us brownies if you want to get a good grade."

I said, "I am auditing this program, so there is no grade. And I don't bake brownies."

I stopped at the Food Lion on the way back to Bill's and bought a box of microwave brownies. I cooked them the next afternoon and took them to the clinic.

"These are so you know I'm not a S.O.B."

CELEBRITY

I was interviewed by Beth Taylor in November 1987 for an article in the *VMCMC Monitor* published in winter 1988 edition below which was also carried by *Collegiate Times*, the official newspaper of Virginia Tech.

Back to the Classroom for Dr. Sam Tate

By Beth Taylor, Public Affairs Intern

Not every retired military major decides to go back to school, but Sam Tate is not an average guy.

Returning to veterinary school after 20 years of active duty in the U.S. Air Force, the retired military veterinarian is taking a combination of senior clerkships and third-year lecture programs at the Virginia-Maryland Regional College of Veterinary Medicine.

"I've never been in clinical practice," Tate said. "It's something I've always wanted to do, and I was getting a little tired of what I was doing in the military. I was ready for a change of pace."

Although ready for something different, Tate is familiar with the academic environment. Between military work in human preventative medicine and public facility sanitation, he found time for numerous professional short courses. Tate said he is somewhat apprehensive about the different pace of the program at Virginia Tech.

"In this particular curriculum it's kind of frightening because I haven't done anything like this in quite a while," he said. It's not as 'hands-on' or physical (as in the military), but more intellectual.

"But the idea of going to school in itself is not frightening because all my life I've been going to school in one way or another," he said. "The military is not an academically sterile environment. There are professional courses and programs you go to all the time. The military is not an academic wasteland."

Although he is in a special program, Tate's day begins much the same as any vet student's. "I start out at 7:50 in the morning and its lecture, lecture, lecture, about eight hours a day," he said. "It's a peculiar set-up," Tate said when asked about his classes. "I'm picking and choosing (the courses) I feel meet my needs." The program Tate is involved in is the first of its kind at the veterinary college.

He plans to take enough "refresher" courses to update his knowledge and be competitive in small- animal clinical practice, he said. "Everyone I've talked to on the faculty and staff has been tolerant as well as helpful," Tate said. "They all said, 'Gee, you've got a lot of guts to do this'."

Tate said his wife Shirley and two sons, Samuel, 21 and Andrew, 17, were equally supportive.

"My wife was a little leery of it to start with," he said. "But she's been with me though all of my academic endeavors. I feel I've done the right thing as far as wanting to go into clinical practice," he said. "Once I made that decision I knew that was what I wanted to do the rest of my productive life."

ANDY AT VMI

Andy was adjusting very well to his senior year at Blacksburg High School. He played kicker on the football team and placed third is his weight class in the region in wrestling. He also got serious about academics and started pulling up his grades. He said to me one day in April, "Dad, I have an appointment at VMI tomorrow. Will you go with me?"

"Sure."

I knew he was serious about this appointment because he was wearing socks.

The dean of admission, a colonel in the VA Militia, met us in his waiting area and invited us into his office for Andy's interview. I declined and said I was along for morale support and would wait. The colonel invited me into his office after he had interviewed Andy. He said, "I have reviewed Andy's transcripts and see he has made a real effort to improve his grades. If he can score twenty-four out of twenty-eight on the ACT, he will be eligible for the summer prep school. It is tuition free; his room and board is the only expense."

I told Andy on the way back to Blacksburg that I would buy him an ACT study guide at the VA Tech book store. He replied, "I already have one, Dad." He scored twenty-six on the test.

We returned to VMI in May for Sam's graduation. I went to the colonel's office to make payment for Andy's prep school. The colonel accepted my check and left me alone in his office as he went to turn in the check. Andy's file lay open on his desk in plain sight. The colonel returned and saw that I was standing close enough to his desk to be able to read the file. I apologized for snooping but was impressed by the comment, "Prospective cadet's father waited outside during the interview."

He explained, "Doctor, you might be amazed by the number of fathers that try to kick my door down to get their sons into VMI. I knew by your action that VMI was what Andy really wanted and was willing to work for it."

Andy chose Marine option for NROTC and was greatly influenced by two successive professors of naval science: Colonel Dabney fought at Khe Sanh and was the son-in-law of Lieutenant General Lewis B. "Chesty" Puller, and Colonel John W. Ripley who received the Navy Cross for blowing up the bridge at Dong Ha on Easter 1972. This is recounted in the book by the same name. Second Lieutenant Andy Tate served on the detail planning Colonel Ripley's retirement ceremony at Quantico Marine Base in the summer of 1992. Andy followed in his brother's footsteps and also did a summer semester at Oxford, again linking up with Paul Barber.

TIGER CRUISE

Meanwhile, Samuel L. Tate, Lieutenant, USN, became the aide to Rear Admiral John Scott Redd, Commander of Cruiser Destroyer Group 12 in Jacksonville, FL. The group deployed to the Persian Gulf with the *USS Dwight D. Eisenhower* (CVN-69) as its flagship to enforce the "no fly zone" in Iraq after Desert Storm. The IKE Battle Group returned in April 1992. Sam's father-in-law, Charlie Fudge, I, and three hundred other sons, daughters, and fathers were flown from Norfolk to Bermuda to meet and return with the fleet on a tiger cruise. During our three-day transit we toured the ship and ate in the admiral's mess. As the admiral's aide, Sam wore an aiguillette on the left shoulder consisting of two loops, gold with dark blue spiral bands. Thus nickname for the aid was "loop." Rear Admiral Redd wanted to spend some time with his son so he told Sam to take Charlie and me to areas of the Ike that we had not seen yet. The aide precedes the admiral, and people expected the admiral to be directly behind. Sam took us to one of the flight-ready rooms. He entered first and someone called, "Attention." I stepped into the room and said, "As you were."

We attended two ceremonies on the *Ike*. The first was thanksgiving for safety because there had not been a single personal injury on the whole deployment in spite of one aircraft incident. The other was the reenlistment of several of the ships company. Rear Admiral Redd spoke at both ceremonies.

Air operations started as we near the Virginia Capes. The various types of aircraft were flown to their home stations in Norfolk and Oceana. We watched from the buzzard's roost, the catwalk outside the flag bridge one deck above the navigation bridge. The next operation was to VERTREP storage boxes by helicopters over several trips. We were approaching the Chesapeake Bay when one of the helicopters returned with a number of journalists. RADM Redd asked me if I recognized any of them. I named the ones I could and what TV stations they were from. They were escorted to the admiral's bridge where he gave a speech. After the reporters left, Rear Admiral Redd turned to me. "Doc, how did I do?"

"You did very well for a speech you have given three times."

Rear Admiral Redd said, "Practice makes perfect."

Sam was responsible for all of Rear Admiral Redd's sea bags, which Sam carried off the ship when we docked in Norfolk. Charlie and I carried Sam's bags as well as our own. Amy, Sam's wife, "kidnapped" Sam to an unknown location. We took Sam's bags home with us. The next day the command master chief called looking for Sam. We told him we didn't know where he was. He asked if we happened to have one of Rear Admiral Redd's sea bags. We looked, and sure enough we did. The master chief said it contained the presents for the admiral's family. It also contained dirty clothes, and Shirley offered to wash them. The master chief said there was no need to do that and he would be over right away to pick it up.

ANDY'S FIRST CLASS YEAR

Andy earned a NROTC scholarship for his first class year (Senior) just as his college fund was empty.

Andy was the Regimental S-3 (training and operation) that year. He was in charge of planning all the parades and ceremonies. Andy arranged to have Gunnery Sergeant Carlos Hathcock, II, USMC, to be a speaker at VMI. Carlos lived across the street in VA Beach from my parents. His story as a sniper in Vietnam is told by Charles Henderson in *Marine Sniper, 93 Confirmed Kills*. 1986. Carlos died February 1999 of MS. Andy very much wanted Sam to be at his graduation. Since Sam was aide to Rear Admiral Scott Redd, Andy knew the only way to get Sam to graduation was to get the admiral there. Andy told the commandant, "I can get a 'fleet admiral' for the Navy commissioning officer." (Andy confused Rear Admiral Redd's position as the IKE Battle Group Commander with that of a fleet admiral, which is a five-star rank and has not been used since WWII.)

The commandant asked, "How so?"

Andy said, "My brother is his aide. It's all worked out; all you have to do is officially invite the admiral."

Below is an excerpt from Rear Admiral Redd's speech.

"Let me give you a real world example which is close to home – a VMI cadet from the class of 1988, now a Navy lieutenant. In the last year he has traveled in nine countries, four continents, three oceans, six seas, five gulfs, and four fjords. One year ago, on a frigate in the Pacific, he participated in the largest victory at sea – ever –in the drug war, confiscating almost six thousand pounds of cocaine en-route the United States. That's over half a billion dollars worth on the street. Three months later he was on an aircraft carrier in the Persian Gulf. As a member of the staff of the commander of Battle Force Zulu, he stood watch in the nerve center of the largest combatant ship in the world, the *USS Dwight D. Eisenhower*. As a watch officer, he personally directed the ships and aircraft of the most powerful naval force at sea anywhere in the world in the intense post-war environment of Desert Storm Operations. Pretty impressive stuff for a twenty-six-year-old lieutenant. That officer, incidentally, is Lieutenant Sam Tate whose brother Andy is being commissioned here today."

Sam administered the commissioning oath to Andy.

It was providence that Major General Robert Buethe, USAF, MC, Deputy Surgeon General, was the Air Force commissioning officer. He was the USAFE Deputy Surgeon when we were at Ramstein, and Shirley was a close friend of his wife.

Jim Richardson published in 1989 his photographic reflection *Virginia Military Institute, The Spirit*. On pages 74-75 is a contemplative Cadet Andy Tate at his study carrel in Preston Library. I had the honor of sewing his academic stars on his uniform just before his graduation parade.

INTERVIEWS

I interviewed in practices in Dublin, Roanoke, Northern VA, the Shenandoah Valley, and Hampton Roads. I made an appointment with Dr. John T. Wise to interview at his Westwood Animal Hospital in Staunton, VA, about a hundred and twenty miles from Blacksburg. I was halfway there when I realized I left my wallet at home. It was a mixed animal practice with four veterinarians and looking for a fifth. Dr. Wise was on a farm call when I arrived, so another vet showed me around. I observed surgery on a goat. Dr. Wise called and said for me to go to the Country Kitchen down the street, order lunch, and he would meet me there. I ate lunch, and Dr. Wise still had not arrived when the hostess brought me the bill. I was embarrassed. I explained I was supposed to meet Dr. Wise and I had forgotten my wallet. She said okay and left me sitting there. I was thinking I was going to be dead meat if Dr. Wise didn't show up. Much to my relief, he did. He ate his lunch as we talked. He was looking for someone to do mostly small animal work but who could fill in on large animals when needed. We decided that the position might not be a good fit for me. He paid for lunch and thanked me for coming. I thanked him for lunch and his consideration. Although I didn't get the position, John and I worked together on the VVMA board when he was president, and we see each other every year at the VVMA Conference.

I was in Woodbridge, VA, when Dr. William P. Knox called and offered me a position at York Veterinary Hospital in Yorktown, VA. He wanted me to cover his practice while he and Joyce were gone for two weeks. He said we could live in his house. Joyce was the sister of Harvey Philips from our work with ticks at ODU. Then we could move to Yorktown and the position would be full-time. My contract with Dr. Knox included one continuing education course to meet the VA license renewal requirements. I chose an off shore course that included sites in Puerto Rico, St. John, Cancun, and Cozumel. We were in Cancun when Desert Storm started on January 17, 1991. I worked for Dr. Knox until I purchased Deer Park Animal Hospital in December 1991.

In January 1992, I received a letter from the Military Personnel Center (MPC), Randolph AFB, TX requesting for retired environment health officers to volunteer to be recalled to active duty. Retired military members are subject to recall for up to ten years after their retirement date. I figured if I volunteer I could be assigned to Langley AFB to back fill the position for the officer deployed to the Middle East. I responded that I would volunteer if it included automatic promotion to lieutenant colonel. That was the last I heard from MPC.

MATCH MADE FROM HEAVEN

Shirley died October 4, 1997, of metastatic breast cancer after an eight-year battle. Margaret "Marty" Griggs, her Bible study leader, was with us the last hours. Both Sam and Andy were stationed in California and had come home with their families a month before when it looked like the end, but their visit seemed to renew her strength. Both did get emergency leave to attend the funeral. My veterinary colleagues kept my practice running for two weeks without charge. Marty Griggs had a ministry of taking meals to people, and she kept me well supplied. Marty sort of adopted me as a brother. She and husband George, a retired AF medical doctor, had me over for dinner frequently.

Our cancer support group counselor steered me to a grief support group. I tried it a couple times. I was the youngest person and one of only two males among a bunch of widows looking for a husband. About February 1998 I confided in Marty that I was ready for female companionship. She gave me the address and phone number of her younger widowed sister, Dianne. I knew about Marty's family because Shirley often shared their prayer requests with me.

My first letter to Dianne contained a photo of all the Tate men at my sister Lou's wedding, writing that I was the one on the end but didn't say which end. I also wrote that I would be going to the Officers Christian Fellowship retreat center, White Sulphur Springs, Bedford, PA, for Easter and would be stopping at Arlington National Cemetery where my parents were buried and could meet for lunch somewhere. We met at the Orleans House across from Arlington Cemetery (it's no longer there). I brought a family photo album, and we talked for about two hours. She gave me a tape on grief by her pastor and an Easter bag full of goodies I couldn't eat. On the flip side of the tape was a speech given at Cherrydale Baptist Church by Brigadier General Graves, an OCF member I was acquainted with. Our dates back and forth included Yorktown and VA Beach on July 4th and a moonlight Potomac River dinner cruise on the *Spirit of Washington* on Labor Day weekend. I took a photo of Dianne with her "yacht" in the background. In October we went to White Sulphur Springs (WSS) for volunteer's period. Our project was to finish painting the suite of rooms dedicated to Shirley. At dawn on Saturday, October 3, I proposed to Dianne at the picnic pond. She said yes. We announced our engagement at breakfast with all the volunteers.

We talked about getting married in June when Sam and Andy would be reassigned to the East Coast. Our friends advised us we weren't getting any younger and that we were getting married, not my sons. We settled on February 4, 1999, based on my clinic schedule. The wedding was at Cherrydale Baptist Church in Arlington. Guests included Dianne's sisters and spouses, my brother and his wife, my cousin, Katie Buethe, several of Dianne's church friends, her best friend Sheila, boss, and the staff from WSS.

Dianne's sisters did all the arranging and organized the reception in Dianne's condo. We honeymooned at the Parsonage B&B in St. Michaels, MD. Katie Buethe had given us a big fruit basket with lots of cheese and crackers, and Dianne's sisters gave us money, which came in handy. We had a commuter marriage until Rob graduated from high school, and he lived in the condo until it was time to go to James Madison University.

In February 2021, we celebrated twenty-two years of marriage!!

DEER PARK

Deer Park Animal Hospital was one of three "shops" in a small strip mall on J. Clyde Blvd. in Newport News. We did grooming and boarding in addition to medicine and surgery. I operated it for thirteen years. I didn't make much money, but I kept six women employed part-time and assisted one in completing veterinary technician's school. My dad said my contributing to the economy was a redeeming quality. My military retirement was what kept us afloat. I served on the emergency clinic board of directors, vice president for one year, and treasurer of the Greater Peninsula Veterinary Association (GPVMA) for six years. I was appointed to represent the GPVMA on the VMMA board of directors, which I'm still serving to the present day.

Clare and John Hubbard were among my best clients. They raised and trained English Mastiffs. All their dogs were named for English poets. Their first dog to be a patient of mine was Tennyson. He was two hundred and twenty-five pounds. He participated in a TV show where dogs run an obstacle course. The last event is to knock down all the towers. All Tennyson had to do was walk though and all the towers fell.

When people would ask what type of practice I had I would respond, "I limit my practice to cats under twenty-five and dogs less than two hundred and twenty-five pounds." When Byron became my patient I had to change my saying to "dogs less than two hundred and fifty pounds." Byron had several skills. He was a trained rescue tracker. His certification was done on the Yorktown Battle-field. The scent track was made by a leather glove. Clare was working with Byron on a twenty-foot leash. Byron found the glove and ate it before Clare could get to him. The judge would not certify Byron because there was no proof he had found the glove. Fortunately for Bryon, he passed the glove two days later, Clare took it to the judge in a baggie. Byron was certified as a tracker.

His other skill was pulling a cart for the patients at the Children's Hospital of the King's Daughters. Byron entered Deer Park one day and immediately crawled under a chair in the waiting room. He stood up with the chair on his back like a howdah on an elephant.

Clare called to say Byron had been vomiting for two days. I palpated his abdomen and it was painful. I did a barium GI X-ray series. He had a blockage in his small intestine. I took him to Pine Meadow Hospital where we could operate with Byron on the horse table. We found a rolled up pair of socks.

I attempted to list the practice with national companies that dealt in prac-tice sales but none would do so because it was not profitable. Dr. Gary Farwell, a veterinarian doing relief work at Freed Animal Hospital and fellow AF vet-erinarian, called me at eight o'clock one morning in 2003.

"Sam, are you still interested in selling your practice?"

"Yes, why?"

Gary said, "I might have a buyer for you. Let's meet for lunch."

At ten o'clock Dr. John Freed called, "Sam, I hear you are selling your practice. What are you planning on doing afterwards?"

"I am not sure, I may have to help Dianne with her organizing business," I said.

John asked, "Would you consider coming to work for us? Can you meet at my house tonight?"

"Sure."

What was going on? Within two hours I got a bite on the sale of the clinic and a potential offer for a full time position. I found out at a lunch that Dr. Farwell was financially backing Dr. John Savell to buy Deer Park. Dr. Savell was at the end of his five-year contract with Dr. Freed and wanted to operate his own practice. I met with Dr. Freed and Dr. Carolyn Kutzer that evening and accepted their position. So John Savell and I essentially changed positions. Dr. John Freed, my "Little Brother" from MSU died June 2021.

FINDER

The owner of Pet Cremation asked me if I would make a house call for euthanasia. It was a twenty-seven-year-old Irish setter that was featured in the *Daily Press* the year before about the dog's twenty-sixth birthday. In that article, the owner had bragged that Finder had never been to the veterinarian and was very healthy. I was very curious to see in what condition Finder would be. Here is the *Daily Press* article about Finder's end.

27-YEAR-OLD DOG'S LIFE ENDS
Owner ends pet's pain and suffering.
By A. J. Plunkett (Daily Press)

HAMPTON
Finder, the dog who found longevity in the love of a good owner, died Friday. He was 27 years, one month and two days old – the equivalent of 145 years of humans. For three days, Finder had been shunning his food, apparently trying to starve himself to death, said Dee Copley owner of the Irish setter who gained fame and several fans a year ago when the Daily Press wrote about the dog's 26th birthday.

Copley said she couldn't stand to see her longtime companion suffer. "Today I said that's it my friend," Copley said. She called Dr. Sam Tate, veterinarian at Deer Park Animal Hospital, and asked that he make a house call.

Tate administered the fatal dose of sedative to Finder as the dog was stretched out on his favorite couch, Copley nearby patting Finder's head as he went to sleep for the final time.

The dog suffered from arthritis in his legs and cataracts in his eyes, but had no other health problems. In the end, she thinks it was just too much for the proud animal not to be able to care of himself.

After the Daily Press wrote about Finder, Copley said she got several calls from fellow pet lovers and Finder even got a few birthday cards. While record books show dogs as old as 29 years, it is rare for dogs to live as long as Finder, animal experts have said.

Finder will be cremated and his remains returned to Copley, she said. "Wherever I am," she said, "his remains will be."

Sadly, the rosy picture the owner painted was not reality. Finder's emaciated body was crawling with fleas. His teeth were rotten, his breath was urinemic (smelled like urine), and his gums were pale. He had the classic symptoms of kidney failure. In kidney failure, urea builds up in the blood stream. It suppressed the production of red blood cells in the bone marrow and the patient becomes anemic. The urea also stimulates the vomiting center and suppressed the appetite center in the brain. The body starts cannibalizing muscle for a protein source. It is a terrible wasting process and not humane for a "natural death." I couldn't help but think that his quality of life could have been better if he had received proper veterinary care all those years. But I kept my thought to myself.

PETS

"Dr. Tate, do you have any pets?" I get that question a lot, including today, July 20, 2020, by a nurse at the health department. People assume a veterinarian has pets. My reply is that I have a forty-two year old cat. I pause to let the statement sink in. Then I continue, "My cat is very low maintenance. I don't have to change its litter pan nor feed it either." It now dawns on them that I am not talking about a live cat. It's a ceramic cat my grandmother gave me for Christmas 1978. She said, "Every veterinarian should have a cat."

When I was a teenager, we had beagles that we trained for rabbit hunting. The first one was Elvis because he was *"ain't nothing but a hound dog."* Then dad got Bell from a hunting buddy. Bell was already pregnant. We kept two of her puppies and named one "Doc," for Dr. Ward, and the other Elvis Junior, Junior for short. We hunted mostly in the Black Water River area of Princess Anne County, now Virginia Beach. My dad lived there with his Uncle Dan and Aunt Hagar after his parents died in February 1936 of the flu.

I don't remember what happened to Elvis, Bell, and Doc, but Junior died of heartworm disease during my first year at MSU.

Then there was Cubby, short for Cub Scout. I bought him from the ranger at Boy Scout camp in Charleston, SC, in 1977. Cubby's mother was a Brittany spaniel and his father was a fence jumper. Cubby traveled with us to Woodbridge, VA, Germany, Goldsboro, NC, Blacksburg, and Yorktown, VA. In 1989, he developed kidney failure, and I had to put him to sleep. I had him cremated and planted a tree in the backyard over his ashes.

Just about the time we were getting used to not stepping on Cubby when we got out of bed, Oxford came into our lives. It was early Thanksgiving morning. Sam knocked on our bedroom door. "Dad, you need to come down to the garage." Sam was home on leave from the Surface Warfare Officer School in Newport, R.I. My thought was that he had an accident with his car. Wrapped in his Navy bridge coat was a beagle. He found the injured beagle on the US 17 just south of Fredericksburg, VA, and just couldn't leave it there. We took the dog to the hospital where I was working. He had multiple lacerations but no broken bones. I surmised he had been attacked by another dog. I patched him up and we named him Oxford for Oxford University in England where both Sam and Andy had attended in the summer abroad program at VMI.

Millie came to us in December 1990 by way of the Animal Aid Society. I owned Deer Park Animal Hospital and provided discounted services for them. Millie was found on the side of Interstate 64 near Williamsburg and was taken by a good Samaritan to a local veterinary hospital. She had a hunt club collar with her name as Millie. The hunt club didn't want to pay to have her broken front leg repaired, so she ended up at Animal Aid. I agreed to fix the fracture if I could adopt her.

I called them my FORD Beagles. People would say they never heard of that breed. I would reply, "Found on the Road Dead. It was a good thing they were a year apart because if it had been the same time, I may not have gotten the right parts on the right dog."

There is a procedure called reverse inheritance. My dad inherited Junior when I went to MSU. He inherited Cinnamon and Pepper when my sister, Lou, joined the Navy. Sam asked me, "Dad, Amy and I are thinking about getting a dog. What breed do you recommend?"

Pointing to Oxford, I replied, "What about this dog?"

Sam said, "Dad, Oxford has lived with you for ten years, don't you think he's yours now?" Reverse inheritance. Well, they adopted Joseph and Jillian and never did get a dog.

Dianne and I married in February 1999 and agreed that when Millie and Oxford died, we would not get any more dogs. Well, Oxford's cataracts progressed to total blindness. His kidneys failed and I put him to sleep. Millie developed both heart and kidney failure, and I put her to sleep a year after Oxford.

Whenever the staff of a clinic where I was working would say, "Dr. Tate, look at this cute beagle. He has only one ear, it will be hard to find a home for him. Can't you take him?"

I said, "Sorry, I have a prenuptial agreement." (The *Daily Press* printed a similar quote in the article below.)

Prior to COVID-19, Dianne and I traveled a lot, including overseas, and we didn't have to board any dogs. Besides, I can always pet someone else's dogs.

Then there was the shaggy dog. Dianne's sister and her husband were moving to Phoenix after living in Poquoson for twenty-five years. Dianne conducted a garage sale in our driveway to help them get rid of some of their stuff. One of the items was a stuffed shaggy toy dog. It sat on its haunches with it front paws in a begging position. We placed him at the end of the driveway with a sign reading, "Free to a good home." He was still there at the end of the sale. So along with the other items the Salvation Army wouldn't take, we put the shaggy dog in a dumpster around the corner. The next day, we were walking Millie and Oxford and passed the dumpster. I looked in. Everything was still there, but the shaggy dog was gone. He found a good home.

MEDICAL RESERVE CORPS (MRC)

I joined the MRC in the spring of 2006. The Peninsula MRC unit's mission is to augment and assist existing community operations during large-scale emergencies, aid in the response to pressing health care needs, improve community emergency preparedness, and build community resilience. The MRC service area is the cities of Hampton, Newport News, and Williamsburg the counties of James City and York, and the town of Poquoson.

I was given the position of volunteer coordinator for veterinary activities and conducted twenty free rabies clinics vaccinating 3,839 dogs and cats. I served as team leader for point of dispensing (POD) in a federal mandated nuclear power plant exercise, support volunteer for flu and back to school vaccination clinics, and COVID-19 call center, and contact tracing. I represented the health department on the Peninsula Disaster Pet Shelter Planning Working Group, and was a Member National MRC Working Group. I was selected to attend the 2009 Integrated Medical, Public Health, Preparedness and Response Training Summit in Dallas, Texas.

I have been a guest instructor at two local high school veterinary assistant programs speaking about zoonotic diseases and disaster preparedness. I did two presentations each day. My goal was that the students I instructed before lunch would not desire to eat lunch, and the ones who met after lunch would wish they had not eaten lunch.

I was the recipient of the following awards:

- MRC 2006 Emergency Preparedness Excellence Award
- MRC Volunteer of the Year 2008, 2012
- MRC Instructor of the Month July 2008
- VA Citizen Corps Superstar Award 2010
- Nominated by MRC for Daily Press Citizen of the Year 2012

I was not selected for Citizen of the Year. However, the *Daily Press* did a feature article on each of the nominees that ran at a later date.

VET SQUARED

RETIRED VETERINARIAN STILL CARES FOR PETS
York's Samuel Tate stays busy in his retirement Working for animal safety
By JENNIFER L. WILLIAMS

Samuel Tate spent his career caring for animals, and now in retirement he works constantly to figure out ways to save them as well. Tate is a prominent face statewide in the area of disaster preparedness for animals. Studies show people are much more likely to evacuate in advance of a storm or in case of a disaster if they can take their pets with them, Tate said.

"I approach the issue from a public health standpoint," Tate said. "The thing is one, if people can't take their pets in an evacuation – particularly people who are transportation dependent – if they can't get on the bus with their dog or their cat, they're not going to evacuate. And then if you don't have a place where they can take their animal, they're not going to evacuate. So that's the public health, public safety side of the issue is getting people to evacuate when they're told to evacuate."

The York County resident serves as Director of the Greater Peninsula Veterinary Medical Association and on the board of directors of the Virginia State Animal Response Team.

He volunteers with the Peninsula Medical Reserve Corps, speaking at events and since 2009 has been in charge of more than 10 free rabies clinics conducted in low-income areas of the Peninsula.

VASART has established pet shelter operations for emergencies statewide including Hampton and Newport News, and Tate is currently working with the team, starting it in York County.

"Dr. Tate's fortitude and passion for animal welfare in and around Hampton Roads has made our communities a stronger, safer, and healthier community," Teresa Blakeslee, Peninsula Medical Reserve Corps coordinator, wrote in an email.

"I am very thankful to have such a dedicated, insightful volunteer serving with the Peninsula Medical Reserve Corps."

After completing veterinary school Tate spent 20 years as an Air Force

Veterinarian and then owned and operated Deer Park Animal Hospital in Newport News for 15 years. Starting in 2007, he used his military and veterinary training to advice on matters of preparedness for pets evacuated with their owners in case of large-scale disasters.

"I volunteer at different various levels, both the local and the state, Tate said. "We're developing disaster pet shelters in conjunction with human shelters, then we are able to accommodate their pets there."

Tate, 71, received the Peninsula MRC Community Emergency Preparedness Excellence Award for 2006, 2007 and 2012 MRC Volunteer of the Year, the 2008 Virginia Veterinary Service Award and the 2010 Virginia Citizen Corps Superstar Award.

He doesn't see animal as patients anymore, and doesn't even have any at home, though dogs are his favorite and he had cats as a child.

"My wife made me promise that once the two beagles I had died, I wouldn't get anymore," Tate said.

RELIEF VET

I worked for Dr. Kutzer full time on an annual contract for two years. Dianne and I decided to apply for the Hampton Roads area representative position with OCF. I changed my practice status to relief work so that I was not tied to a contract if we were selected. It also gave me the flexibility to help Dianne with major projects in her WORK OR DI business.

After eighteen months of delays and deliberation by OCF we were not selected for the position, but we remained in the volunteer roles supporting the area rep.

I was working some clinics one or two weeks at a time all over the Hampton Roads. I got tired of the tunnel traffic and cut back to Freed and Armistead one day a week each. They were both in Hampton and only two miles apart. Dr. Gary Farwell was also working both hospitals on different days. Both hospitals provided service to the Hampton Animal Control. I was working at Freed's when they brought in a mature female pit bull with a festering wound from the shoulder to the elbow. I gave an estimated of six hundred dollars for treatment.

The vet tech said, "Dr. Tate, they won't approve that. They have a two hundred dollar limit."

"Yes they will."

"Why?" she asked.

I explained, "Because it's me doing the treatment."

"Why are you so sure?"

"Because the last four animals they brought in I had to euthanized at $50 each, thus saving them six hundred, which they can now spend on this dog."

The Animal Control Office called and said, "Dr. Tate, we got approval to treat."

CHOW

Chow was an adult male mix-breed Chow Chow. He had been a patient at Freed Animal Hospital for several years. His visits were for annual physical exams, vaccines, heart worm and intestinal parasite tests. He was brought to the hospital with severe bleeding from the mouth at about three in the afternoon. His owners told me that their home had been burglarized. One of the items stolen was a hand gun, which was apparently used to shoot Chow. My examination revealed a groove-like laceration the length of the tongue and an exit wound just caudal (rear) of the mandible (jaw bone). I sedated Chow with an inter-muscular injection in order to place an IV and intubated him to start gas anesthesia. I sutured close the wound in his tongue which stopped the bleeding. I flushed the exit wound and left it open to drain. I turned off the gas anesthesia and removed the tracheal tube as he was waking up. I had not anticipated what happened next. He started having difficulty breathing due to swelling in the pharynx. I could not get the tracheal tube back in past the swelling. We turned Chow over on his back and I performed a tracheotomy. We did not have a tracheotomy tube so I used a standard tracheal tube instead. Since it was closing time for the hospital, I called the emergency veterinary clinic and transferred Chow there. Unfortunately, he died during the night.

A Hampton police detective interviewed me the next day. He wanted to know the extent of Chow's injuries and if they were consistent with a gunshot wound. I stated that they were. I also suggested how they could catch the burglar.

"Issue a press release stating that in the course of the dog's treatment, he bite someone. Since he died, he tested positive for rabies. Then wait for someone to show up at the emergency room wanting treatment for rabies."

The detective replied, "We can't issue that kind of misinformation."

The *Daily Press* carried an article about the incident. The owners were quoted as saying how gentle Chow was. It was not my place to contradict them in their grief. Besides, some dogs can be very nice at home and be very difficult in the hospital.

RACCOON

I was performing relief services at Armistead Avenue Animal Hospital. A Hampton Animal Control Officer (ACO) brought in a raccoon in a wire transport cage. It obviously had a broken rear leg, probably having been hit by a car.

I asked, "Do you know what is wrong with this raccoon?"

The officer said, "You are the vet. You tell me."

"I'll tell you what is wrong with it. Someone did not run over it enough to kill it. Now you bring it to me to kill it."

Sometimes a little levity relieves the stress of having to euthanize an animal, but not with an owner.

I continued to do relief work two days a week until my seventieth birthday in December 2011, at which time I was not retired but "no longer gainfully employed."

EMERGENCY RESPONSE

My first experience in Virginia with hurricane response and recovery was with Hurricane Isabel on September 2003. Isabel churned through the Caribbean as a category 5 hurricane. It stalled off the East Coast for several days, during which the Hampton Roads was pounded by northeast winds reaching 105 miles per hour and producing a storm surge of seven to eight feet. The storm surge caused extensive flooding in the Hampton Roads. There was two to three feet of water in the buildings on Langley AFB and the runway was awash with water. Isabel made landfall on the North Carolina Outer Banks as a category 2 hurricane on September 18. There was a mandatory evacuation of low areas of the Hampton Roads including Langley AFB and Bethel Manor military housing. Captain Erick and Jicks Wallman, a couple we were mentoring, evacuated to Camp Pickett in Blackstone, VA.

Eric and Jicks returned before base housing was cleared for occupancy. They arrived at our house before attempting to get into Bethel Manor. Although we had no electricity, we had natural gas for cooking and hot water. We told them they could stay with us if they could not get into their quarters. They returned about a half hour later. Jicks said, "Mother, there was a young enlisted family at the gate that has nowhere to stay. They have a little boy and the mother is pregnant. Do you think they can stay here for a couple of days?"

We had a guest room with a double bed, a hide-a- bed sofa in the living room, and a coach in the sunroom. So, we said go get them. Eric said, "They are outside in their car." So, we had a full house for three or four days.

Freed Animal Hospital had several pecan trees on the property that had been blown down, blocking the parking lot and dog exercise yard. I took Erick with me to help Dr. Kutzer clear the parking lot. We used snow shovels to pick up the immature pecans still in their green husks. Dr. Kutzer had a brand new chainsaw. I checked the chain oil reservoir; it was empty, and Dr. Kutzer had not bought any chain oil. I went to Home Depot to get some and was back in about an hour. I put the oil in the saw and pulled the starter cord - nothing. I tried several more times - nothing. I opened the gas tank - empty.

I asked Erick, "I thought you filled the gas tank while I was gone?"

Erick said, "I thought you filled it before you left."

Dr. Kutzer asked, "How did you two ever make it in the Air Force?"

I was still doing relief work at Freed's in August 2011 when Hurricane Irene threatened VA. I received an activation notice from the Medical Reserve Corps (MRC). I called the coordinator for my assignment. I was to report to the Grafton High School to be the leader of the pet shelter team. I arrived at the school to find that not only was I the leader, I was the team. The pet shelter equipment was stored in two pods. One had been delivered from the storage yard, but it didn't have the items we needed first to set up the shelter. Two more MRC volunteers, who had practiced shelter set up with me before, arrived. We finally got the other pod about ten o'clock that evening. The county

EMT supervisor was my neighbor, and he assigned two firemen to help. We got the pet shelter set up in one hour.

It wasn't until the next day when the storm got closer that we received some animals - two cats and two dogs from two families. I asked one owner if his animals were on any medication. He went pale.

I asked, "What's the matter?"

He said, "I forgot my insulin."

He had arrived in a taxi, so the EMTs took him back to his trailer in an ambulance to get his insulin.

VIRGINIA STATE ANIMAL RESPONSE TEAM (VASART)

When I started getting involved in disaster planning for pets, there would be people at meetings boasting about their participation on the Gulf Coast in response to Hurricane Katrina. Although they had good intentions, they self deployed, which is no longer allowed. They would ask me what disaster had I responded to.

My reply was, "The last disaster I responded to was called a war."

Hurricane Katrina in August 2005 followed by Rita in September were quintessential events that raised the nation's consonance to the plight of animals in disasters. The PETS Act of October 2006, enacted by congress, authorized "FEMA to provide rescue, care, shelter, and essential needs for individuals with household pets and service animal following a major disaster or emergency." Virginia passed its own legislation effective July 1, 2007 directing VDEM to "develop an emergency response plan to address the needs of individuals with household pets and service animals in event of a disaster and assistant and coordinate with local agencies in developing such plans."

The Memorandum of Understanding (MOU) between Virginia Veterinary Medical Association (VVMA), Virginia Federation of Humane Societies (VFHS), and the Commonwealth of Virginia (Virginia Department of Agriculture and Consumer Services (VDACS) and Virginia Department of Emergency Management (VDEM), and Virginia- Maryland College of Veterinary

Medicine (VMCVM)) was signed on November 15, 2006. The purpose of the agreement was to establish a unified and broad scope coordinated assistance in establishing pet-friendly human shelters and facilities that will accept pets in response to the Governor's declaration of a state of emergency. The VVMA was to take the lead in establishing the state animal response team (SART). I was the signatory for the VVMA.

Dr. Don Butts was the emergency coordinator for VDACS and former state veterinarian. We had served together in the AF. He called and wanted my help with a plan to deal with the evacuation of owners and pets from the Hampton Roads. I sent an email to the heads of all state agencies and non-governmental organizations as potential stakeholders requesting a meeting to be held at VDEM. I specifically stated that I had no authority to neither request such a meeting nor task any agency but that I was only trying to help Dr. Butts. Well, that created such a stir that VDEM set a date and hosted the meeting after clarification from Dr. Butts. In two months the state pet shelter task force completed the Commonwealth of Virginia Pet Evacuation and Shelter Plan and sent to the governor for signature in May 2007.

VASART held its initial training summit August 2-3, 2007 in Richmond, VA, facilitated by the NCSART, which originated the SART program in 1999 after Hurricane Floyd. VASART was now officially established and ready to roll. I assumed duties of secretary from the executive director in January 2008.

The thought crossed my mind in early 2008 that what I had been doing in disaster preparedness was the kind of activities the VVMA gives an award for. A committee selects the recipient in November, and it's a secret until the presentation at the annual conference in February. I was packing for the conference and asked Dianne if I should take my sport jacket or my suit. She said my suit. That light bulb went on again. It came the night of the awards banquet, and Sam and his family showed up with the story that they were in Charlottesville and decided to drive to Roanoke (120 miles). Then my brother Stratton and his wife showed up from VA Beach (295 miles). The VVMA presented me with the 2008 Service Award.

VASART hosted Noah's Wish in-field training and VDACS first pet shelter exercise at the Rockingham County Fair Grounds June 27-28, 2009. I was seated at picnic table for lunch with Dr. Butts and Dr. Wilkes, the state veterinarian, when the commissioner of agriculture asked me, "Dr. Tate, what is your role in all this?"

I said, "I am an unpaid employee of VDACS. When Dr. Butts doesn't have the funds to hire someone, he calls me?"

I thought both Drs. Wilkes and Butts would choke on their sandwiches.

VASART mission includes assisting localities in establishing community animal response teams (CART). I have participated in the organization and training of seventeen pet shelter teams, eleven of which are CARTs. These teams have responded by operating pet shelters in eight declared state of emergency since 2008. VA has been able to obtain Homeland Security grants to purchase thirty-nine pet shelter supply trailers.

VASART was also proactive in dealing with livestock in disaster by hosting seven technical large animal emergency rescue (TLAER) courses in three years. The program instructed firemen and other first responders how to adapt the rescue equipment and techniques they use for human rescues to animal rescues.

I have been a speaker on disaster preparedness for many organizational conference including VVMA, Virginia Federation of Humane Societies, Virginia Association of Animal Control and Care, VA VOAD, VA State Employees Disaster Preparedness Expo, U.S. Navy Disaster Preparedness Expo, USDA Disaster Preparedness Expo, D.C. Council of Governments, and US Justice Department. I have also served as an augmentee to emergency support function 11 (agriculture) in the VA Emergency Operation Center.

VETS WITH A MISSION (VWAM) 2013

Colonel Doug Braendel and I met in Germany in the 1980s. He was stationed at the US Army Medical Center, Landstuhl, while I was at Ramstein. We served in the Boy Scouts and attended chapel and Officers Christian Fellowship (OCF) together. He and Cammie moved to Manns Choice, PA, when he retired from the army. We would see them often when we attended the OCF Retreat Center at White Sulphur Springs. He convinced me to return to Vietnam with him on a medical mission sponsored by VWAM in June-July 2013. VWAM was started in 1998 by a group of Vietnam veterans to promote reconciliation with the Vietnamese people and emotional healing of veterans through humanitarian medical missions. The team assembled in San Francisco and flew to Ho Chi Minh City (Saigon). There we had two days to acclimate and sightsee.

The first day we looked for sites around Bien Hoa where Doug had been stationed. Our guide was Sergeant Phong, a former soldier in the Army of the Republic of Vietnam (ARVN), who Doug met on previous trips. I was amazed at the change in the countryside. What was once wide open space between Saigon and Bien Hoa now was urban sprawl as if the two cities had become one. What had been a large US Army and USAF base at Bien Hoa had been developed into a huge industrial park. Sergeant Phong told us that much of the clothing for export was made there. I thought of the hiking boots I was wearing that I bought in Montana. Doug was using a topographic map from the 1960s to locate sites. We found where the Black Horse Regiment had its base. But it was now an active Vietnamese Army base and a restricted area.

The next day, Sergeant Phong took us by hydrofoil down the Saigon River to Vung Tau, where I had attended the 7th AF Medical Conference, and Doug served with an evacuation hospital. The former site of the hospital is now a commercial heliport. Just down the street was the house where Doug was billeted. We also visited the Grand Hotel, Back Beach, and the lighthouse. We had pizza at the "Good Morning, Vietnam" restaurant (named for the 1987 movie starring Robin Williams). We returned to Saigon in time to meet Chuck Ward, Executive Director of VMAM, and Dr. Bill Jenkins at the roof top restaurant of the Rex Hotel. There we were, four Vietnam veterans where the "Five o'clock Follies," the briefing for foreign correspondents, were held during the war.

The next morning, the team flew to Da Nang where we stayed at the five-star Furama Resort on China Beach. We had the rest of the day off to enjoy the beach and the pool. That evening, we met for a briefing on how the clinics would be conducted and received our assignments. Doug and I were in patient services. It was our job to provide security and to facilitate patient flow.

Actually this was my third trip to Da Nang. My first trip was on an aeromedical evacuation flight in March 1968. A C-130 squadron at Tuy Hoa provided the aircraft and air crew for the in-country air-evac for the northern sector. The Da Nang detachment of the 903rd Aero-Medical Evacuation Squadron provided the flight nurses and technicians. Their daily mission started at Tuy Hoa. They would pickup patients at Phu Cut and unload them at Da Nang. They then preceded north Hue/Phu Bai, Quang Tri, and Dang Hoi. They would unload those patients at Da Nang, pick up a fresh medical crew, and return to Tuy Hoa. The medical crew would spend the night in our dispensary and repeat the cycle the next day. They always welcomed other medics to ride along to help with patients. It was a convenient way to get to the base exchange at Da Nang. Technical Sergeant McGuire and I did just that. I do not remember what I bought. But I do remember the female Viet Cong patient we helped.

My second trip to Da Nang was with Captain Dan Adona to get an R&R flight to Hong Kong mentioned in "Uniform Snafu."

Our first clinic was in Hoa Hai, a southern district of Da Nang just beyond Marble Mountain. It was a two-story building. We conducted our clinic on the second floor while the Vietnamese medical staff conducted a well baby clinic on the ground floor. Our main purpose was to find patients to whom we could provide life-changing procedures, specifically heart surgeries. In order to do so, we had to screen whomever the local council sent to us. So, we saw a lot of older adults with aches and pains who usually were dispensed non-steroidal, anti-inflammatory medication. We did identify three children who needed heart surgery, paid for by VWAM at the Hue University Hospital. Eyeglasses were dispensed to those who needed them and everybody received dental care information and a toothbrush kit. We did not have a dentist on this team, so no dental procedures were performed.

Our interpreters were a special group and half of them were Christians. Some had even chosen interesting nicknames like "Typhoon" (Thuong) and "Porcupine" (Hanh). Linh worked in the pharmacy. Tammy, a Vietnamese-American student nurse, was my interpreter. Then there was "Bond, James Bond." We shared a seat on the van one day. He was listening to music with his iPod. He asked me what kind of music I liked. I replied, "Traditional hymns like 'Amazing Grace.'" I proceeded to tell him the story of John Newton who was the captain of a slave ship before becoming a Christian and Anglican clergyman. The next morning, James had "Amazing Grace" on his iPod. He wore a T-shirt, the first day of clinic, printed with, "Let Me Tell You About Jesus." He did not wear it again. I think Chuck asked him not to wear it out of concern that the secret police would intervene in some way.

Several times we were visited by men in civilian shirts and slacks who looked around and then asked to be examined. They were the local secret police. We learned that agents were interviewing our patients after they left the clinic to see if we were handing out bibles or telling the patients about Jesus.

Two pediatric cases stand out. The first as a six-year-old boy that had a treatable viral infection as an infant, but without treatment, he was mentally disabled. The second was eight year old Phuoc who developed hydrocephalus (water on the brain) because he did not receive a shunt as an infant. The team spent three days at Hoa Hai Clinic.

The team then had a four-day weekend off. Chuck Ward pre-arranged a guide and driver for Doug and me to go to Tuy Hoa, two hundred miles south of Da Nang, to where I was stationed. One thing that impressed me was how one town was connected to the next by a thin ribbon of buildings on each side of the road with rice paddies behind them. The thatched and corrugate tin roofed huts of the 1960s were replaced by three and four-story buildings. On the ground floor were various kinds of businesses, while the upper floors were living quarters. That was the pattern I saw throughout the cities and towns. But what impressed me the most on our road trip was rice spread out on the verge of blacktop road to dry. It was the practice even in the towns. Is that why one should wash the rice before cooking?

Doug and I shared a room at the modern four-star hotel, Gen Delux in Tuy Hoa next to a theme park. It boasted of having four theme restaurants, but only one was open because it was the off-season for tourists. We were each given a menu and we discussed what we might order. We soon realized we each had a different menu from one of the four restaurants.

The next day, we crossed over the Da Rang River to see the area of Tuy Hoa Air Base, part of which is the commercial airport, while the rest is a restricted military base. I was able to peer over the stone wall to take a photograph of the concrete air craft revetments that were built after I left in 1968. What had been the refugee village north of the base were now houses as described above. We then proceeded south to Vung Ro Bay. This was the port through which the air base was supplied. I had visited there in 1968 with the Junior Officer Council. We had a rest stop at a Vietnamese Navy Memorial in a small cove. It commemorated the sinking of naval trawler carrying weapons to the Viet Cong on February 16, 1965. On display was a map of the sea borne supply routes prior to 1966. It was here that our guide revealed that his uncle was Viet Cong.

The countryside between Tuy Hoa and Vung Ro Bay had very little development. It was mostly rice paddies and salt ponds. However, the railroad bridges were repaired and the train now runs all the way from Hanoi to Saigon.

On the way back to Tuy Hoa City, I wanted to find the boat builders at Don Toc village where we held our first rabies clinic. They had moved from the bank of Da Rang River to the beach where the river flows into the South China Sea. They were now building the large Ha Long Bay square head fishing boats instead of the small sampans of the 1960s.

I told our guide that on the return trip I wanted to take photographs of water buffaloes. North of Qui Nhon. Highway 1A forks to the right. A few miles further, our driver did a u-turn. I thought maybe we took the wrong fork. The guide said, "No, we are going back for you to photograph water buffaloes."

We drove back about a half a mile to a field with a small herd of buffaloes, which included a couple of calves. I got my photos and we continued north to Da Nang.

The next three days we conducted a clinic at Hoa Hip Nam in the northwest part of Da Nang. Bill Jenkins was our only medical doctor, so we were not able to screen as many patients as we did at Hoa Hai where we had two doctors. It was 104 degrees Fahrenheit on the second day, and we screened 104 patients. I was stationed on the ground floor porch. I bent over to speak to a young woman who brought her grandmother. Just then, my foot broke through the tile floor. Fortunately, I was not hurt and my photo made the VWAM daily blog.

My station was next to where eye glasses were dispensed. The boxes of reading glasses were arranged according to strength. I watched as two well-dressed women were independently fitted with glasses of different optics. After they moved away from the table, they compared frames and traded glasses. The team triaged 403 patients at that clinic.

A VMAM tradition is a banquet on the night before departure. A ceremony is held for the veterans where finches are released representing each veteran releasing any negative emotions about their wartime experience in

Vietnam. The rest of the team wrote phrases of appreciation on the back of our wartime photos that we had sent as part of our applications.

Most of the team departed the next day. Doug remained for a few days to visit with Tony and Cindy Brewer who operated Orphan's Voice Orphanage. Dr. Jenkins remained to be part of the next team. I shared a room with Steve Scott, RN, triage coordinator, overnight in San Francisco. He was able to get an earlier flight to Miami than originally planned. So, he departed before I woke up but left me a note. My flight left an hour before a Boeing 777 from Seoul hit the sea wall and crashed on the runway. Some of the team members who had flights later that day did not get out until the next day. I returned home with a severe case of bronchitis and dehydration and needed treatment in the emergency room. I still have a mild cough as a result.

VWAM 2017

In August 2015, Dianne and I became sponsors for the International Maritime Officers' Course (IMOC 54) at the USCG Training Center Yorktown. We requested the two Vietnamese officers because of my association with Vietnam. We sponsored two more Vietnamese officers in the next class, IMOC 55, in the spring of 2016 and another two that fall in IMOC 56. By that time, I developed a desire to serve on another mission to Vietnam. This time I took Dianne with me. The trip was scheduled for March 17-April 2, 2017 to avoid the heat issues experienced with the previous missions in July.

The east coast team members assembled in Atlanta for the flight to Seoul, Korea, and then onto Da Nang. Again we stayed at the Furama Resort. We had the next day, Sunday, off to recover from the long flight and to acclimate to the time difference. We had emailed Lt. Son Doan Hong Doan, Vietnam Coast Guard, who was one of our first IMOC students, as to when we would be in Da Nang. Son met us at the Furama and took us sightseeing around Da Nang. We stopped at Pham Van Cong Beach to photograph the fishing boats anchored offshore. The next stop was Linh Ung Pagoda and Lady Buddha on Son Tra Mountain (Monkey Mountain to us veterans). The Lady Buddha is a 220-feet tall, white stature that can be seen for miles. Son then drove along Tran Hung Dad Street that parallels the Han River as it flows into Da Nang Bay. We stopped at a spot to photograph the Song Han Bridge (also called the Sail Bridge) and Dragon Bridge. The dragon has a head at both ends and on Friday nights, the heads belch fire from their mouths. Unfortunately, we were not there on a Friday to see it. I did not have the opportunity to see it in 2013 either.

Son then took us to his home to meet his wife, young daughter, and his wife's parents. His wife is a sales representative for a seafood company, has an MBA, and traveled to the US quite often. We sat down to a typical Vietnamese meal of seafood Son's mother-in-law had prepared. We started with pho (a soup). The main dish was a whole baked fish, eyeballs and all. After dinner and conversation, Son drove us back to the Furama.

We left the next day on our road trip to Hue. The team members who had been there before took the express route through the tunnel in the Annamite Range. The rest of us took the scenic route over the Hai Van Pass (ocean cloud pass). At the top is a fourteenth century brick gate. Alongside of it are French fortifications. There is also a war memorial commemorating the victory of the People's Army of Vietnam (PAVN) over the ARVN in 1975 to gain entry into Da Nang. We arrived at the Imperial Hotel in Hue in the afternoon. After a swim in the roof top pool, we went to dinner at the Mandarin Café around the corner from the hotel. It was the unofficial HQ of VWAM in Hue. We ate most of our evening meals there while in Hue. They also catered all our lunches at the clinic sites, even a far away as A Luoi. The café was also the place to drop off our laundry (less expensive than the hotel), buy bottled water, and make tour arrangements. The owner Cu Phan (Mr. Cu) was former ARVN and a world-renowned photographer. Many of his photos are on display in the café.

The hotel provided a private buffet breakfast for us at 5:30 – 6:15 A.M. (No one else would get up that early). We then had devotions and team meeting. We boarded the vans and departed at seven o'clock for the clinic sites about fifty minutes from Hue. We spent two days each at the hamlets of Quang Thai and Quang Loi. The clinic buildings were designed by the US Army Corps of Engineers in 2001 and had plaques in English and Vietnamese stating that fact.

It was at Quang Thai that I started teaching the Vietnamese how to brush their teeth. Dianne wrote an article about it for the *VVMA Town and County Call* Issue 11 summer 2017.

One Health – An Example By Dianne L. Tate

In March, Dr. Sam Tate, of the VVMA Board of Directors, participated in his second medical mission to Vietnam. Being a Vietnam veteran, he was on the team Vets With A Mission; a Christian humanitarian group started by Vietnam veterans and has been serving the people of Vietnam for 29 years.

At the first team meeting in Da Nang, Vietnam, our dental coordinator, Dr. Tom Love, explained that the number one health issue of the Vietnamese people is poor oral hygiene (Fig. 1). Since our dental team of three dentists, three dental assistants, and three Vietnamese dental student interpreters would all be engaged in performing dental procedures, he needed a volunteer to teach oral hygiene. Dr. Tate said as a veterinarian he had taught owners how to brush their pet's teeth, he could certainly teach humans how to brush theirs.

He had to overcome the language barrier because all the interpreters were assigned to other tasks. One interpreter provided the Vietnamese phrase for "after you eat" which in English sounds like "sow key an." He chose a set of chopsticks and a glass to convey the motions of eating followed by actually brushing his teeth. (Fig. 2, 3). He stashed the chopsticks and toothbrush in his sweatband for easy access, which became a real attention-getter (Fig. 4)

The dental team had a toy dragon that Dr. Tate used as a model when teaching children (Fig. 5). Dr. Tate said his greatest satisfaction of the whole mission was when he saw a young boy showing his younger friends how to brush "Dragon's" teeth (fig. 6). Then an amazing thing happened. A young girl started teaching her girlfriends (Fig. 7).

Over the seven day of the clinics Dr. Tate educated 434 patients. Dianne Tate is the wife of Dr. Tate and served in the pharmacy on this mission.

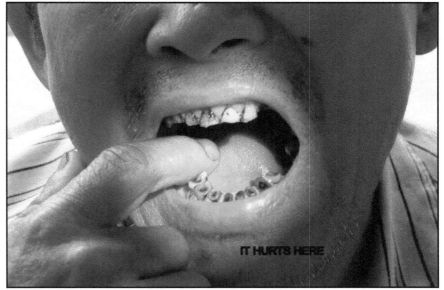

Fig. 1

Fig. 2

Fig. 3

Fig. 4

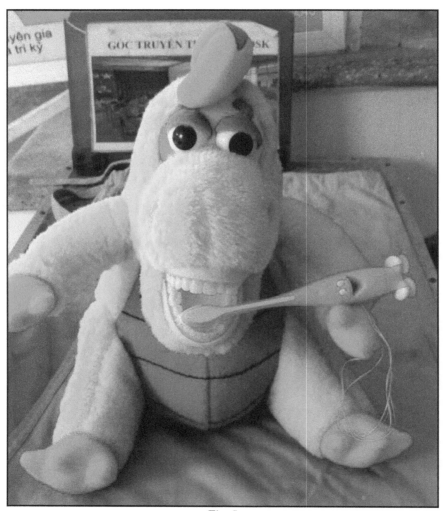

Fig. 5

Fig. 6

Fig. 7

253

A large canopy had been set up in the courtyard, under which was the patient waiting area and triage. Dental procedures were performed in three rooms on the first floor and the pharmacy was in the fourth room at the opposite end. The first floor porch was used as a waiting area for dental patients. That is where I conducted my dental hygiene demonstration. The room on the second floor over the pharmacy was used for ophthalmology. The medical exam rooms were over dentistry. The second floor balcony was used for patient waiting area. This was the lay out at all three facilities on this mission.

We had a much larger team than in 2013. There were fifty-two members composed of four medical doctors and one medical student, five triage nurses, three dentists with three dental assistants, one pharmacist with three assistances, an ophthalmologist, and eight patient services personnel. We also had fourteen Vietnamese interpreters, of which one was a medical student and three were dental students. The team was completed by the support of six Vietnamese drivers, the team leader, assistant team leader, the in-country coordinator, and a Vietnamese doctor assigned by the government. Among the team members were sixteen Vietnam veterans.

While at dinner Saturday night at the Mandarin Café, I was arranging a group tour of the Hue Citadel. I was trying to explain to Mr. Cu's daughter that we wanted to rent eleven pedicabs. She did not understand what I meant by "pedicabs" until I drew a picture of three wheels. Her eyes lit up as she exclaimed, "Cyclos!" It is a bicycle frame with a two-wheeled passenger seat in front. Sunday morning, eleven of them were lined up in front of the Imperial Hotel. We climbed aboard and off we went, crossing the Hong River (also known as the Perfume River.) We followed the river bank to the street that ran between the moat and the canal. We entered the walled city via the Dong Ba Gate where the US Marines fought in 1968 to gain entrance. We made a rest stop at what we were told was a shrine but was also a jewelry store. We then went on to Hein Nhen Gate to the Citadel where we met our tour guide. We spent most of the day touring the Citadel, the ancient capital of Vietnam, and the residence of the emperor until 1945. We walked the several blocks to the military museum and saw the outdoor display of US military equipment captured from the ARVN. We took a cab from there back to the hotel.

Bud Bruton, a forward air control (FAC) pilot during the war, made reservations for us that night at the Tinh Gia Vien Restaurant, which specialized in decorative dishes. Bud knew the owner during the war. She had won many culinary awards for her presentation of food in the shapes of various animals. We were privileged to have a private dinner hosted by her daughter in traditional dress.

Monday morning was the same routine as before. We left at seven o'clock for A Luoi, twenty-seven miles west of Hue as the crow flies. It took us two hours on the mountainous and winding Route 49. We made one stop in Hong Ha to deliver medical supplies to the Floyd Olsen Memorial Clinic (FOMC).

Captain Olsen was a US Army helicopter pilot who crashed April 21, 1968, near Hong Ha, Thua Thien Hue province. The bodies of him and his crew were never recovered. Captain Olsen's family built a clinic in 1996. VWAM accepted responsibility for the facility in 2005. The structure had succumbed to the ravages of time and climate. VWAM completed construction of the new $108,000 FOMC in November, 2011.

Significant places near A Luoi are the A Shau Valley, A Bia Mountain (Hamburger Hill) and the Ho Chi Minh Trail. Our accommodations were at the Thanla Quang Guest House. Our rooms were outfitted with mosquito nets for our beds. We were there during a cold spell and did not have the mosquito problem that the previous team experienced. The clinic was about fifteen minutes from the guest house. Again it was the standard two-story structure. I also noticed that there were army posts across the road from all the clinics we operated. A unique characteristic about our patients at A Luoi is that they were from several different ethnic tribes. We conducted the clinic for three days. We demobilized the operation by service area with triage leaving first. Dianne and I were in the fifth van to leave, which broke down on a steep upgrade. The last van to leave picked us up. It was very cramped but better than walking. The decision had been made that morning that we not go back to Hue but directly to the Furama in Da Nang. We arrived about eleven o'clock at night to find Dianne and I had one of the honeymoon suites.

The team accomplished very significant humanitarian services. We examined 1,137 medical patients, 378 dental patients, performed seventeen cataract surgeries, dispensed 249 pairs of eyeglasses (reading or prescription), and provided eighteen mobility aids including a self-propelled cart, wheelchairs, walkers, crutches, and canes. VWAM also paid for fifty-one special lab tests performed at the University of Hue Hospital.

The next day was for R&R. We went to the pool in the morning. A group of us hired one of our team drivers to take us in a van to Hoi An, a major Southeast Asia seaport in the sixteenth and seventeenth centuries, about forty-five minutes south of Da Nang. We were dropped off at the Yaly Culture Center where on the second floor one could be fitted for tailored clothing. We proceeded down Nguyen Duy Hieu Street lined with many buildings with shops of the ground floor and living quarters on upper floors. We arrived at the Central Market with its many stalls. We were immediately approached by several shopkeepers. All Dianne wanted was a souvenir refrigerator magnet. Of course, I was taking photographs as we went. The sixteenth century Japanese bridge is a favorite location for wedding pictures, and I photographed newlyweds being photographed. Women were waiting in boats at the river bank to take tourist on the river. The river front had many historic houses that were converted to restaurants and shops.

There was a rehearsal on a stage in the park for a pageant performed nightly that week. The conductor was wearing a US 8th Air Force T-shirt. After an afternoon of sightseeing and shopping, fourteen of us met for dinner at the "Good Morning, Vietnam" Italian Restaurant. We had a private "upper room" on the second floor. The hit of the night was the tipsy glass that our drinks were served in. The glass had a slight convex bottom that caused it to lean and tip. We walked back to the cultural center where our driver met us for the ride back to the Furama.

The next day was more R&R. We enjoyed the pool and a massage. That evening we had our traditional VWAM farewell banquet and release of the finches.

POST MISSION TOUR

I had arranged a post mission tour to Hanoi for myself, Dianne, and Allison Burngardas through the same company that booked everything for VWAM. Allison was one of our triage nurses. We had also served together on the VWAM 2013. She still owes me a steak dinner for me claiming her excess bag so she did not get charged for it. Our plane departed Da Nang earlier than scheduled so when we arrived in Hanoi Airport, I had to borrow a phone to call our guide, Mr. Thang, to pick us up.

The first thing he wanted to do was take us to lunch. All our meals were prepaid, and he made sure we got our money's worth whether we were hungry or not.

He then took us to the Hilton Hanoi Opera, named so because it was across the street from the opera house and not to be confused with the "Hanoi Hilton," which is actually Hoa Lo Prison where the American POWs were held. He picked us up an hour later for a tour of Ho Chi Minh's mausoleum and vestige in the Presidential Palace Area. The former Indochina's General Governor Place was too ostentatious for Ho, so he lived in rooms that were the servant's quarters House #54 from 1954 to 1958. He then moved to the house on stilts with open four sides and had a bomb shelter next to it.

Our next stop was the Lotus Water Puppet Show. The stage is actually a pool. The puppets are on poles and operated by puppeteers in the pool behind a curtain. Musicians sit on platforms on each side of the pool. Small world - Lieutenant Hoang Trung Bui, Vietnam Coast Guard, IMOC 59, March-June 2018, told us his mother was one of the musicians we saw perform at the puppet show. After the show, it was time to eat again. Mr. Thang took us downtown Hanoi where the traffic was really congested.

The next day we left for the hundred-mile drive to Ha Long Bay. The road was under construction most of the way. Lieutenant Bui told us the super highway was complete. We made two rest stops. The first one was Hong Ngoc, which was like an outlet mall for paintings, marble sculptures, and clothing made on the spot. I was interested in a ten-foot marble sculpture of a mermaid swimming with four dolphins. It would not fit in the van. Our next stop, just before Ha Long Bay, was the Legend Pearl. We viewed a demonstration on cultured pearls and given the opportunity to purchase all types of pearl jewelry in the showroom. I did buy Dianne a mother of pearl bracelet made out of the oyster shells.

Onto Ha Long Bay where we boarded a tender to convey us to our junk boat. Dianne was apprehensive about spending the night on a junk, when we were planning the trip, until I showed her pictures of them on the web. They are actually modern cruise ships designed to look like a junk. The accommodations are very spacious. In fact, our bathroom on the junk was larger than our entire cabin on the *American Queen* steamboat on the Mississippi River.

Ha Long Bay is famous for its rock islands and is UNESCO World Heritage Site. There are 1969 rock islands in the bay. They are limestone islands subject to sea erosion. The largest ones are topped by rainforests. Dianne accused me of photographing all of them when really I took only 170 photographs and five movies.

Our cruise included the Vung Vieng fishing village where everyone lives in floating houses or boats. We boarded six-passenger boats rowed by women standing in the stern. We also disembarked at Vung Ha Beach. We could wade but not swim. We returned to the junk and anchored for the night and had a massage and buffet dinner. The next day we toured Thien Cahn Son Cave with its mineral stalactite and stalagmite formations before heading back to the dock.

Mr. Thang took us to a modern day shopping mall on the way back to Hanoi. Dianne bought a couple of items in the 40,000 VN Dong (two-dollar) store while I photographed shoppers. Allison bought two bags of spirits, which we had difficulty packing for the trip home. Mr. Thang wanted to show us a market in Hanoi. It was so crowded we walked down the middle of Ngo Quiyen Street. There were shops on both sides with wares displayed on the sidewalks. We entered the market through to food section with all kinds of dried foods on display and live turtles. Inside the main building on two floors were hundreds of stalls, each specializing in one item. Allison wanted to buy silk which was on the second floor. It was displayed in stacks that went almost to the ceiling. I still had some sites on my list and we had an evening departure the next day. Mr. Trang said we had plenty of time and would pick us up at 10:30 in the morning. He immediately took us to the Sen Tayho buffet restaurant. I asked why so early. He said we had to beat the tour buses. There were ten buffet lines, each with a category of food and one for just desserts. From there went to Van Meu, the eleventh-century Temple of Literature where mandarins were educated to the level of present day doctor of philology (Ph.D.). I took pictures of the Khue Van Pavilion at the Third Court Yard to match the brass plate given to us by Lieutenant Tuan Qhang Pham, IMOC 55.

Our next and final site was Hoa Lo Prison, "Hanoi Hilton." It was built by the French in 1886-1901. Much of was demolished in the 1990s and replaced by a high rise government building and the Somerset Grand Hotel.

What remains is a two-story gatehouse with two one-story wings. These rooms displayed exhibits of the atrocities committed by the French on Vietnamese political prisoners.

Behind the gatehouse is a two-story building, and on the second floor is a photo gallery of the humane treatment of the American POWs.

Our trip to the airport was slow going because of the heavy rush hour traffic. It was the most motor scooters I have ever seen. We had plenty of time before our flight to Seoul, Korea. We spent most of it adjusting the contents of Allison's three suitcases to get them under the maximum weight. We succeeded with two. She explained to the agent that the third suitcase contained medical instruments used on a humanitarian medical mission. The extra weight was excused.

We arrived in Seoul, Korea, to find team members Dr. Robert Swan and his wife Jean waiting for the same flight to Atlanta. He was a dentist, retired USN, and she was a dental technician. They had remained in Da Nang to be on the next VWAM team. I was watching the flight progress on the monitor when I noticed we were circling over Ohio. Finally they announced we were diverted to Dulles Airport in Washington, D.C. because of tornado warnings in Atlanta. We spent three hours on the plane at Dulles. If we could have gotten off, retrieved our suitcases, and rented a car, we could have been home by the time the flight proceeded to Atlanta. We arrived at Atlanta about five o'clock in the afternoon to find it packed with people. The lights had been dimmed in a section of the train concourse and people were sleeping there. We finally departed at four in the morning for the two and a half hour flight to Newport News, Virginia.

Our total travel time from Hanoi to our front door in Yorktown was forty hours.

Shirley, 2nd Classman (Junior) Regimental Operations Sergeant Andy
and Dr. Tate, Parents' Weekend, VMI. October 1990.

Medical Reserve Corps instructor, Dr.
Tate, presenting disaster preparedness
information, 2008.

Virginia State Animal Response Team
instructor, Dr. Tate, presenting
emergency pet sheltering course. 2009.

President, Dr. Steven Karras (left), and President Elect, Dr. Tomas Massie (right), present the Virginia Veterinary Medical Association Service Award to Dr. Samuel Tate. February 2008.

Dr. Tate and Dianne, Ayres Rock, Australia. 2015.

Dr. Sam Tate, Sgt. Phong, and COL. Doug Braendel at Vung Tau Lighthouse. Back Beach is in the background.

Four Vietnam Veterans at Rex Hotel. (Left to right) Chuck Ward, USN; Dr. Bill Jenkins, US Army; Doug Braendel, US Army; and Dr. Sam Tate, USAF. June 2013.

Transfer of patients from the Green Bird to the Blue Bird, 903d Aero-Evacuation Squadron, Da Nang, March 1968.

Dr. Sam Tate and RVAN veteran, Hoa Hai Clinic, Da Nang.

Little girl with dental kit provided by Dr. McKinley Price, Newport News, VA. June 2013.

VWAM Interpreters.

Linda Avery teaching English; Thuong "Typhoon" teaching Vietnamese.

US student nurse, Tammy holds young Vietnamese patient.

Left to right: Hanh "Porcupine" (dental hygiene), Linh (pharmacy), Han (glasses), and Tammy (patient services).

Farmers drying rice on the asphalt of Route 1A south.

Dr. Sam Tate and COL. Doug Braendel at
Vung Ro Bay filled with floating houses.

Vung Ro Bay, 1968.

Don Toc villagers building a Ha Long Bay square head boat on the beach at Tuy Hoa.

Dr. Sam Tate reaching to touch   Sunset over Tuy Hoa. See the eagle?
a water buffalo.

Joette Ward with finches, symbolic of our emotions.

Vietnam Veterans with their war time photos. (Left to right) Dr. Sam Tate, Doug Braendel, Nurse Rhea McCarthy, Chuck Ward, Mike Connolly, Nurse Steve Scott, and Dr. Bill Jenkins. Vets with a Mission banquet, Furama Resort, Da Nang. July 2013.

Lady Buddha, Son
Tra Mountain.

Dragon Bridge, Han River Da Nang.

Left to right: Dr. Sam Tate, Dianne, Lt. Son Doan, wife and daughter. March 2017

Quang Thai Clinic, ground floor.

Triage in the courtyard, (left to right) nurses Steve Scott, Leone Dipboye and Monica Treta.

Dr. Tom Love supervises dental student performing extractions.

Left to right: Pharmacy assistants Sloane Robinson, Dianne Tate and Joette Ward. March 2017.

Quang Tai Clinic, second floor.
Dr. Rodger examines foot of patient who lost his toes in an accident.

 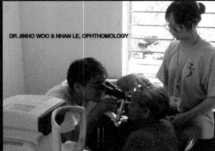

4th year medical student, Page Cummings, examine patient with Vietnamese medical student/interpreter.

Dr. Jinho Woo with interpreter Nhan Le evaluate patient with cataracts.

SAM & DIANNE, NOON BREAK, QUANG LOI

Quang Loi Clinic.
Dr. Sam Tate and Dianne on noon break.

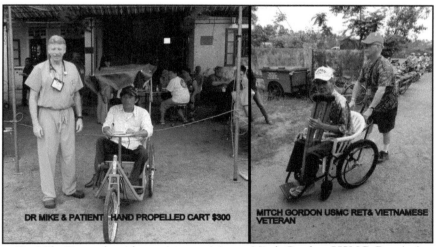

DR MIKE & PATIENT HAND PROPELLED CART $300

MITCH GORDON USMC RET& VIETNAMESE VETERAN

Dr. Mike Bernardo with a patient receiving a hand propelled cart.

Mitch Gordon, USMC, Ret. Assists a Vietnamese veteran with a new wheelchair.

271

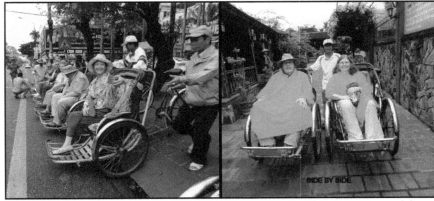

Eleven cyclos lined up in front of Imperial Hotel. Dr. Hai Huang, DDS, in first and Dr. Sam Tate in second.

Dr. Sam Tate and Dianne prepared for a rainy day.

Their tour group enters the walled city of Hue by the Dong Ba Gate.

Sculptured food served at Tinh Gia Vien Restaurant. Hue.

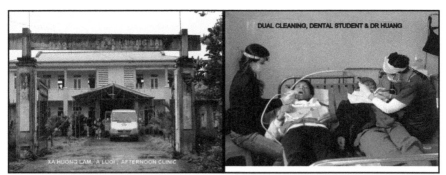

Xa Huong Lam Clinic, A Luoi. It rained all three days.

Vietnamese dental student/interpreter and Dr. Huang perform dental cleanings side by side.

Triage nurses, Erin Hammes and Steve Scott, confer on a patient.

Dianne Tate under the mosquito net.

Newlyweds posing at the 16th Century Japanese Bridge.

French Colonial houses on Tan Ky Street, Thu Bon River.

Fourteen VWAM team members meet for dinner in the "upper room" of the "Good Morning Vietnam" Italian Restaurant. Hoi An.

Vietnam Veterans at VWAM farewell banquet.

POW-MIA chair for Captain Floyd Olsen and all other unaccounted for service members. Da Nang. April 2017.

Ho Chi Minh's Mausoleum.

Ho Chi Minh's house on stilts. Hanoi.

Our junk, Victory Star.

Dianne displays our suite

Dr. Tate and the amazing large bath room. Ha Long Bay.

Dragon's Tooth, one of 1969 rock formations in Ha Long Bay.

Sunset at Thien Son cove

278

Vegetable shop, Ngo Quiyen Street.   Allison Bungardas contemplates
                                              buying silk.

Main court of Hang Da Market. Hanoi.

Khue Van Pavilion, Third Court Yard, 11th Century Van Mieu Temple of Literature.

Gate house of Hoa Lo Prison, "Hanoi Hilton".

FACES OF VIETNAM

OWNER, TINH GIA VIEN RESTAURANT, HUE

CASSAVA LEAVES, KO-TU TRIBE

WAITING FOR DR MIKE

EPILOGUE

My son Sam and I attended the OCF East Coast Leaders' Conference at White Sulphur Springs in January 2020. Sam asked me several deep, reflective questions on the way home. He asked if there was anything I could be doing that I was not doing.

I replied that I had thought about writing down the many stories I retold about my experiences but just never got started.

I was at the medical desk in the health department's COVID-19 call center April 13-16. Incoming calls were infrequent, and I was getting bored. I started writing my stories on blank sheets of paper. I continued the project at home during the forty-eight days of "lockdown." Some nights I would have so many stories going around and around in my mind that I couldn't sleep. I would get out of bed and write them down until I grew sleepy again.

My story would not be complete without reliance on my Lord and Savior, Jesus Christ. I attended Sunday school and church at the nearest Protestant church wherever we lived. My grandmother Falconer (Gonie) sang in the choir at Royster Memorial Presbyterian Church in Norfolk, VA. I was baptized there. My son Sam and his wife Amy were married there in 1988. Gonie lived three houses from us on Louisiana Drive, and I would ride with her to church in her wooden paneled station wagon.

I was in the front seat one cold rainy Sunday. As we turned left from Louisiana Drive onto Granby Street, the front passenger door opened and I was ejected from the station wagon into the middle of the street in the path of an oncoming car. It stopped just before hitting me. I was wearing a hooded winter coat which cushioned my impact with the pavement. I jumped up, got back in the station wagon, and went on to church even though Gonie was distraught.

I accepted Jesus as my Savior through a Catechism class at the Congregational Christian Church in Somerset, MA, in 1954. My knowledge of the Bible and faith grew as a charter member of Christ Presbyterian Church in Virginia Beach, VA. I was a member of the youth group and Sunday school class along with Bill Wheeler. Bill and I were also in the Boy Scouts, and I took very seriously the twelfth point of the Scout Law, a scout is reverent.

I attended a local church in East Lasing, MI, my freshman year at MSU and with Shirley after our wedding, a practice we continued my entire military career. I have taught both high school and adult Sunday school in civilian churches and military chapels. As I mentioned before, I was introduced to Officers Christian Fellowship at Ramstein, Germany. I rededicated my life to Christ and His service. That, combined with my thirty years of Scout experience, has instilled in me an obligation of service to others. I have served as an usher, elder, fund council chair, parish council president, and local and regional OCF leader.

I went on a tour of the Holy Land in 2014. Chaplain MacDonald baptized me in the Jordan River as confirmation of my service. But my most significant experience was our visit to Shiloh. I felt a strange sensation as I stood on the site where the tabernacle was. This is the very spot where God called the judge and prophet Samuel for a lifetime of service, I Samuel 3. I continue my spiritual walk through Bible studies in the chapel adult Sunday school class, Bible Study Fellowship, and OCF.

This is not THE END but the extent of my recollections to this point, May 30, 2020.

P. S.

I was reactivated by the MRC on July 10 to assist in the communicable disease section. My assignment was to prepare contact tracing packets using patient positive COVID-19 test results printed from the VA Department of Health (VDH) reportable disease system. The packets were then distributed to the investigators doing the contact tracing. The VDH reporting system contained positive reports for various communicable diseases and sometimes they would be printed along with the COVID-19 cases. I established a rapport early on with the nurses by calling their attention to a stool sample report positive for shigella (the cause of dysentery). They were glad to have a veterinarian paying attention to detail. A week later, I found a positive report for Legionnaire's disease. On another occasion, I found a positive TB report. I told the nurse who printed the reports. She said she had printed the reports late the day before knowing that it was in the pile by did not have time to look for it. Besides, she knew that I would find it in the morning.

Another advantage of being a veterinarian was that I could in good conscience use the "doctor's phone line" in requesting patients' phone numbers that were omitted in the reports from the testing facilities.

The staff was also appreciative that I was volunteering every day. The patients' surnames became so familiar that I was able to recognize family cluster that were reported several days apart. By doing so, the reports were sent to the same investigator, reducing duplication of effort.

Another aspect of attention to detail was identifying reports that needed to be prioritized for the investigators. There were several categories:

- Age – children five years and under and adults sixty-five and older
- Health care providers
- First responders – EMS, firefighters, and police
- Jails – staff vs. inmates (three jails in the area)
- Nursing homes – staff vs. residents (required a special form)

Also being a military veteran and an area resident for thirty-two years, I could recognize the reporting military testing facilities by their addresses or phone numbers when the names of the facilities were missing from the reports.

When I started in July, I worked four and half to five-hour shifts, seven days a week, twenty-three days straight until August 1. The health department employees were working six days a week, rotating days off. So I scaled back to six days a week.

I was processing about three hundred reports per shift for six jurisdictions in the Peninsula Health District. Some days, when I arrived at nine in the morning, there would be a pile of reports on my desk that were printed since eight in the morning. It would take me to 11 or 11:30 to catch up.

By late August, the number of test being performed increased but the positivity rate was falling to around six percent. By late September, there was significant decline in reports. On September 28, I processed about twenty. On the 29th, I had only seven and on the 30th, only one. When I completed my shift on September 30th, the section chief thanked for my dedication and hard work.

The inter-phase between the state and local systems would be automated on October 1, so I was no longer needed for that task. All total, I volunteered sixty-three days providing 315 hours of service valued at about four thousand dollars. I also trained six volunteers, including two medical doctors and a nurse to work the afternoon shift. I was called back in January 2021, when the vaccines became available, to perform special projects and vaccination scheduling.

On February 25, 2021, I was selected to receive the 2021 CVM Distinguished Veterinary Alumni Non-Practitioner Award from the Michigan State University College of Veterinary Medicine.

MILITARY OFFICER RANKS

Air Force, Army, Marine Corps (abbreviations)	Navy, Coast Guard
01 Second Lieutenant (2d Lt, 2LT, 2ndLt)	Ensign (ENS)
02 First Lieutenant (1st Lt, 1LT, 1sLt)	Lieutenant Junior Grade (LTJG)
03 Captain (Capt, CPT, Capt)	Lieutenant (LT)
04 Major (Maj, MAJ, Maj)	Lieutenant Commander (LCDR)
05 Lieutenant Colonel (Lt Col, LTC, LtCol)	Commander (CDR)
06 Colonel (Col, COL, Col)	Captain (CAPT)
07 Brigadier General (1 star) (Brig Gen, BG, BGen)	Rear Admiral lower (2 star) (RDML)
08 Major General (2 star) (Maj Gen, MG, MajGen)	Rear Admiral upper (2 star) (RADM)
09 Lieutenant General (3 star) (Lt Gen, LTG, LtGen)	Vice Admiral (3 star) (VADM)
010 General (4 star) (Gen, GEN, Gen)	Admiral (4 star) (ADM)

Veterans Employment Toolkit Handout, www.va.gov/vetsinworkplace

CPSIA information can be obtained
at www.ICGtesting.com
Printed in the USA
BVHW022312030422
633182BV00001B/1